VM/CMS

VM/CMS

A User's Guide

Paul Chase

WILEY

JOHN WILEY & SONS

New York □ **Chichester** □ **Brisbane** □ **Toronto** □ **Singapore**

This book was formatted by the author using IBM's
Document Composition Facility and printed on an IBM
3820 printer.

IBM, VM, VM/SP, VM/CMS, VM/XA, VM/IS, VM/370,
CMS, AIX, MVS, DOS, DCF, and SCRIPT are trademarks
of International Business Machines. VMS is a trademark of Digital Equipment Corporation. UNIX is a
trademark of American Telephone & Telegraph.
VMSECURE is a trademark of VM Software
Incorporated.

Library of Congress Cataloging in Publication Data:

Chase, Paul.
    VM/CMS: a user's guide / Paul Chase.
       p.   cm.
    Bibliography: p.
    ISBN 0-471-50170-0 (pbk.)
    1. VM/CMS (Computer operating system) I. Title.
QA76.76.063C455 1989
005.4'429 — dc19   88-26069
                                          CIP

Printed in the United States of America

10 9 8 7 6 5 4 3 2 1

Contents

Preface

Virtual Machine/Conversational Monitor System (VM/CMS) is a general purpose interactive operating system that runs on computers that range in capacity from minicomputers such as the IBM 9370 to supercomputers such as the IBM 3090. Other names by which VM/CMS is known include VM/SP, VM/XA, VM/IS, VM/370, VM and CMS.

Most people use VM/CMS for one or more of the following activities:

- **Data Processing** involves running programs that take one set of data as input and produce another set of data as output. Common examples of data processing are:

  - Accounting

  - Inventory

  - Payroll

  - Billing

  - Forecasting

  - Statistics

  - Graphics

- **Text Editing** involves the use of a utility program called an **editor** for the creation of new files and the modification of old files.

- **Text (Word) Processing** involves embedding commands within text that will format the text in certain ways to produce documents such as:

  - Reports

  - Letters

  - Articles

  - Books

  - Announcements

  - Forms

- **Communicating with Other Computer Users** involves sending notes, files and messages to other computer users located either on your system or on other systems to which yours is connected.

- **Program Development** is a preliminary step in data processing whenever the program that processes the data has not been written. It usually involves several, sometimes repetitive, steps:

  1. Define the goal that a program is supposed to accomplish.

  2. Choose an appropriate language in which to write the program.

  3. Write the program.

  4. Compile the program.

  5. Fix compilation errors.

  6. Repeat steps four and five until there are no compilation errors.

  7. Identify any data that is to be input to or output from the program.

  8. Execute the program.

  9. Fix any execution errors.

  10. Repeat steps seven through nine until there are no execution errors.

For Whom is This Book Intended?

This book is intended for anyone with the need and the motivation to learn VM/CMS. Everyone from the casual system user to the professional programmer should find it useful. This book presents the material that anyone learning VM/CMS needs for a comprehensive understanding of how to accomplish tasks with VM/CMS and how the system works.

The Scope of This Book

The scope of this book is limited to the VM/CMS operating system. There is no discussion of application software and the separately purchased software products that might be encountered on a VM/CMS system. Thus, there is no coverage of document formatting with SCRIPT, database management with SQL/DS, or programming with languages such as FORTRAN or COBOL. The batch and tape commands native to VM/CMS are also omitted.

Programming and applications on VM/CMS are discussed in another text, *VM/CMS: A Guide to Programming and Applications*, also written by me.

Differences between VM/CMS Systems

When using this text in conjunction with your VM/CMS system, there are three considerations of which you should be aware:

  1. VM/CMS is not implemented identically on each of the machines on which it runs. The basic VM/CMS system is almost always modified and enhanced to conform to the needs of its users and the preferences of those who manage and maintain it. Differences may relate to:

- How the system is accessed.

- The version of VM/CMS currently running on the system.

- The availability and use of real input and output devices.

- The HELP facility.

- How batch and tape processing are done.

- How you are charged for using system resources.

- How you communicate with other computer users.

- Which products are available and how they are used.

2. A wide variety of different video display terminals can be used with VM/CMS. These terminals differ in terms of which keys perform specific functions. There are special purpose keys, such as program function keys, program attention keys, terminal management keys and cursor movement keys, that differ between terminal types. For this reason, this book will usually refer to the *function* that a key performs, leaving the reader to consult with those who support the system to determine the *actual key* that performs the function.

3. The kinds of application software found on a VM/CMS system depend mostly on the needs of those who use it. An institution engaged in business applications will have products, such as COBOL, related to business activities, whereas a facility engaged in scientific applications will have products, such as FORTRAN, for scientific applications. This book, however, is concerned solely with the VM/CMS operating system; there is no discussion of application software that runs on VM/CMS.

Releases of VM/CMS

Since its introduction, there have been several new releases of VM/CMS affording new features and enhancements. This text describes VM/CMS up through Release 5. The only major difference between Release 5 and Releases 3 and 4 is the availability of a primitive windowing system in Release 5 that will not be discussed in this text.

Other Documentation

This book makes no attempt to comprehensively document the VM/CMS system. It discusses the material that most people will need in working with VM/CMS. The extent to which a specific command or topic is described depends on the general usefulness of the command or topic. While many commands are described completely, some are only partially described and others are not discussed at all.

The most complete description of VM/CMS is available in literally hundreds of manuals written by and available from IBM. The following list identifies some of the more useful documentation. The number in parentheses following each title is a reference number with which to order the document from IBM:

- **CMS User's Guide (SC19-6210)**
  This is a general purpose introduction to VM/CMS. Unfortunately, much of the material, such as that on DOS, is irrelevant to using VM/CMS.

- **Application Development Guide (SC24-5247)**
  This is an introduction to developing and running FORTRAN and COBOL programs on VM/CMS. The reader is assumed to be familiar with FORTRAN or COBOL but unfamiliar with VM/CMS.

- **CP Command Reference for General Users (GC19-6206)**
  This contains complete descriptions of all CP commands. Commands are ordered alphabetically. This manual is not tutorial.

- **CMS Command Reference (SC19-6209)**
  This contains complete descriptions of all CMS commands, EDIT subcommands and macros, DEBUG subcommands, EXEC Control Statements and HELP Format Words. Commands are ordered alphabetically. This manual is not tutorial.

- **System Product Editor Command and Macro Reference (SC24-5221)**
  This contains complete descriptions of all XEDIT commands and XEDIT macros. Commands are ordered alphabetically. This manual is not tutorial.

- **System Product Editor User's Guide (SC24-5220)**
  This is a general purpose introduction to XEDIT and writing XEDIT macros.

- **EXEC 2 Reference (SC24-5219)**
  This provides a complete description of the EXEC2 language as well as some tutorial information.

- **System Product Interpreter Reference (SC24-5239)**
  This provides a complete description of the REXX (Restructured Extended Executor) language. This manual is intended for experienced programmers.

- **System Product Interpreter User's Guide (SC24-5238)**
  This is a general purpose introduction to REXX and writing REXX programs.

- **Terminal Reference (GC19-6206)**
  This discusses the types of IBM terminals supported by VM/SP.

- **System Messages and Codes (GC19-6206)**
  This describes the messages and codes produced by VM/SP as well as an explanation of why each message occurs and what you must do to correct an error.

Other Learning Resources

Many organizations have one or more individuals who act as consultants to system users. Consultants are typically there to help you help yourself — not to do your work for you. Their primary role is usually to point you in the direction of documentation and other resources that will enable you to do your work. Find out what kinds of consulting resources are available within your organization. The consultants should be able to tell you:

- How to access the system.

- Which version of VM/CMS is currently running on your system.

- How to use your type of terminal on the system.

- What programs and products are available on the system.

- What real input and output devices are available and how to use them.

- How to use the HELP facility.

- How batch and tape processing are done if they are available.

- How you are charged for using system resources.

- How you communicate with other computer users.

The Organization of This Book

This book consists of fifteen chapters organized into five parts:

- **Part I: The VM/CMS System**
  Read the chapters in Part I in their order of occurrence and then proceed to Part II.

  - **Chapter 1: A Conceptual Overview of VM/CMS**
    This chapter introduces the Virtual Machine concept and other terminology that is used throughout the book. It also discusses the syntax used to present commands.

  - **Chapter 2: Accessing and Leaving VM/CMS**
    This chapter discusses the procedures and commands used to access and leave the system.

  - **Chapter 3: Becoming Acquainted with VM/CMS**
    This chapter discusses the different environments on the system as well as how to enter commands, interrupt commands, interpret messages from the system and use your terminal effectively.

  - **Chapter 4: CMS Disks and CMS Disk Files**
    This chapter discusses the characteristics of CMS disks and CMS disk files.

- **Part II: Creating and Editing Files with XEDIT**
  This is probably the most important part of the book for two reasons:

1. Most of your time on VM/CMS will be spent using the XEDIT editor to create and edit files.

2. Some of the most frequently used facilities on VM/CMS are controlled by XEDIT. The more facile you are with XEDIT, the better you'll be at taking full advantage of these facilities.

Read the chapters in Part II in their order of occurrence and then proceed to either Part III or Part IV. Reading Chapters 7 and 8 may be postponed until later.

- **Chapter 5: Becoming Acquainted with XEDIT**
  This chapter is designed to give you an understanding of XEDIT and how it works. This chapter should be read both before and after you've read the other three chapters concerned with XEDIT.

- **Chapter 6: Performing Common Editing Tasks with XEDIT**
  This chapter is concerned with the kinds of editing tasks that you will perform most often.

- **Chapter 7: Special Topics in XEDIT**
  This chapter is a heterogeneous collection of useful, but less common, editing commands and tasks.

- **Chapter 8: Customizing the XEDIT Environment**
  This chapter is concerned with modifying the XEDIT environment so that it better suits your needs and preferences.

- **Part III: Working with Disk Files**
  This part is concerned with managing and manipulating disk files. Read the chapters in this part in their order of occurrence and then proceed to Part IV if you haven't already.

  - **Chapter 9: Working with Disk Files**
    This chapter is concerned with activities such as copying, renaming, erasing, comparing and printing files.

  - **Chapter 10: Managing Disk Files**
    This chapter is concerned with facilities that enable you to keep track of your files and conveniently work with them. This chapter will be easier to understand if you are familiar with the material on creating and editing files in Part II.

- **Part IV: Communicating with Other Computer Users**
  This part is concerned with sending electronic communications to and receiving them from other computer users. After this part, proceed to Part V.

  - **Chapter 11: Communicating with Other Computer Users**
    This chapter is concerned with sending notes, files and messages to and receiving them from other computer users.

- **Part V: Special Topics in VM/CMS**
  The chapters in this part can be read in any order after a reading of Part I.

- **Chapter 12: Managing Your Virtual Machine**
  This chapter is concerned with making both temporary and permanent changes to your VM/CMS account.

- **Chapter 13: Virtual Devices and Spooling**
  This chapter details the characteristics of virtual devices and spool files and how to work with them.

- **Chapter 14: Customizing the CP/CMS Environments**
  This chapter is concerned with customizing the CP/CMS environment so that it better suits your needs and preferences.

- **Chapter 15: Diagnosing and Correcting Problems**
  This chapter is concerned with how to diagnose problems when they occur and what to do to solve them.

How to Use This Book

Since this book was written to be tutorial, the material in any one section usually depends on the material in previous sections. What this means is that you will derive maximum benefit from this book if you read the sections within a chapter in their order of occurrence.

To assist those who are new to VM/CMS and those who want to get going quickly, each section is labeled according to whether the material in that section is of primary or secondary importance:

- Sections of primary importance contain information that is necessary for a basic understanding and effective use of VM/CMS. Omitting one of these sections may result in a loss of continuity when you are reading subsequent material. Everyone should read these sections. They are labeled:

  First Reading

- Sections of secondary importance contain information that is not immediately necessary for an understanding of VM/CMS but which is, nonetheless, important. Return to these sections when you have the time and the interest. Omitting one of these sections should not result in a loss of continuity when you are reading subsequent material. They are labeled:

  Second Reading

Numerous practical exercises and examples are included throughout the book. You are strongly encouraged to perform the examples yourself and, whenever useful, to adapt them to your own work.

There are sections that you *can* and *should* skip over. For example, this text discusses the use of two types of video display terminals with VM/CMS: IBM display terminals and ASCII terminals that *emulate* IBM display terminals.

- If you are using an IBM display terminal, there is no need for you to read the sections and comments concerning ASCII terminals.

- If you are using an ASCII terminal or a personal computer to emulate an ASCII terminal, there is no need for you to read the sections and comments concerning IBM display terminals.

You may also find that there are sections or even entire chapters that are beyond the scope of your immediate needs; if so, skip them for the time being and come back to them if and when you need them.

Some information appears more than once. This is done when the information is important, relevant in more than one section and you may have missed it in another section.

Reader Comments

If you have comments regarding any aspect of the content, organization or style of this book, I would appreciate hearing from you. Please address your feedback to:

Paul Chase
c/o John Wiley & Sons
605 Third Avenue
New York, NY
10158-0012

Acknowlegdments

Several people generously contributed their time and expertise in reviewing and criticizing this book.

- Carol Silverman read the book from the perspective a new VM/CMS user once in a draft form and once again in a finalized form. Her insights and recommendations made this book significantly better.

- Richard Peters and Mike Friedman read the book from a technical standpoint. They pointed out my errors and misconceptions, offered useful examples and suggested other topics.

Special thanks are extended to Richard Eusebio and the IBM Corporation for providing the IBM 3820 printer on which this book was printed.

I'm also grateful to the management and staff of Information Systems and Technologies at the University of California at Berkeley for their encouragement and support throughout the writing of this book.

Paul Chase

Berkeley, California
November 1988

Part I
The VM/CMS System

Chapter 1
A Conceptual Overview of VM/CMS

Introduction

An operating system is a collection of programs running on a computer that determines how the computer interacts with the outside world. The operating system accepts input from a console connected to the computer. A computer operator or user communicates with the computer by entering instructions on the console in the language of the operating system. The operator might enter a command instructing the computer to print a file or to copy a file from one disk to another. If the operating system *understands* the command, it performs the action requested. If the operating system does not understand the command or if the command simply cannot be carried out, the operating system sends the operator a message indicating the nature of the problem.

An operating system also controls and organizes these kinds of activities on the computer:

- Access to the machine is monitored and controlled to ensure that the machine is used only by those authorized to do so.

- Access to information on the machine is monitored and controlled to ensure that programs and data are used only by those authorized to do so.

- Convenient access to devices enables computer users to communicate quickly and effectively with peripheral devices, such as disks and tapes attached to the computer.

- Resource management allows more than one person to use the machine simultaneously by scheduling resources so that conflicts do not arise when two or more users request the same resource, such a printer.

- Usage data is maintained to keep track of who used the machine, what they used it for and how long they used it.

VM/CMS (Virtual Machine/Conversational Monitor System) is an operating system that is the subject of this book.

1.1 Of Real Machines and Virtual Machines

The concept of a *virtual* machine is best understood in terms of a *real* machine, what the components of a real machine are and what those components are supposed to accomplish.

Most real computer systems have certain components in common:

- An **Operator Console** is a terminal that the computer operator uses to manage and otherwise control the operations of the machine.

- **Software** is a set of instructions that enables the computer user to communicate with the computer system and tell it what to do. A **program** is a set of instructions that accomplishes a specific task. An **operating system** is a collection of programs that controls and organizes the computer's activities.

- **Input Devices** enable a computer user to get information *into* the computer. On some computing systems, the card reader is an input device.

- **Memory** is where the programs and data currently being worked on are stored.

- A **Central Processing Unit (CPU)** interprets and executes the instructions that comprise a computer program.

- **Bulk Storage Devices** are used to store large quantities of information. Because memory is limited in its capacity to store information, these devices serve as an extension of memory. The most common storage device is the **direct access storage device (DASD)** known as a **disk**. Information stored on a disk can be *directly* accessed in a very short period of time. The direct method of accessing information on a disk is contrasted with the sequential method of accessing information stored on magnetic tape, another common storage device.

- **Output Devices** enable the computer user to get information *out of* the computer. The printer is one of the most common output devices. On some computing systems, the card punch is another.

When you access your system, **Virtual Machine System Product (VM/SP)** creates a computing environment for you called a **Virtual Machine (VM)**. A VM is a simulation of a real machine. VM/SP simulates the resources of the real machine in such a way that each user seems to have a complete system independent of other users. This means that, as a user, you have all the components of a computing system. VM/CMS provides each system user with a virtual machine by sharing the resources of the real machine:

- The video display terminal you use functions as the **Virtual Console** of your VM. Your virtual console enables you to communicate with and control your VM.

- The real CPU is shared among users so that each VM has a **Virtual CPU**. The system shares CPU time between users by running one user's program for a short time, then running a second user's program for a short time and so forth until it returns to the first user, where the cycle begins again.

- The real memory is shared among users so that each has **Virtual Memory** — also referred to as **Virtual Storage**. Your virtual memory is where your programs are stored when they are running and files are stored when you are editing them. Virtual storage is accomplished by substituting disk storage for real storage. The system divides a program that is executing into sections called **pages**. Only those pages immediately necessary for program execution reside in real memory. The other pages are stored on disk until they are needed. The process of moving pages from disk storage to real storage is called **paging**. By substituting disk storage for real storage, the system seems to have more memory than it actually does, which enables you to run programs that are larger than the system's real storage capacity.

- A real disk is shared among users by dividing it into smaller segments called **Virtual Disks**, each of which belongs to a specific VM. Your disks are the devices on which you store your programs and data.

- Real input devices are shared among users so that each user has **Virtual Input Devices**. Your **Virtual Reader** is a virtual input device used to get files *into* your VM. When other computer users send you electronic mail, it is stored in your virtual reader.

- Real output devices are shared among users so that each user has **Virtual Output Devices**. Your **Virtual Printer** and **Virtual Punch** are virtual output devices used to get files *out of* your VM. When you send mail and data to other computer users, you do so with one of your virtual output devices.

The virtual machine concept is both elegant and useful. In the past, a computing system offered a single environment in which to work. A single system running VM/SP allows many users to run VMs independent of each other, each of which can run different operating systems. Different users on the same system might be simultaneously running CMS, DOS, MVS or AIX operating systems. VM/SP also affords the opportunity of developing and testing a new version of an operating system, including VM, without compromising normal system usage. Thus, VM/SP acts as a **host operating system** that supports **guest operating systems** on its virtual machines.

1.2 Two Main Parts to Your Virtual Machine

There are two parts to your virtual machine:

- The Control Program

- The Conversational Monitor System

The Control Program (CP)

The Control Program is the operating system that controls the *real* machine and its resources such as the *real* memory and *real* input/output devices. CP handles the connection between your VM and the real machine. These are the CP commands you'll use most often:

- LOGON accesses your VM.

- LOGOFF leaves your VM.

- QUERY determines the status and configuration of your VM and virtual devices.

- DEFINE and LINK change the configuration of your VM.

- SET changes the characteristics of the CP environment.

- SPOOL changes the characteristics of your virtual input and output devices.

The Conversational Monitor System (CMS)

A VM only becomes useful when an operating system is loaded into virtual memory to run it. While there are several different operating systems that run VMs, the Conversational Monitor System is the most commonly used. CMS is an operating system running under CP that controls your *virtual* machine and its resources such as *virtual* memory and *virtual* input/output devices. CMS performs tasks on your VM. These are the CMS commands you'll use most often:

- XEDIT creates and edits files.

- FILELIST and LISTFILE manage disk files.

- COPYFILE, ERASE, RENAME, PRINT, PUNCH and TYPE work with disk files.

- RDRLIST manages reader files.

- PEEK, DISCARD and RECEIVE work with reader files.

- EXEC and RUN run programs.

- QUERY determines the status of the CMS environment.

- SET changes the status of the CMS environment.

- NOTE, SENDFILE and TELL enable you to communicate with other users.

1.3 Configuring Your Virtual Machine

When your account is set up on the VM/CMS system, an entry is made in the **CP User Directory** that identifies your VM and specifies how your VM is to be configured when you access the system. Among other things, the directory includes:

- The userid that identifies your account.

- The password that authorizes use of your account.

- How you are charged for system usage.

- The privilege class of your account.

- How your VM is normally configured.

- How you can change the configuration of your VM if necessary.

When you log onto the system, a VM is configured for you according to the specifications in the CP user directory. Your VM is set up to have:

- Virtual storage of a specific size.

- A virtual printer.

- A virtual punch.

- A virtual reader.

- The disks that belong to your VM.

- The disks that belong to other VMs that you are authorized to access.

- The CMS operating system that is loaded.

- Other control information.

1.4 Command Syntax

This section describes the syntax that will be used to describe commands. The general structure of commands is:

cmdname   [operands...]   [(options...]

where **cmdname**   is a string of one to eight letters that is the name of the command to be executed. A command name is usually descriptive of the function the command performs.

operands   are one or more operands that specify *what* the command is to operate on. Depending on the function a command performs, it may require several operands or none at all.

(is a left parenthesis that separates the operands from the options. A left parenthesis is only used if one or more options are specified.

options   are one or more optional operands that specify *how* the command is to operate by modifying the function the command performs. The options on a CMS command usually follow a left parenthesis.

...   are ellipses to indicate that more than one operand or option may be specified.

[ ]   are square brackets around an operand or option to indicate that it is *optional* and does not have to be specified unless the function the command performs is to be *modified* in the manner specified by the operand or option.[1]

The operands most frequently used on commands are CMS file identifiers. Accordingly, file identifiers will be be used throughout this section to provide examples of command syntax. File identifiers are discussed in detail in the chapter *CMS Disks and CMS Disk Files*. Briefly, a CMS file identifier consists of three parts:

- A Filename (fn)

- A Filetype (ft)

- A Filemode (fm)

---

[1] The brackets, vertical bar and ellipses are only used here to present command syntax. When you actually enter a command, you should *not* use them.

The Importance of Order for Operands and Options

The order in which operands are specified is very important. If operand1 and operand2 are both specified, operand1 must precede operand2.

The order in which options are specified is usually not important. After the left parenthesis that separates operands from options, options may appear in any order.

Example:

The following syntax indicates the order in which you specify the filename, filetype and filemode as operands:

    fn ft fm

This indicates that:

- The filename must be first.

- The filetype must be second.

- The filemode must be third.

Using Square Brackets to Indicate an Operand is Optional

Some commands that use a file's filename, filetype and filemode as operands represent the fileid as:

    fn ft [fm]

This indicates that specifying the filemode, which corresponds to the disk on which the file is stored, is optional.

Nesting Operands to Indicate Dependencies between Them

If one operand enclosed in brackets is *nested* within another operand that is also enclosed in brackets, the outer operand must be specified if the inner operand is specified:

    [operand1 [operand2]]

This indicates that:

- Both operands are optional.

- If **operand2** is specified, **operand1** must also be specified.

Example:

Some commands that use a file's filename, filetype and filemode as operands represent the fileid as:

[fn   [ft   [fm]]]

This indicates that:

- Specifying any part of the fileid is optional.

- If the filemode is specified, the filetype must also be specified.

- If the filetype is specified, the filename must also be specified.

Alternative Operands

Many commands have operands that are *alternatives* to each other, that is, you may specify one of the operands *or* another, but only one can be specified.

A vertical bar | between two operands indicates that the operands are alternatives to each other:

- When choosing one of the alternatives is *optional*, the alternatives are enclosed in brackets with the default alternative appearing in *bold italics*:

  [*operand1*|operand2]

  The **default alternative** is automatically implemented if you don't specify one. You only need to specify an alternative if it is not the default alternative. Thus, if neither operand1 or operand2 is specified and operand1 appears in bold italics, operand1 takes effect. The default mode of a command's operation is how that command operates in the absence of any modifying operands.

- When choosing one of the alternatives is *mandatory*, the alternatives are not enclosed in brackets:

  operand1|operand2

  You *must* specify one of the alternatives. Otherwise, the system will display an error message and the command will not be executed.

Example:

ON and OFF are often alternative operands that either engage or disengage some function.

- When choosing one of the alternatives is mandatory, they are presented as:

Command Syntax   §   9

ON|OFF

- When choosing one of the alternatives is optional and ON is the default, they are presented as:

[ON|OFF]

Example:

FILELIST is a CMS command that displays a list of the files on any disk to which you have access. You can then work with a file by entering the appropriate command next to the file.[2] The following syntax indicates how you specify which fileids are to be included in the list:

FILELIst   [fn|* [ft|* [fm|*A]]]

This indicates that:

- Specifying any part of the fileid is optional. If the fileid is omitted:

  - The filemode is assumed to be A.[3]

  - The filetype is assumed to be * which means *all* filetypes.

  - The filename is assumed to be * which means *all* filenames.

- If the filemode is omitted, is assumed to be A. If the filemode is specified, the filetype must also be specified.

- If the filetype is omitted, it is assumed to be * which means *all* filetypes. If the filetype is specified, the filename must also be specified.

- If the filename is omitted, it is assumed to be * which means *all* filenames.

Notice that:

```
FILELIST fn ft A    is equivalent to    FILELIST fn ft
FILELIST fn  * A    is equivalent to    FILELIST fn
FILELIST  *  * A    is equivalent to    FILELIST
```

---

[2] If you enter the FILELIST command and want to leave the FILELIST display, either press the PF3 key or type in QUIT after the arrow at the bottom of the screen and press ENTER.

[3] Each user has a disk, known to CMS as his A-disk, on which files can be stored.

10 § A Conceptual Overview of VM/CMS

The Importance of Blanks in Commands

Blank characters, typed by pressing the space bar, are important in entering commands. While a blank may appear to be nothing, it is a character that serves the important function of separating command names from operands and operands from each other.

- At least one space must separate the command name from the first operand.

- At least one space must separate each operand from the next.

- At least one space must separate each option from the next.

- If options are specified, spaces are optional between the last operand and the left parenthesis and between the left parenthesis and the first option.

Abbreviating Commands

Uppercase characters indicate the shortest possible abbreviation of a command name or operand.

Example:

In the previous example with FILELIST, notice also that FILEL, FILELI and FILELIS are all valid abbreviations for FILELIST.

Chapter 2
Accessing and Leaving VM/CMS

Introduction

To use VM/CMS, you must arrange to have an account set up on the system for you. There is a CMS system administrator in your organization who is responsible for setting up new accounts and making changes to existing accounts. Determine who this person is and request an account from him.

When your account is set up, you should receive:

- A Userid
- A Logon Password
- A System Name

When you go to access the system for the first time, be sure that you know your userid, your password and the name of the system to which you've been assigned. You'll find that accessing the system for the first time will be considerably easier if you have the assistance of someone who is already familiar with doing so.

The Userid

The userid is a name, such as CHASE, that identifies your account on the system. A userid is *public* in that anyone using the system can find out what other userids are currently using the system.

The Logon Password

The password is a string of characters, such as 10USNE1, that is required to use your account. A logon password is *private* in that it should only be known to those authorized to use the account and to those who administer the system. By keeping your password secret, you can restrict access to your account, since only those who know both your userid and password can use your account.

The System Name

The system name is the name of the VM/CMS system to which you've been assigned. The system name may only be necessary if you are part of an organization with more than one computing system. If this is the case, you may have to specify, at some point, the name of the system you want to use.

2.1 Communicating with VM/CMS

The usual means of communicating with VM/CMS is through a video display terminal. While many different types of terminals can be used with VM/CMS, this text will only discuss the use of those that can be used as **display terminals**. The IBM 3275, 3276, 3277, 3278, 3279, 3179 and 3192 terminals, hereafter referred to as **IBM display terminals**, are examples of display terminals. Display terminals have **full-screen** capabilities whereby a user can enter and edit text in any permissible input area and then send all new and edited text to be processed as a whole when the ENTER key is pressed. This mode of communicating with a computer system differs from that, typical of ASCII terminals, in which each character is sent to the computer as it is typed on the keyboard.

All video display terminals have at least two parts in common:

- A keyboard to enter characters.

- A video screen to display the characters.

The Keyboard

The keyboard enables you to send a command to the system:

1. Type the command on the keyboard.

2. Press the ENTER key.

While the terminal keyboard *resembles* that of an ordinary typewriter, there are important differences.

The following keys function in the same way on a terminal keyboard as they do on a standard typewriter keyboard:

- Lowercase letters a − z.

- Uppercase letters A − Z.

- Numbers 0 − 9.

- Special characters such as , . / ´ ; * ( ).

- Space bar.

- Shift and shift lock keys.

The following are keys that you'll find on the keyboard of a display terminal but not on a typewriter. They are discussed in more detail in the next chapter.

- **Cursor Movement keys** enable you to move the cursor. Four of these keys usually have arrows on them indicating the direction the cursor is moved when the key is pressed.

- **Program Function (PF) keys** execute commands assigned to them.

- **Edit Control keys** enable you to edit text in any input area using the cursor.

- **Program Attention (PA) keys** execute commands assigned to them.

- **Terminal Management keys** enable you to control what is displayed on the screen.

The Screen

The video screen displays the commands you type on the keyboard and the results of those commands when they are executed. The video screen on most terminals displays 24 lines with 80 columns in each line. There is a small illuminated object on the screen called the **cursor** which shows where the next character will be displayed on the screen. The cursor normally appears as the underscore (_) character or as a small rectangle.

2.2 ASCII Terminals

An ASCII terminal is a type of terminal that conforms to the standards of the **American Standard Code for Information Interchange (ASCII)**. One of those standards is the character set used by ASCII terminals. The character set used by VM/CMS is known as **Extended Binary Coded Decimal Interchange Code (EBCDIC)**. All printable ASCII characters have a corresponding EBCDIC character except two:[1]

- The EBCDIC cent (¢) usually displays as the ASCII backslash (\).

- The EBCDIC logical not (¬) usually displays as the ASCII caret (/\).

ASCII terminals differ from display terminals in several significant ways but many ASCII terminals can be made to *emulate* display terminals by a device known as an **ASCII Controller** which is located between the ASCII terminal and the VM/CMS system. The ASCII Controller functions to make a specific ASCII terminal *emulate* an IBM display terminal by tailoring the characteristics of an IBM display terminal to those of the specific ASCII terminal.

ASCII terminals can differ widely among themselves in various ways:

- The characters supported.

- Keyboard organization.

- How actions are effected on the screen.

- The number of special function keys provided.

If you are using an ASCII terminal, consult with either those who support your system or someone who is familiar with the type of terminal you are using to find out:

- The name that identifies your terminal type to the ASCII controller.

- How your terminal type is used to emulate a IBM display terminal.

On an ASCII terminal, there are three important keys not found on the keyboard of a display terminal:

- CTRL

- ESC

- RETURN

CTRL is like a special shift key. It is used in conjunction with another key to override that key's usual meaning and give it a new meaning. The CTRL key

---

[1] The ASCII characters used to represent EBCDIC characters is somewhat system dependent. On an IBM 9370, the EBCDIC backslash and caret default to the ASCII backslash and caret.

is used frequently on ASCII terminals to perform the functions of special purpose keys, such as the edit control keys on IBM display terminals. For example, pressing the CTRL and M keys simultaneously is equivalent to pressing
the ENTER key.

ESC is like a special shift key. It is also used in conjunction with another key
to override that key's usual meaning and give it a new meaning. The ESC key
is used frequently on ASCII terminals to perform the functions of special purpose keys, such as the edit control keys on IBM display terminals.

RETURN serves the same function as the ENTER key on an IBM display terminal.

2.3 Using a Personal Computer as a Terminal

You can use a personal computer as a display terminal if you have:

- Terminal Emulation Software

- A Modem

- A Serial Port

Terminal emulation software enables the PC to imitate a specific type of terminal. There are many terminal emulation programs available both commercially and in the public domain. The software you should obtain depends on the types of ASCII terminals supported on your system. Contact those who support your system and ask what software they recommend for terminal emulation.

A modem is a device that sends and receives data over ordinary telephone lines. The telephone system sends audio signals whereas computer communications are in binary digits. The modem converts transmissions of binary digits into audio signals and audio signals into binary digits.

A serial port is an accessory that enables the PC to send data to and receive it from other devices.

2.4 Connecting to the System

The way that you access VM/CMS depends on the type of terminal that you are using and how it is connected to the system. Accessing the system from an ASCII terminal is different than from an IBM display terminal. If you are using an ASCII terminal, you may have to go through one or more intermediate steps, such as:

- Specifying the computer system you want to use.

- Specifying the type of terminal you are using.

Regardless of what type of terminal you are using, begin by turning on the power to the terminal.

Using an IBM Display Terminal

If you are using an IBM display terminal, you should see a display that identifies the system as **VM** after the terminal warms up. Clear this display by pressing the ENTER key. You are ready to log on when the system displays the message:[2]

```
Enter one of the following commands:

    LOGON userid        (Example:  LOGON VMUSER1)
    DIAL userid         (Example:  DIAL VMUSER2)
    LOGOFF
```

The system might also display a message in the lower right corner of the screen:

```
CP READ
```

Using an ASCII Terminal

Many computing facilities have more than one type of computing system available. In fact, it's not uncommon to have not only different *types* of systems but also several systems of the same type. When this is the case, it is obviously more convenient for a user to be able to access *any* one of these different systems from the same terminal than having to have a different terminal to access each system or even type of system. If you are at such a facility, you may find that the terminal you are using is an ASCII terminal and that when you turn your terminal on, a message appears asking you to specify the *computer system* you wish to use. At this time, you should type in the name that identifies your VM/CMS system and then press the RETURN or ENTER key. If

---

[2] Some systems may present you with a panel to enter your userid and password.

there is no message, contact those who support your system and ask about the correct procedure for connecting to the system.

IBM display terminals are connected to the VM/CMS system through a different kind of controller than ASCII terminals. Because ASCII terminals differ from each other, the ASCII Controller will display a message requesting that you enter the type of terminal that you are using. At this time, you should enter the type of terminal you are using and press ENTER or RETURN. If you don't know what type of terminal you are using or don't know how to specify the type, ask someone who is familiar with the terminal and the system.

Once you've entered a recognized terminal type, you should see a display that somehow identifies the system as **VM**. Clear this display by pressing the ENTER key. You are ready to log on when the system displays the message:

```
Enter one of the following commands:

    LOGON userid          (Example:  LOGON VMUSER1)
    DIAL userid           (Example:  DIAL VMUSER2)
    LOGOFF
```

The system might also display a message in the lower right corner of the screen:

```
    CP READ
```

2.5 Logging On: Accessing the System

The procedure by which you identify yourself to the system is referred to as logging in or logging on. Logging on is a two step process:

1. Entering your userid.

2. Entering your password.

Entering Your Userid

LOGON is the command you use to enter your userid. Type in the word LOGON followed by your userid and press the ENTER key.

Command Format:

> **Logon**   **userid**

where **userid**   is your userid.

System Messages:

If you do not enter your userid correctly, the system displays the message:

        DMKLOG053E userid NOT IN CP DIRECTORY

If this should happen, enter the LOGON command again, correctly specifying your userid.

Example:

Suppose your userid is CHASE. To access the system, type in the LOGON command followed by CHASE and press ENTER. Since LOGON can be abbreviated as L, the following are equivalent:

        LOGON CHASE
        L CHASE

Entering Your Password

Once you enter your userid correctly, the system requests that you enter your password:

        ENTER PASSWORD (IT WILL NOT APPEAR WHEN TYPED):

Type in your password and press the ENTER key. Your password will not be displayed on the screen as you type it on the keyboard. This is a security precaution to prevent someone else from seeing your password.

System Messages:

- If you enter your password incorrectly, the system displays the message:

```
DMKLOG050E LOGON UNSUCCESSFUL--INCORRECT PASSWORD
```

  If this should happen, you must enter *both* the LOGON command and the password again.

- The system does not allow a userid to be logged on more than once at the same time. Consequently, if someone else is currently using your userid, or if you've left yourself logged on elsewhere, the system will display the message:

```
DMKLOG054F ALREADY LOGGED ON.
```

  - If you share your userid with someone and that person is currently logged on, you can use the CP MESSAGE command, discussed in the chapter *Communicating with Other Computer Users*, to send him a message requesting that he log off the account so you can use it.

  - If your userid is being used by someone not authorized to do so, contact those who administer your system and change your password as soon as possible.

- When you enter your password correctly, you are logged onto the system and the log message is displayed. The parts of the log message and their significance are discussed in the section *The Log Mes-*

```
LOGON CHASE
ENTER PASSWORD

LOGMSG - 11:44:37 PST MONDAY 02/08/88
*
* The system will be down on Saturday 02/13/88 for routine maintenance.
*
FILES: 001 RDR, NO PRT, NO PUN
LOGON AT 13:00:14 TUESDAY 02/09/88

VM/SP CMS RELEASE 5




                                                      VM READ
```

Figure 2.1 The screen layout when logging on.

sage at the end of this chapter. Figure 2.1 shows the screen as it might appear when the userid CHASE logs on. If the log message should fill the screen, the lower right corner of the screen will display the message:

MORE...

Press the CLEAR key to continue.

2.6 Loading CMS into Virtual Memory

Most systems automatically load CMS into virtual memory for you when you log on. After you've logged onto the system, check the message displayed in the lower right corner of the screen.

- Your system automatically loads CMS if one of these messages is displayed:

  ```
  VM READ
  RUNNING
  MORE...
  ```

- Your system may not load CMS if this message is displayed:

  ```
  CP READ
  ```

  You must load CMS by entering the command:

  ```
  IPL CMS
  ```

  The message in the corner should change to one of these:

  ```
  VM READ
  RUNNING
  MORE...
  ```

The messages displayed in the lower right corner of the screen are discussed in the section *The Areas of the Screen and Their Uses in CP and CMS* in the next chapter.

Your First Command

Once CMS is loaded into virtual memory, you are ready to enter your first command.

1.   Type in the command:

     ```
     MSG * ARE WE HAVING FUN YET?
     ```

2.   Press ENTER or RETURN.

2.7 Logging Off: Leaving the System

The procedure by which you leave the system is referred to as logging out or logging off.

LOGOFF (**LOGout** is a synonym) is the CP command that you should normally use to leave the system when you've finished your work.

You should *not* end a session by simply turning the terminal off. If you do so, you may find that your VM remains logged on but you are unable to communicate with it from the terminal. Usually when this happens, CP automatically logs your VM off the system. Under unusual circumstances, however, your VM can remain logged on indefinitely, incurring charges for connect time. If this should happen, contact those who support your system and request that your userid be forced off the system.

Command Format:

LOGoff   **[HOld]**

where **HOld**   retains the connection between the terminal and the system. If **HOLD** is omitted, the connection is dropped. This option is convenient if you are accessing the system through a dial-up and you plan to log onto the system again soon because then the connection is held and you don't have to dial the phone number again.

System Messages:

The system responds to the LOGOFF command by displaying a message which includes:

- The date and time when you are leaving the system.

- How long you were logged onto the system (connect time).

- How much virtual CPU time you used.

- How much total CPU time you used.

Message Format:

      LOGOFF AT time zone weekday date
      CONNECT=ctime VIRTCPU=vtime TOTCPU=ttime

where **ctime**   is the amount of time you were connected to the system. The time is expressed in the format **hours:minutes:seconds**.

vtime	is the amount of virtual CPU time you used. The time is expressed in the format **minutes:seconds.hundredths of seconds**.
ttime	is the total CPU time you used. The time is expressed in the format **minutes:seconds.hundredths of seconds**.

Exercise:

If you are currently logged onto the system, use LOGOFF to leave it:

```
LOGOFF   HOLD
```

2.8 The Log Message

The log message is a message displayed to anyone logging onto the system.

The Date and Time the Log Message was Last Updated

The first line of the log message displays the date and time the log message was last updated.

Message Format:

>   **LOGMSG - time zone weekday date**

where **time**   is the time of day on a 24 hour clock in the format **hours:minutes:seconds**.

      zone   is the time zone in which the computing system is located.

      weekday   is the day of the week.

      date   is the month, day and year in the format **month/day/year**.

Example:

In Figure 2.1, the log message was last updated on February 8, 1988 at 11:44 AM.

The Body of the Log Message

Next, the body of the log message appears. It includes information about:

- When the system is scheduled to be unavailable.
- New products that are available.
- Any changes to old products.
- Any problems that system users should be aware of.
- Any other information that is relevant to using the system.

The Spool Files in Your Virtual Devices

After the body of the log message, the system displays information about any spool files residing in your virtual devices.

Message Format:

FILES: **n RDR   n PRT   n PUN**

where **n**   indicates the number of spool files in each device. If **n** is 0, the word NO is substituted for **n**.

RDR   is the virtual reader.

PRT   is the virtual printer.

PUN   is the virtual punch.

Example:

In Figure 2.1, there is one file in the virtual reader, no files in the virtual printer and no files in the virtual punch.

The Time and Date of Your Logon

Finally, the system displays the actual date and time that you are logging on.

Message Format:

LOGON AT time zone weekday date

where **time**   is the time of day on a 24—hour clock in the format **hours:minutes:seconds**.

zone   is the time zone in which the computing system is located.

weekday   is the day of the week the logon is taking place.

date   is the date in the format **month/day/year**.

Example:

In Figure 2.1, the logon is taking place on Tuesday February 8, 1988 at 1:00 PM.

Chapter 3
Becoming Acquainted with VM/CMS

Introduction

The VM/CMS system is *conversational*:

- You communicate with VM/CMS by entering commands that it recognizes.

- VM/CMS communicates with you by displaying system messages.

The system's response to one of your commands depends on whether the command is executed successfully:

- If the command executes successfully, the system displays a response known as the ready message to indicate that it is ready for your next command.

- If the command cannot be executed, the system displays an error message describing the problem, followed by the ready message.

It is **very important** that you pay close attention to the system's response to your commands. If you make a mistake, the system's response to that mistake is usually diagnostic of what you've done wrong and what you must do to redress the problem.

You continue to enter commands until you've finished your work. Such a system is contrasted with a **batch** system, in which you submit *all* the commands at once to be processed when the system has sufficient resources available. The batch system then schedules the running of your job according to the availability of the system resources your job requests. Depending on the availability of these resources, your job may be processed immediately or it may be processed hours later.

3.1 Environments in VM/CMS

From a practical standpoint, the VM/CMS system consists of three basic environments:[1]

- The CP Environment

- The CMS Environment

- The XEDIT Environment

While each environment has its own set of commands which it recognizes, there is a hierarchical relationship between the environments, represented in Figure 3.1, that determines what happens to a command that is not recognized in the environment in which it is entered:

- In the CP environment, *only* CP commands are recognized. If you enter any command other than a CP command in the CP environment, CP displays a message indicating that the command is not a CP command:

  Unknown CP Command

- In the CMS environment, CMS executes CMS commands and normally[2] sends unrecognized commands to CP. If the command is a CP command, CP will attempt to execute it. If CP does not recognize the command, CMS displays a message indicating that the command is neither a CP or CMS command:

  Unknown CP/CMS Command

- In the XEDIT environment, XEDIT executes XEDIT commands and normally[3] sends unrecognized commands to CMS. If CMS recognizes the command, CMS executes it. If CMS does not recognize the command, it sends it to CP. If CP does not recognize the command, XEDIT displays a message indicating that the command is not a CP, CMS or XEDIT command:

  No Such Subcommand

---

[1] Applications running on VM/CMS, such as ISPF, may afford other environments.

[2] *Normal*, in the context, refers to the default setting of the IMPCP function of the CMS SET command, which determines whether CMS sends unrecognized commands to CP.

[3] *Normal*, in this context, refers to the default setting of the IMPCMSCP function of the XEDIT SET command, which determines whether XEDIT sends unrecognized commands to CMS.

Determining Which Environment You are In

The environment your VM is in is indicated by the status message displayed in the lower right corner of the screen.

- The status messages displayed in the CP and CMS environments are discussed in the next section, *The Areas of the Screen and Their Uses in CP and CMS*.

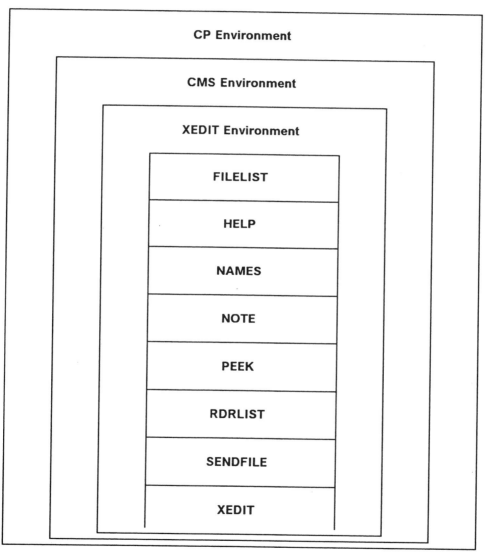

Figure 3.1. Environments in VM/CMS.

- The status messages displayed in the XEDIT environment are discussed in the section *The Areas of the Screen and Their Uses in XEDIT* in the chapter *Becoming Acquainted with XEDIT*.

When you are using VM/CMS, it is important that you know which environment your VM is in because **the environment you are in determines**:

- *Which* commands are recognized.

- *How* commands should be entered to be recognized.

3.2 The Areas of the Screen and Their Uses in CP and CMS

In the CP and CMS environments, the screen is divided into three parts:

- The Command Input Area

- The Output Display Area

- The Status Message Area

Each of these areas serves a special function explained below. Figure 3.2 shows the locations of these three areas.

The Command Input Area

The command input area is the two lines at the bottom of the screen. The cursor is automatically positioned in the first column of the first of these two lines. This is the area where you enter CP and CMS commands. If a command is longer than the 80 columns in the first of the two lines, continue it on the second line up to but not into the status message area. *Do not enter commands any place other than the command input area.* The other areas of the screen are **protected areas**, which means that if you try to enter *anything* in either the output display area or the status message area, the keyboard will lock to prohibit you from doing so and the terminal may sound an alarm. If necessary, use the RESET key to unlock the keyboard.

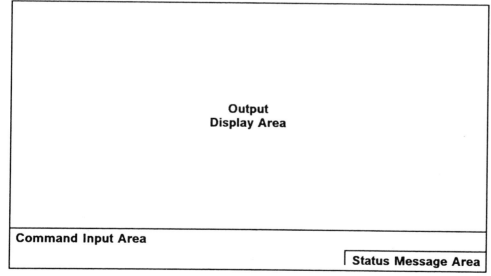

**Output
Display Area**

Command Input Area

Status Message Area

Figure 3.2 The three areas of the terminal display in the CP and CMS environments.

The Areas of the Screen and Their Uses in CP and CMS § 33

The Output Display Area

The output display area is the area above the command line. This is where the system displays the results of commands. Remember that this area is protected so you cannot write on this part of the screen. Demonstrate this to yourself by moving the cursor to anywhere in this area and trying to type something.

The Status Message Area

The status message area is the lower right corner of the screen. This is the area in which the system status message is displayed. The **status message** indicates the environment your VM is in and what it is doing. This information can be useful if you make a mistake or otherwise run into difficulties.

These are the status messages and their meanings:

VM READ indicates that:

- You are in the CMS environment.

- CMS is waiting for you to enter either a command or a response to a command.

- Messages from other users, responses from commands just issued but not yet completed and output from programs are *not* displayed until the status is changed to RUNNING, which can be done by either entering a command or pressing the ENTER key without a command.

RUNNING indicates that:

- You are in the CMS environment.

- CMS is either working on something or waiting for you to enter a command.

- If you've just entered a command, the results of that command will appear in the output display area as soon as the command is completed.

- If another user sends you a message, the message will appear in the output display area as soon as it is received.

MORE... indicates that:

- You are in the CMS environment.

- The output display area is full and there is more information to be displayed.

- The next screen will *automatically* be displayed in 60 seconds.

- ▪ To clear the output display area and display the next screen of information, press the CLEAR key or PA2 key.[4]

- ▪ To *hold* the present screen and not have the next screen displayed, press the ENTER key. The status message will then change to HOLDING.

HOLDING indicates that:

- • You are in the CMS environment.

- • The output display area is full and there is more information to be displayed.

- • The present display will be held *indefinitely*.

  - ▪ To clear the present screen and display the next one, press the CLEAR key or PA2 key.

  - ▪ To change the status message to MORE..., press the ENTER key.

CP READ indicates that:

- • You are in the CP environment.

- • CP is waiting for you to enter a command.

  - ▪ If you are in the process of logging on, CP is waiting for you to enter your userid or password.

  - ▪ If you have already logged on, you can enter the CMS environment either by entering BEGIN or IPL CMS. The difference between these commands will be discussed later.

NOT ACCEPTED indicates that:

- • You are in the CMS environment.

- • The command you just entered was not accepted because the terminal buffer is full. When the system is ready for another command, the status message changes to RUNNING.

---

[4] The CLEAR key and PA2 key may not be labeled as such. Contact those who support your system to determine which keys function as such).

The Areas of the Screen and Their Uses in CP and CMS § 35

3.3 The CP Environment

The CP environment is used to perform various kinds of tasks:

- Obtain system status information such as:

    - Whether a file has been printed yet.

    - How heavily the system is being used.

    - Who else is using the system.

- Obtain VM status information such as:

    - Whether there are files in any of your virtual devices.

    - Which disks you are currently linked to.

    - The current size of your virtual storage.

- Change the configuration of your VM in ways such as:

    - Increasing your virtual memory.

    - Accessing another user's minidisk.

    - Accessing a temporary minidisk.

    - Changing the way virtual printer files are handled.

- Manage the resources of the real machine.

Entering the CP Environment

You initially enter the CP environment when you log onto the system.

After you've logged on, you can also enter the CP environment from either the CMS or XEDIT environments with the command:

CP

When executing a CP command, always remember that *you do not have to be in the CP environment to execute a CP command*. Since XEDIT sends unrecognized commands to CMS and CMS sends unrecognized commands to CP, you can enter a CP command from either the CMS or XEDIT environments and CP will eventually try to execute the command.[5]

---

[5] Special precautions are necessary, however, if the CP command has the same name as a command recognized in the environment in which it is entered. For more information, refer to the sections on *Controlling Command Interpretation and Execution* in the chapters *Customizing the XEDIT Environment* and *Customizing the CP/CMS Environment*.

If you should enter the CP environment from CMS or XEDIT:

- You can return to the environment from which you entered CP, *continuing* what you were doing before, with your VM configured as it was before entering CP with the command:

  BEGIN

- You can enter the CMS environment, *terminating* whatever you were doing prior to entering CP, by loading the CMS operating system into virtual memory again, discussed next.

3.4 The CMS Environment

The CMS environment is used to perform these kinds of tasks:

- Working with files.

- Compiling, debugging and executing programs.

- Formatting documents.

- Communicating with other system users.

Entering the CMS Environment

You enter the CMS environment when the CMS operating system is loaded into virtual memory by a process called an **Initial Program Load (IPL)**. Most systems perform an **automatic IPL**, which means that CMS is *automatically* loaded after you've logged on. Exceptions to this will be discussed later. To determine whether your system performs an automatic IPL, examine the status message in the lower right corner of the screen after you've logged on.

- Systems that perform an automatic IPL display one of these status messages:

```
VM READ
RUNNING
MORE...
HOLDING
NOT ACCEPTED
```

- Systems that do not perform an automatic IPL display the status message:

```
CP READ
```

IPL (Initial Program Load) is the CP command that configures your VM according to the entry for your VM in the CP User Directory and loads CMS into virtual memory. On systems that do not perform an automatic IPL, you must explicitly execute the IPL command to enter the CMS environment.

Command Format:

    IPL   **CMS**

The PROFILE EXEC

An important part of the process of loading CMS is the execution of a special program that assists in defining your CMS environment by executing commands that perform the kinds of tasks that are normally carried out each time you log on, such as:

- Defining the characteristics of your virtual console.

- Defining the characteristics of your VM.

- Assigning commands to program function keys.

- Accessing disks that belong to you.

- Accessing disks that belong to other users that you're authorized to access.

The program is stored in a file called PROFILE EXEC. The PROFILE EXEC is special in that the commands in it are executed automatically as part of an IPL CMS command. Don't tamper with this file until you know what you're doing. The PROFILE EXEC is discussed in more detail in the chapter *Customizing the CP/CMS Environments*.

3.5 The XEDIT Environment

The XEDIT environment is used to create new files and make changes to existing files. XEDIT is also responsible for controlling the FILELIST, HELP, NOTE, PEEK, RDRLIST and SENDFILE commands, to be discussed later. Since these commands are controlled by XEDIT, you have many of the capabilities of XEDIT at your disposal when using them. The XEDIT environment is discussed in detail in Chapters 5 through 8.

Entering the XEDIT Environment

The usual way of entering the XEDIT environment is by entering the XEDIT command specifying the name of a new file to be created or an existing file to be changed. If the file to be edited already exists, XEDIT reads a copy of the file from disk into virtual storage, which is a temporary storage area. All changes to the file are made to the copy in virtual storage. To make the changes permanent, you must write the copy in virtual storage to disk.

The XEDIT environment is also entered when you use one of the commands controlled by XEDIT such as FILELIST, HELP, NOTE, PEEK, RDRLIST and SENDFILE.

3.6 The Cursor and Cursor Movement Keys

The cursor is a small illuminated object that shows where the next character will be displayed on the screen. As characters are entered, the cursor moves to the right. When the cursor reaches the end of a line, it then moves to the first column of the next line.

The shape of the cursor depends on the type of terminal that you are using. On many terminals, the cursor appears as an underscore (_) character. On other terminals, the cursor appears as a small rectangle.

Moving the Cursor

It is frequently necessary to move the cursor from one location on the screen to another. This is done by means of **cursor movement keys** which move the cursor in several different ways. Four of the cursor movement keys usually have arrows on them. The arrow on each key indicates the direction in which the cursor is moved when the key is pressed.

The *functions* performed by cursor movement keys are discussed next. The *actual key* that performs a given function usually depends on the type of terminal that you are using. Consult with those who support your system to determine which keys actually perform the various cursor movement functions on the type of terminal that you are using. If you are using an IBM display terminal, refer to the IBM publication *Terminal Reference (GC19-6206)* for complete information about the cursor movement keys. Once you determine which key performs each cursor movement function on your type of terminal, write it into Table 3.1 for future reference.

Cursor Up   moves the cursor up one column each time you press the key. The key that performs this function is usually labeled by an arrow that points up: ↑

Cursor Down   moves the cursor down one column each time you press the key. The key that performs this function is usually labeled by an arrow that points down: ↓

Cursor Left   moves the cursor to the left one column each time you press the key. The key that performs this function is usually labeled by an arrow that points left: ←

Cursor Right   moves the cursor to the right one column each time you press the key. The key that performs this function is usually labeled by an arrow that points right: →

Tab Forward   moves the cursor to the first column of the *next* input area. The key that performs this function is often labeled by a right arrow pointing at a vertical bar: →|

The Cursor and Cursor Movement Keys § 41

Tab Backward   moves the cursor to the first column of the *present* input area if the cursor was not originally in the first column. If the cursor was originally in the first column, the cursor moves to the first column of the *previous* input area. The key that performs this function is often labeled by a left arrow pointing at a vertical bar: |←

New Line   moves the cursor to the first column of the next unprotected line. The key that performs this function is often labeled by a vertical bar with an arrow at its base that points to the left: ←|

Home   moves the cursor to the first column of the first unprotected area on the screen.

Exercise:

One by one, experiment with each of the cursor movement keys in order to become facile in moving the cursor.

1. Press each key *once* to see how the cursor moves.

2. Press each key several times in succession.

3. Hold each key down and observe the cursor's movement. Notice where it reappears if it goes off the edge of the screen.

4. When the cursor is not in the command input area, press ENTER to move the cursor from wherever it is on the screen to the first column of the command input area.

Cursor Movement Key Assignments

Function Performed	Key Assigned	Function Performed	Key Assigned
Cursor Left		Cursor Right	
Cursor Up		Cursor Down	
Tab Forward		Tab Backward	
New Line		Home	

Edit Control Key Assignments

Function Performed	Key Assigned	Function Performed	Key Assigned
Delete Character		Erase EOF	
Enter Insert Mode		Leave Insert Mode	
Erase Input Areas		Reset	

Program Function Key Assignments

Function Performed	Key Assigned	Function Performed	Key Assigned	Function Performed	Key Assigned
PF1		PF9		PF17	
PF2		PF10		PF18	
PF3		PF11		PF19	
PF4		PF12		PF20	
PF5		PF13		PF21	
PF6		PF14		PF22	
PF7		PF15		PF23	
PF8		PF16		PF24	

Program Attention Key Assignments

Function Performed	Key Assigned	Function Performed	Key Assigned	Function Performed	Key Assigned
PA1		PA2		PA3	

Table 3.1 The correspondence between display terminal functions and the actual keys that perform those functions. Once you determine the actual key that performs each function, write that key into the table for future reference.

3.7 Editing Text with the Edit Control Keys

Edit control keys enable you to edit text in *any* valid input area using the cursor. These keys allow you to:

- Delete a character.

- Delete characters from the cursor to the end of the line.

- Clear input areas.

- Insert characters between others.

- Type over characters.

Unlike the line editing symbols, discussed later, you cannot change the settings of these keys.

To edit text with an edit control key:

1. Use the cursor movement keys to move the cursor to the area of the screen where text is to be changed.

2. Use the appropriate edit control key.

The remainder of this section discusses the **functions** performed by the edit control keys. The **actual key** that performs a specific function depends on the type of terminal you are using. Contact those who support your system to determine which keys perform each edit control function on the type of terminal that you are using. If you are using an IBM display terminal, refer to the IBM publication *Terminal Reference (GC19-6206)* for more information about the edit control keys. Once you determine which key performs each editing function on your type of terminal, write that key into Table 3.1 for future reference.

Deleting a Character

DELETE CHARACTER removes the character under which the cursor is placed.[6] When a character is deleted, the characters to the right of the cursor are shifted to the left. On an IBM display terminal, the key that performs this function is usually labeled DEL but may also be labeled by a lowercase 'a' with a crooked line through it.

Exercise:

1. Type the FILELIST command in the command input area with a space between FILE and LIST:

---

[6] If the cursor on your terminal displays as a rectangle instead of an underscore, superimpose the cursor on the character rather than placing it under the character.

FILE LIST

2. Move the cursor between the letter E and the letter L:

FILE_LIST

3. Press the key that performs the DELETE CHARACTER function once to remove the space and again to remove the letter L.

Deleting Characters from the Cursor to the End of the Line

ERASE EOF (**EOF** stands for **End Of Field**) deletes all characters on a line from the cursor to the end of the current input field. This is a convenient way to erase part of a line. On an IBM display terminal, the key that performs this function is labeled ERASE EOF.

Exercise:

1. Type the FILELIST command in the command input area.

2. Move the cursor under the second I:

FILELIST

3. Press the key that performs the ERASE EOF function.

Clearing Input Areas

ERASE INPUT clears *all* input areas on the screen.

- In the CP and CMS environments, this key clears the command input area. This is convenient if you decide that you no longer want to execute a command that you've begun to type in.

- In the XEDIT environment, this key clears the command input area, the file area and the prefix area. The contents of the screen that were cleared were not, however, erased from the file, they were simply cleared from the screen. To display again that which was cleared, press the CLEAR key.

On IBM display terminals the key that performs this function is labeled ERASE INPUT.

Exercise:

1. Type the FILELIST command in the command input area.

2. Press the key that performs the ERASE INPUT function.

Inserting Characters between Others

INSERT MODE puts your terminal into insert mode, which allows you to insert new characters *between* existing contiguous characters. When you are in insert mode, if you place the cursor under a character and then begin typing in new characters, the characters to the right of the cursor are pushed to the right without being replaced. If you try to push the right-most of the preexisting characters past the end of the input area, the keyboard will lock to prohibit you from doing so and the terminal may sound an alarm. If necessary, use the RESET key to unlock the keyboard. On IBM display terminals the key that performs this function is usually labeled INS MODE but may also be labeled by a lowercase 'a' with a caret over it.

Exercise:

1. Type the FILELIST command in the command input area.

2. Move the cursor under the second I:

    FILEL̲IST

3. Press the key that switches your terminal to insert mode.

4. Press the space bar one or more times.

5. Remove the space(s) with the key that performs the DELETE CHARACTER function.

Overstriking: Typing over Characters

END INSERT removes your terminal from insert mode, allowing you to type over and replace characters. While in insert mode, the character under the cursor and to its right are pushed to the right as new characters are entered. To type over and replace the characters, you must end insert mode. On IBM display terminals, the key that performs this function is labeled RESET.

Exercise:

1. Type the FILELIST command in the command input area.

2. Move the cursor under the second I:

    FILEL̲IST

3. Assuming you are in insert mode, press the key that switches your terminal out of insert mode.

4. Press the space bar one or more times.

3.8 Executing CP and CMS Commands

To **execute a command**, you must normally do two things:

1. Type the command on the keyboard.

2. Press the ENTER key.

Be sure that you enter commands in the command input area. If you attempt to enter one anywhere else on the screen, the keyboard will lock to prohibit you from doing so and the terminal may sound an alarm. If necessary, use the RESET key to unlock the keyboard.

Enter commands in either uppercase or lowercase. Commands entered in lowercase are converted to uppercase.

Entering Successive Commands

Once you enter a command, you do not have to wait for it to complete before enter another command. Commands entered before the command now executing has completed are stored in the **terminal buffer**, which is a temporary storage area of a limited capacity. As soon as the command now executing is completed, commands in the terminal buffer are executed on a first-in first-out (FIFO) basis. If you try to enter more commands than the terminal buffer can accommodate, however, the system displays the status message:

        NOT ACCEPTED

When the system is ready for another command, the status message will change to:

        RUNNING

Null Lines

If you press the ENTER key without typing a command, you enter a null line which has these special meanings:

*   If you enter a null line when the status message is RUNNING, the status message changes to VM READ.

*   If you enter a null line when the status message is VM READ, the status message changes to RUNNING and the system indicates that you are in the CMS environment by displaying the message:

        CMS

- If you enter a null line when the status message is CP READ, the status message remains unchanged but the system displays the message:

```
CP
```

Forcing CP to Execute a Command Immediately

#CP is a special CP command that tells CP to execute the command that follows it *immediately, regardless* of any other command that is being executed.

Command Format:

      #CP   **[command]**

where **#**   is the character normally defined to be the logical line end character. If another character is defined to be the logical line end, use it instead.

      command   is a CP command to be executed. If the command is omitted, your VM enters the CP environment.

Examples:

- Suppose you've started a program running that is going to take a long time to complete and you want to do something else in the meantime, such as log onto another userid and work on something else. You can disconnect your terminal from your VM and let the program continue running with the command:

```
#CP DISCONN HOLD
```

The DISCONN command is discussed in more detail in the chapter *Managing Your Virtual Machine*.

- Suppose you've started a program running that you have to stop because it's not doing what it is intended to do. Entering #CP without a command will stop the program and place you in the CP environment:

```
#CP
```

To return to CMS to correct the program, you must load CMS into virtual memory again:

```
IPL CMS
```

3.9 System Messages: the Response to Commands

When you press the ENTER key after typing a command, the command disappears from the command input area and is displayed in the output display area followed by a ready message and an error message if the command could not be executed.

Example:

MSG is a CP command that you can use to send a message to another system user who is currently logged onto the system.

- If the user is currently logged on, the message is displayed on the user's terminal.

- If the user is not logged on, an error message is displayed on your terminal.

Suppose you have a friend whose userid is AVATAR and you want to send a message to arrange a meeting:

        MSG AVATAR CAN WE MEET AT 3 PM TODAY ?

- If AVATAR is logged on, the message is displayed on AVATAR's terminal and the system displays a ready message on your terminal similar to:

        Ready; T=0.02/0.01 18:07:36

- If AVATAR is not logged on, the system displays an error message and then a ready message on your terminal similar to:

        DMKCQG045E AVATAR NOT LOGGED ON
        Ready(00045); T=0.02/0.01 18:07:36

The above error message and ready message will be discussed in detail in the next two sections.

3.10 The Ready Message

Unlike some operating systems, CMS does not display a prompt at the beginning of the command input area to indicate that it is ready for you to enter your next command. CMS does, however, display a message, known as the **ready message**, *after* it has finished processing a command to inform you that it is *ready* for your next command.

Message Format:

> **Ready[7] (retcode); T= vtime / ttime time**

where **retcode**   is the return code, to be discussed later in this section.

       vtime   is the virtual (CMS) CPU time the command used. The time is expressed in seconds in the format **seconds.hundredths of seconds**.

       ttime   is the total (CMS + CP) CPU time the command used. The time is expressed in the format **seconds.hundredths of seconds**.

       time   is the current time of day expressed in the format **hours:minutes:seconds**.

Example:

In the previous example using MSG:

- Ready(00045); T=0.02/0.01 18:07:36 is the ready message.

- 00045 (in parentheses) is the return code.

- 0.02 is the virtual CPU time the command required to execute.

- 0.01 is the total CPU time the command required to execute.

- 18:07:36 is the current time of day on a 24 hour clock.

The Return Code

The return code is a number that indicates whether a command executed successfully and, if not, why it could not be executed. The return code is *only displayed* if a command is not executed successfully:

- A return code of 0 indicates that the command executed successfully.

---

[7] On releases of VM/CMS before Release 5, the letter *R* is displayed instead of the word *Ready*.

- A return code less than 0 indicates that the command is not recognized.

- A return code greater than 0 indicates that the command was recognized but was probably not executed because of some error that depends on the nature of the problem.

Example:

In the previous example using MSG, notice that:

- When the command did not execute successfully, the return code was 45.

- When the command executed successfully, the return code was not displayed since it was 0.

3.11 Error Messages

If you enter a command the system does not recognize, it displays an error message, discussed in the section *Environments in VM/CMS*, that depends on the environment you are in.

If you enter a command that the system recognizes but cannot execute for some reason, the system displays an error message consisting of two parts:

- A Message Identifier

- A Message Text

The Message Identifier

The message identifier uniquely identifies the error that has just occurred and consists of four parts.

Message Format:

pppmmmnnns

where **ppp** is the **prefix**.

- If the prefix is **DMK**, the message originated from CP.

- If the prefix is **DMS**, the message originated from CMS.

mmm is the **module code**. The module code consists of three letters abbreviating the name of the module that generated the message.

nnn is the **message number**. The message number is a three digit number identifying the error that has occurred.

s is the **severity type**. The severity type is a single letter indicating the nature of the error:

- **I** for Information.

- **W** for Warning.

- **E** for Error.

- **S** for Severe error.

- **T** for Terminal error.

Example:

In the above example using MSG, DMKCQG045E is the message identifier with these components:

- DMK is the prefix.

- CQG is the module code.

- 045 is the message number.

- E is the severity type.

The Message Text

The message text is a brief description of the error which might also include recommendations as to how to correct the error.

Example:

In the above example using MSG, AVATAR NOT LOGGED ON is the message text. The message text indicates that messages cannot be sent to AVATAR at this time since he is not logged on.

HELP with System Messages

If the nature of the problem is not apparent from the message text, use the HELP facility for a more detailed explanation of the problem as well as the corrective action to be taken. To display the HELP file for a given error message, enter HELP followed by the message identifier, omitting the module code which is the the fourth, fifth and sixth characters.

Command Format:

> **HELP**   **pppnnns**

where **pppnnns**   is the message identifier omitting the module code.

Exercise:

In the above example using MSG, the message identifier was DMKCQG045E. Display the information for this message identifier:

> HELP DMK045E

How to use the HELP facility is discussed in detail later in this chapter.

- To scroll forward, press PF8.

- To scroll backward, press PF7.

- To leave HELP and return to CMS, press PF3.

For more information about diagnosing and correcting problems refer to the chapter *Diagnosing and Correcting Problems.*

3.12 Program Function Keys

An alternative to entering a command by typing it in on the keyboard and then pressing the ENTER key is to assign the command to a **Program Function (PF)** key. Once a command has been assigned to a PF key, you can execute the command just by pressing the PF key. Assigning a frequently used command to a PF key is a convenient way to execute the command because the command can then be executed in a single keystroke. The system allows you to assign commands to 24 PF keys.

A convenient way to assign commands to PF keys automatically whenever you log on is to make the assignments part of your PROFILE EXEC. How to assign CP and CMS commands to PF keys is discussed in the chapter *Customizing the CP/CMS Environments*.

The Keys Assigned to Function as PF Keys

The actual keys that function as PF keys depend on the type of terminal that you are using. Contact those who support your system to determine which keys on your type of terminal function as PF keys.

- On IBM display terminals, the PF keys are usually labeled PF1, PF2, PF3, and so forth.

- On ASCII terminals, the PF keys are often labeled F1, F2, F3, and so forth, but may not be explicitly labeled at all.

Once you determine which keys function as PF keys on your type of terminal, write them into Table 3.1 for future reference.

The Commands Assigned to PF Keys

The commands assigned to PF keys depends on the environment you are in:

- In CP and CMS, PF keys are not normally assigned commands, but those who support your system may have done so for you.

- In FILELIST, HELP, NOTE, PEEK, RDRLIST, SENDFILE and XEDIT, PF1 through PF12 are assigned commands that are covered in the sections that discuss these commands.

In any environment, however, you can determine which commands have been assigned to which PF keys by entering:

    QUERY   PF

Exercise:

Use the QUERY PF command to determine whether commands have been assigned to PF keys in CP and CMS on your system.

Program Function Keys § 55

Retrieving Previous Commands

The CP and CMS commands you enter are stored in a buffer (temporary storage area) of a fixed size. **RETRIEVE** is a keyword that retrieves commands from this buffer and displays them in the command input area with the cursor positioned at the end of the command. Commands are retrieved in the opposite order they were executed:

- One execution of RETRIEVE displays the previous command.

- Two executions of RETRIEVE display the command prior to the previous command.

Retrieving a previous command is useful if you have to execute the command again or if the command was misspelled, incomplete or otherwise in error because you can edit the command using the edit control keys to correct the mistake without typing the entire command again.

Because the buffer is relatively small, the number of previous commands that you can *retrieve* depends on the length of the commands. More commands can be retrieved if they were short than if they were long.

Only one copy of each command is stored in the buffer. If you enter a command that is identical to another entered earlier, it is not stored in the buffer again.

RETRIEVE is only useful, however, when assigned to a PF key. Assigning a command to a PF key is discussed in the chapter *Customizing the CP/CMS Environments.*

Exercise:

Demonstrate the use of the RETRIEVE command:

1. Assign the RETRIEVE command to PF1:

   ```
   SET  PF1  RETRIEVE
   ```

2. Enter the command:

   ```
   MSG * TESTING 1 2 3
   ```

3. Press the PF1 key to retrieve the previous command.

4. Press the PF1 key again to retrieve the command before that.

3.13 Program Attention Keys

Program Attention (PA) keys perform functions that depend on the environment in which they are used. In most environments their functions are fixed and you cannot change the commands assigned to them. Execute the command assigned to a PA key by pressing the PA key. There are three PA keys: PA1, PA2 and PA3.

These are the functions assigned to the PA keys in the CP/CMS environment:

- PA1 is assigned to execute the #CP command which causes an attention interrupt, terminating whatever you were doing and places you in the CP environment.

- PA2 is assigned to clear the output display area. This differs from the CLEAR key which clears both the output display area *and* the command input area.

- PA3 is not assigned a function.

In the XEDIT environment and environments controlled by XEDIT, such as HELP, PA keys may have different commands assigned to them.

The Keys Assigned to Function as PA Keys

The actual keys that function as PA keys depend on the type of terminal that you are using.

- On IBM display terminals, PA keys are usually labeled PA1, PA2 and PA3.

- On ASCII terminals, PA keys are not labeled as such. Contact those who support your system to determine which keys function as PA keys on your type of terminal.

Once you determine which keys function as PA keys on your type of terminal, write them into Table 3.1 for future reference.

Exercises:

- Demonstrate the use of the PA1 key by pressing it. Notice the change in the status message. What does the message mean? Return to what you were doing before pressing PA1 with the command:

  BEGIN

- Demonstrate the use of the PA2 key:

  1. Enter the command:

      QUERY TIME

  2. Press the PA2 key.

3.14 The HELP Facility and How to Use It

The HELP facility provides extensive online documentation for command syntax and error messages. This section is primarily concerned with using the HELP facility to display command syntax. Using the HELP facility to display error messages is discussed in the section on *Error Messages*.

If you don't know the name of a command, have forgotten the exact spelling of a command name or are unsure of a command's syntax, you can access this information through the HELP facility. The information available through the HELP facility for CP, CMS and XEDIT commands is the same information that is available in IBM's printed command references.

The HELP system is organized into a multi-level hierarchy.

- The first level of the hierarchy is a menu of components within HELP. The components include CMS, CP, DEBUG, EDIT, EXEC, EXEC2, XEDIT and REXX. In Release 5 of CMS, TASKS is also a component.

  - Enter this level from outside of HELP by entering the HELP command, omitting either the name of a component or a command.

  - Return to the environment from which you entered HELP by pressing PF4.

  - Return to this level from the second level by pressing PF3.

- The second level of the hierarchy is a menu of commands or topics within a component.

  - Enter this level from the first level by placing the cursor under any character of the component name for which you want help and pressing the ENTER key.[8]

  - Enter this level directly from outside of HELP by entering the HELP command, specifying the name of the component or topic.

  - Return to the first level by pressing PF3.

  - Return to the environment from which you entered HELP by pressing PF4.

  - Return to this level from the third level by pressing PF3.

- The third level of the hierarchy is the HELP file for a specific command or topic within a component.

---

[8] If the cursor on your terminal displays as a rectangle instead of an underscore, superimpose the cursor on the menu selection rather than placing it under the menu selection.

- Enter this level from the second level by placing the cursor under any character of the command name or topic for which you want help and pressing the ENTER key.

- Enter this level directly from CMS by entering the HELP command, specifying the command name or topic.

- Return to the second level by pressing PF3.

- Return to CMS by pressing PF4.

Command Format:

Help   [component] [*MENU*|command|HELP] (options

where **component**   displays a menu of the commands within this component. The components include **CMS, CP, DEBUG, EDIT, EXEC, EXEC2, XEDIT** and **REXX**. In Release 5 of CMS, **TASKS** is also a component. Specify the component only when you want to restrict the files that HELP searches to those in that component. If the component is omitted and you specify a command name, HELP searches all components and displays a menu of all commands with that name. Once in a component menu, you can display the HELP file for a selection in the menu by moving the cursor under any character of the selection and pressing the PF1 key.

MENU   displays a menu of commands within a component if a component is specified or a menu of components if no component is specified. To display a MENU of the commands within a component, move the cursor under any character of the component name and press the PF1 key.

HELP   displays information about using the HELP facility.

command   is the name of a specific command. The name can be abbreviated. To display a menu of all command names that begin with a certain string of characters, end the character string with an asterisk, as in **command***.

options   are discussed below.

System Messages:

If you enter a HELP command correctly but HELP is unable to find a file that matches your request, HELP displays an error message:

```
HELP cannot find documentation matching 'name'.
Type " HELP * " for a list of all menus.
Ready(00028);
```

Options Controlling What Information is Displayed

[*ALL*|FORMat|PARMs|DESCript|OPTions|NOTEs|ERRors]
[*BRIef*|DETail|RELated][9]

ALL   provides all the information available.

FORMat   provides only the command syntax.

PARMs   provides only a description of the command's operands.

DESCript   provides only a description of the command's function.

OPTions   provides only a description of the command's options.

NOTEs   provides only usage notes and examples for the com-
               mand.

ERRors   provides only the error messages and responses for the
               command.

BRIef   provides a brief description of the command, command
               syntax without options, an example and, if applicable,
               how to obtain detailed and related information.

DETail   provides all the information available for the command.

RELated   provides a menu of topics related to the command.

Program Function Keys in HELP

Which commands are assigned to which PF keys depends on the version of
CMS and the version of the HELP facility you are using. The commands assigned to PF keys are displayed near the bottom of the screen:

```
PF1=Sel  PF2=Top PF3=Quit     PF4=RETurn  PF5=Locate PF6=?
PF7=BAck PF8=Fwd PF9=PF Help PF10=Back/2 PF11=Fwd/2 PF12=CURsor
```

The number after PF is that of a program function key and the name after the
equals sign is the command executed when the corresponding PF key is
pressed:

PF1   displays the HELP information for the menu selection the
               cursor is placed under.

PF2   Moves the display to the top of the HELP file.

---

[9]   These three options are not available in releases of CMS before Release 5.

PF3	Quits the present level of HELP and returns you to the previous level.
PF4	Returns you directly to the environment from which you entered HELP without going through the previous levels of HELP.
PF5	Moves the cursor to the string of text in the menu you've typed on the command line.
PF6	Displays the command previously executed on the command line.
PF7	Scrolls the display backward one full screen.
PF8	Scrolls the display forward one full screen.
PF9	Executes the command previously executed again.
PF10	Scrolls the display backward a half screen.[10]
PF11	Scrolls the display forward a half screen.[11]
PF12	Moves the cursor from the command line to the menu or from the menu to the the command line, depending upon its current position.

Searching for Text and Moving around in HELP

The HELP facility is controlled by the XEDIT editor. Many of the commands useful in XEDIT for searching for text and moving around in a file are also available in HELP:

- LOCATE searches for text.

- UP moves the display up the number of lines you specify.

- DOWN moves the display down the number of lines you specify.

- TOP moves the display to the top of the file.

- BOTTOM moves the display to the bottom of the file.

These commands and their syntax are described in the chapter *Becoming Acquainted with XEDIT*.

---

[10] PF10 is undefined on Release 5 of CMS.

[11] PF11 is undefined on Release 5 of CMS.

The Command Line in HELP

The command line is the second line from the bottom of the screen. It begins with the arrow:

====>

Use the command line to execute XEDIT commands and others not assigned to PF keys.

Exercise:

This exercise is intended to demonstrate the use of XEDIT commands in moving around and searching for text in HELP.

1. Display the HELP file for the FILELIST command:

    HELP   FILELIST

2. Use DOWN to move the display down five lines:

    ====> DOWN   5

3. Use UP to move the display up five lines:

    ====> UP   5

4. Use LOCATE to search forward in the file (from the present location in the file toward the end of the file) for the word 'Options':

    ====> /Options

5. Use LOCATE to search backward in the file (from the present location in the file toward the top of the file) for the word 'Options':

    ====> -/Options

    Notice that the only difference between searching forward and searching backward is that a minus sign is used to indicate a backward search.

6. Press PF8 to scroll forward.

7. Press PF7 to scroll backward.

8. Press PF3 to leave HELP.

Working with HELP Menus

When you enter the HELP command specifying a request, HELP searches all files for one that matches the request.

- If a single match is found, HELP displays the file for that request.

- If more than one match is found, HELP displays a menu of the matches found.

The first few lines of a menu contain instructions describing how to display one of the HELP files available from the menu.

Exercises:

- Display a menu of the different SET commands with:

  HELP SET

  HELP displays a menu that includes three selections:

  - One for the CP SET command.

  - One for the CMS SET command.

  - One for the XEDIT SET command.

  Choose one of the three selections by moving the cursor under it and pressing PF1. When finished with the selection, press PF3 to return to the menu. When finished with the menu, press PF3 to return to CMS.

- Display the HELP file for the XEDIT SET command with:

  HELP XEDIT SET

- Display a menu of all commands that begin with FILE:

  HELP FILE*

Help with Tasks and Related Topics

The HELP facility on Release 5 of CMS includes a menu selection called TASKS that is useful if you know what you want to do but don't know which commands to use. Release 5 HELP also includes references to which commands are related to a particular topic.

Exercise:

1. Display the menu of task topics available:

   HELP TASKS

The HELP Facility and How to Use It § 63

2.   Choose one of the selections in the menu and work with it.

Moving the Cursor in a HELP Menu

The TAB FORWARD, TAB BACKWARD and PF12 keys provide convenient ways to move the cursor in a menu.

- If the cursor is on the command line:

    - TAB FORWARD moves the cursor to the first selection in the menu.

    - TAB BACKWARD moves the cursor to the last selection in the menu.

    - PF12 moves the cursor to its previous location in the menu.

- If the cursor is in the menu:

    - TAB FORWARD moves the cursor to the next selection.

    - TAB BACKWARD moves the cursor to the previous selection.

    - PF12 moves the cursor back to the command line.

The LOCATE command (assigned to PF5) is convenient for moving the cursor to a specific selection in a menu.

1.   Type the selection on the command line.

2.   Press PF5 to move the cursor to the selection.

3.   Press PF1 to display the HELP file for the selection.

Exercise:

Display the menu of CMS commands with:

    HELP CMS

One of the commands in the menu is FILELIST.   Move the cursor to the FILELIST selection:

1.   Type the word FILELIST on the command line:

    ====> FILELIST

2.   Press PF5 to move the cursor under FILELIST.

3.   Press PF1 to display the HELP file for FILELIST.

3.15 Line Editing Symbols

Line editing symbols are characters defined by CP to enable you to edit text in the command input area. The characters that define the line editing functions have no special meaning outside of command input areas, such as the file area in the XEDIT editor.

Line editing symbols are important for editing text on line mode terminals. On display mode terminals, however, editing text is more convenient with the edit control keys. In fact, the only line editing symbols useful on a display terminal are the logical line end and the logical escape.

This section discusses the functions of the line editing symbols and their normal settings.[12] Those who support your system may have either disabled certain line editing functions or used other symbols to perform the functions. To determine your line editing assignments, use the command:

```
QUERY TERMINAL
```

The Logical Line End

is the character that normally represents the logical line end.

The function of the logical line end is to enable you to put more than one command on the same command line. Accomplish this by placing a # character *between* each of the commands. The # character serves to *logically* separate one command from the next.

Example:

TIME is an option on the QUERY command that displays the date, time of day, elapsed virtual CPU time and elapsed total CPU time. By issuing the command

```
QUERY TIME
```

immediately before and after you execute a command, you can determine the amount of time the command required to execute by taking the difference between the times reported. You could do this for the IPL CMS command by entering three separate command lines:

```
QUERY TIME
IPL CMS
QUERY TIME
```

Or, you could enter all three commands on the same command line:

---

[12] *Normal*, in this context, refers to the default settings of the CP TERMINAL command.

```
QUERY TIME#IPL CMS#QUERY TIME
```

The Logical Line Delete

¢ is the character that normally represents the logical line delete.[13]

The function of the logical line delete is to remove a *logical* line of text. A **logical line** is the string of characters between the last line end and the present location of the cursor. Accomplish this by placing a ¢ character *at the end* of the text to be deleted. This is useful if you've typed in a command which you either recognize to be in error or just don't want to execute. You can delete the command by placing a ¢ at the end of it.[14]

Examples:

- The following command is not executed:

  ```
  QUERY TIME¢
  ```

- Of the following, only the QUERY TIME command would be executed:

  ```
  FILELIST¢QUERY TIME
  ```

- Of the following, both QUERY commands would be executed, but FILELIST would be ignored:

  ```
  QUERY TIME#FILELIST¢QUERY TIME
  ```

The Logical Character Delete

@ is the character that normally represents the logical character delete.

The function of the logical character delete is to delete a character. Accomplish this by placing the @ character immediately *after* the character to be deleted. If several consecutive characters are to be deleted, place as many @ characters as there are characters to be deleted after the last of the characters to be deleted.[15]

Example:

The following commands are equivalent:

---

[13] On an ASCII terminal, the symbol may be the backslash.

[14] Deleting a line may be easier using the ERASE EOF key or the ERASE INPUT key.

[15] Deleting characters is usually easier using the DELETE CHARACTER key.

```
K@QUERY THY@@IME
QUERY TIME
```

The Logical Escape

″ is the character that normally represents the logical escape.

The function of the logical escape symbol is to escape or override the meaning of another logical line editing symbol. Accomplish by placing the ″ symbol immediately *before* the line editing symbol whose special meaning is to be ignored.

Example:

The following command is interpreted as display a list of all files on the A-disk with a filename of #DIRE:

```
FILELIST "#DIRE *
```

Defining Other Characters to be Line Editing Symbols

TERMINAL is a CP command that enables you to:

- Define another symbol to perform a specific line editing function.

- Turn off a line editing function.

- Turn on a line editing function that has been turned off.

LINEDIT is a function of the CP SET command that controls whether *all* line editing functions are turned ON or OFF.

The CP TERMINAL and CP SET commands are both discussed in the chapter *Customizing the CP/CMS Environments*.

3.16 Command Search Order

When you enter a command, the system begins an ordered search for the command in the environment in which the command was entered. When the command is located, the search is terminated and the command executed. The following is the order in which the system searches for a command entered in the CMS environment:

1. Is the command an Immediate Command?[16]

    *   If so, execute it.

    *   If not, go to the next step.

2. Is the command an Exec?[17]

    *   If so, execute it.

    *   If not, go to the next step.

3. Is the command a synonym or abbreviation for an Exec?

    *   If so, substitute the real Exec name and execute it.

    *   If not, go to the next step.

4. Is the command a CMS command name?

    *   If so, execute it.

    *   If not, go to the next step.

5. Is the command a synonym or abbreviation for a CMS command?

    *   If so, substitute the real CMS command and execute it.

    *   If not, go to the next step.

6. Is the command a Module?[18]

    *   If so, execute it.

    *   If not, go to the next step.

---

[16] An Immediate Command is a command that is processed *immediately* in spite of any other commands that might be executing or waiting to be executed. Normally, commands are processed in the order you enter them.

[17] An Exec is a command stored in disk file. The file has a filetype of EXEC and a filename the same as the Exec name.

[18] A Module is a command stored in a disk file. The file has a filetype of MODULE and a filename the same as the Module name.

7. Is the command a synonym or abbreviation for a Module?

- If so, substitute the real Module command and execute it.

- If not, send the command to CP for execution.

Example:

SYNONYM is a CMS command that can be used to display the system-defined and user-defined synonyms and their abbreviations that are currently in effect. SYN is the shortest allowable abbreviation for SYNONYM. Suppose you enter the command:

        SYN

The system would conduct this search:

1. CMS would search for and fail to find an Immediate Command called SYN.

2. CMS would search for and fail to find an Exec called SYN.

3. CMS would search for and succeed in finding that SYN is a synonym for SYNONYM. CMS would then search for and fail to find an Exec for which SYN is either a synonym or abbreviation.

4. CMS would search for and fail to find a CMS command name called SYN.

5. CMS would search for and succeed in finding that SYN is a synonym for SYNONYM. CMS would then search for and succeed in finding that SYN is an abbreviation for SYNONYM and the SYNONYM command would be executed.

3.17 Virtual Storage Capacity

Virtual storage is a temporary storage area that the system uses to store programs when you run them and to store files when you edit them. When you log onto the system, your virtual storage capacity is defined to be of a certain size. The capacity is measured in number of bytes and is usually expressed in terms of thousands of bytes (kilobytes) or millions of bytes (megabytes):

- A **Kilobyte (K)** is 1024 bytes.

- A **Megabyte (M)** is $(1024 \times 1024) = 1048576$ bytes.

Thus, 1024K and 1M are equivalent.

Determining the Size of Your Virtual Storage

STORAGE is an option on the CP QUERY command that determines the size of your virtual storage:

Command Format:

> Query   STORage

Changing Your Virtual Storage Capacity

Your virtual storage size can be changed either temporarily or permanently using the procedures described in the chapter *Managing Your Virtual Machine.*

3.18 Interrupting the Execution of a Command or Program

When you are running a program or executing a command, you can interrupt the program or command either temporarily or permanently.

- A temporary interrupt allows you to resume execution of the command or program.

- A permanent interrupt halts execution and returns your VM to CMS.

On a display terminal, use the PA1 key to send an **attention interrupt**:

- Press PA1 *once* to send an attention interrupt to CP. You enter the CP environment and the status message changes to CP READ.

  - Resume execution with the command:

    BEGIN

  - Halt execution and return to CMS with the command:

    IPL CMS

- Press PA1 *twice* to send an attention interrupt to CMS. The status message changes to VM READ.

  - Resume execution by pressing the ENTER key. The status message changes to:

    RUNNING

  - Halt execution and return to CMS with the **HX** (Halt EXecution) Immediate Command:

    HX

The ENTER key can also be used to send an attention interrupt. When your VM status is RUNNING, press the ENTER key once to change your VM status to VM READ.

- Resume execution by pressing the ENTER key. The system status changes to:

  RUNNING

- Halt execution and return to CMS with the HX Immediate Command:

  HX

Interrupting Output to the Terminal

HT (**H**alt **T**yping) is an Immediate Command that will stop output being displayed on the terminal by a command or program. To execute the command:

1. Type HT on the keyboard when the screen fills and the status message changes to MORE...

2. Press ENTER.

Exercise:

This exercise is intended to demonstrate the use of the HT Immediate Command.

1. LISTFILE is a command that will display a list of files to which you have access. Begin the display of all files to which you have access with the command:

   LISTFILE * * *

2. When the screen fills and the status message changes to MORE..., use the HT Immediate Command to stop the display.

Resuming Output to the Terminal

RT (**R**esume **T**yping) is an Immediate Command that will resume output to the terminal that was halted with the HT Immediate Command. To execute the command:

1. Type RT on the keyboard.

2. Press ENTER.

3.19 Obtaining Information

Several commands are available to provide information about the system and who is using it, your virtual machine and its characteristics, your virtual devices and their characteristics, and your files and their characteristics. These commands are briefly mentioned in this section. More complete descriptions are available elsewhere in this book.

Information about Commands and Problems

HELP provides information about:

- How to interpret error messages and correct problems.

- How to accomplish certain tasks.

- What commands are available.

- What commands are related to other commands.

- The function each command performs.

- Command syntax.

QUERY SYNONYM USER provides user-defined synonyms and abbreviations for commands.

QUERY SYNONYM SYSTEM provides system-defined synonyms and abbreviations for commands.

CP QUERY PF provides the assignments of program function keys.

Information about Disk Files

FILELIST and **LISTFILE** provide information about files on disks to which you have access.

Information about Disks

QUERY DISK provides CMS information about the disks to which you have access.

QUERY SEARCH provides the order in which disks are searched for a file.

CP QUERY DASD provides CP information about the disks to which you have access.

Information about Spool Files

CP QUERY FILES provides the number of spool files in all your virtual input and output devices.

RDRLIST and **CP QUERY RDR ALL** provide information about the files in your virtual reader.

CP QUERY PRINTER provides information about files in your virtual printer.

CP QUERY PUNCH provides information about files in your virtual punch.

Information about Virtual Devices

CP QUERY UR provides information about the characteristics of your virtual printer, virtual reader and virtual punch.

CP QUERY TERMINAL provides information about your terminal's characteristics.

CP QUERY C provides information about your virtual reader.

CP QUERY D provides information about your virtual punch.

CP QUERY E provides information about your virtual printer.

CP QUERY CONSOLE provides information about your virtual console.

Information about the System

CP QUERY TIME provides the time, the date, how long you've been on the system, the virtual CPU time you've used and the total CPU time you've used.

INDICATE provides information about system resource utilization.

CP QUERY USERS provides the number of users on the system.

CP QUERY NAMES provides the userids of all users on the system.

CP QUERY LOGMSG provides information about:

- When the system is scheduled to be unavailable.
- New products that are available.
- Any changes to old products.
- Any problems that system users should be aware of.
- Any other information that is relevant to using the system.

Chapter 4
CMS Disks and CMS Disk Files

Introduction

A **file** is a collection of information stored on some device. A metaphor often used to develop the concept of a file is that of a cabinet in which folders are kept. Each folder contains information about a specific topic. For example, each folder might contain a history of the sales made to a specific company, where each sale made is a separate record and each time another sale is made another record is added to the folder. Each folder also has a unique label distinguishing it from other folders in the cabinet.

Most files contain one of three types of information:

- A **data file** usually contains information that is to be further processed or analyzed. For example, each record might correspond to a sales transaction, with the following information recorded: customer name, customer number, sales date, salesperson, part number, part price, part quantity and delivery date. This data can then be used to generate bills or gather information about sales, inventory, etc.

- A **program file** contains a set of instructions that directs the computer to carry out some task. The task might be to take the data file described above as input, determine how many of each part have been sold and produce an inventory report.

- A **text file** contains information such as a report, a letter or other document intended to be read by someone.

Example:

The following might be an example of the file of sales transactions discussed above. Notice that the file contains six records.

```
ABCD Inc.   02/05/88   PBC   7-3684     0.50   100   02/08/88
ABCD Inc.   01/23/88   DEF   6-5279    10.00    15   01/23/88
ABCD Inc.   12/12/87   PPB   2-1321   100.00     4   12/15/87
ABCD Inc.   12/05/87   PBC   7-3684     0.50    10   12/05/87
ABCD Inc.   11/13/87   KAL   5-2233     5.50    35   11/13/87
ABCD Inc.   10/22/87   BYU   4-2345    39.55    10   10/25/87
```

Storing Files on Disk

If the information in a file is to be used by a computer, it must be stored on a device from which the computer can read. The devices typically used to store files include card decks, magnetic tapes and disks. Accordingly, the files stored on these devices might be called card files, tape files and disk files, respectively. The only storage devices with which this text will be concerned are disks. The files you will be creating, editing and working with will simply be called files.

A disk is sometimes referred to as a **direct access storage device (DASD)** because:

- A disk is a storage device for files.

- A file stored on a disk can be accessed directly.

CMS disks are accessed in either of two ways:

- **Write Access** to a disk allows you to read files from and write files to the disk.

- **Read Access** to a disk allows you only to read files from the disk.

Each CMS user has at least one disk to which he has write access. This disk is known as the **A-disk**.

4.1 The CMS File Identifier

The first thing to learn about CMS disk files is that each file has a unique **file identifier (fileid)** that consists of three parts:

- A Filename
- A Filetype
- A Filemode

When you specify a fileid:

- The filename *must* be first.
- The filetype *must* be second.
- The filemode, when necessary, *must* be third.

Use at least one blank to separate the filename from the filetype and at least one blank to separate the filetype from the filemode.

Example:

Consider the fileid:

PROFILE EXEC A2

- PROFILE is the filename.
- EXEC is the filetype.
- A2 is the filemode.

The Filemode (FM)

The filemode consists of a letter followed by a number.

- The letter is known as the **mode letter** and corresponds to the disk on which the file is stored. Files stored on your A-disk have a mode letter of A.

- The number is known as the **mode number** and corresponds to something that is special about the file. The mode number *does not* contribute to the uniqueness of a fileid. Thus, two files cannot have the same filenames, filetypes and mode letters differing only in their mode numbers.

  Mode numbers are integers between zero and five:

  0 means that the file is private. Only those who have write access to a disk can read files on that disk with a mode number of 0. Mode 0 should not be used for security; it is not a protection.

The CMS File Identifier § 77

1 is normally assigned if you omit a mode number. All files with a mode number of 1 on a disk can be read by anyone with read or write access to that disk.

2 is essentially the same as a mode number of 1 except that a mode number of 2 is not the default.

3 means that the file is to be erased after it is read. Be *very* careful with this one! In fact, you should not normally use this mode number. It is used by language compilers and utility programs for temporary files that are to be erased after they have been read. By assigning temporary files a mode number of 3, you do not have to erase them by an additional command after they have been read.

4 indicates that the file is in OS simulated data set format. Binary files, such as those written out from unformatted WRITE statements in FORTRAN programs, have a mode number of 4.

5 is essentially the same as a mode number of 1 except that a mode number of 5 is not the default.

When it is necessary to specify a filemode, it is usually necessary only to specify the mode letter. You only need to specify the mode number when you are creating a new file and you want it to be something other than the default.

Your primary disk is known as your A-disk. Each of the files stored on your A-disk has a mode letter of A. Many commands do not require you specify a filemode when it is the letter A.

The Filetype (FT)

The filetype usually indicates the type of records in a file as well as the characteristics of the file.

Many application programs on VM/CMS *require* that the files they process have a specific filetype that is often the same as the product name. These are known as **reserved filetypes**. Table 4.1 is a list of the most common reserved filetypes and some of the characteristics assigned to them.

The filetype can be any combination of letters, numbers and these special characters:[1]

- The Dollar Sign ($)

- The Pound Sign (#)

- The Minus Sign (−)

---

[1] Special characters are printable characters that are neither letters nor numbers.

- The Plus Sign (+)

- The At Sign (@)

- The Underscore (_)

- The Colon (:)

No more than eight characters may appear in a filetype. Blank characters cannot be part of a filetype, since blanks are used to separate a filename from a filetype and a filetype from a filemode. When the # character is defined to be the logical line end and the @ character is defined to be the logical char-

FILETYPE	Logical Record Length	Record Format	Trunca-tion Column	Case of Letters	Tab Stops
$EXEC	80	Fixed	72	Upper	1,4,...25,31,...79,80
$XEDIT	80	Fixed	72	Mixed	1,4,...25,31,...79,80
ASSEMBLE	80	Fixed	71	Upper	1,10,16,30,35,...70
BASDATA	156	Variable	156	Upper	1,7,10,15,...120
BASIC	156	Variable	156	Upper	1,7,10,15,...120
COBOL	80	Fixed	72	Upper	1,8,12,20,...80
DIRECT	80	Fixed	72	Upper	1,5,...75
EXEC	130	Variable	130	Mixed	1,4,...25,31,...79,80
FORTRAN	80	Fixed	72	Upper	1,7,10,15,...30,80
FREEFORT	81	Variable	81	Upper	9,15,18,23,...38,81
JOB	80	Fixed	80	Upper	1,5,...75
LISTING	121	Variable	121	Upper	1,5,...120
MACLIB	80	Fixed	71	Upper	1,10,16,30,35,...70
MACRO	80	Fixed	71	Upper	1,10,16,30,35,...70
MEMO	80	Variable	80	Mixed	1,5,...120
MODULE	80	Variable	80	Mixed	1,5,...120
NAMES	255	Variable	255	Mixed	1,5,...120
NETLOG	255	Variable	255	Mixed	1,5,...120
NOTE	132	Variable	132	Mixed	1,5,...120
NOTEBOOK	132	Variable	132	Mixed	1,5,...120
PASCAL	72	Variable	72	Mixed	1,5,...75
PLI	80	Fixed	72	Upper	4,7,...25,31,...79,80
PLIOPT	80	Fixed	72	Upper	4,7,...25,31,...79,80
SCRIPT	132	Variable	132	Mixed	1,5,...120
TEXT	80	Fixed	80	Mixed	1,5,...80
UPDATE	80	Fixed	71	Upper	1,10,16,30,35,...70
VSBASIC	80	Fixed	80	Upper	7,10,15,...30,80
VSBDATA	132	Variable	132	Upper	1,5,...120
XEDIT	255	Variable	255	Mixed	1,4,...25,31,...79,80
Most Others	80	Fixed	80	Upper	1,5,...80

Table 4.1 The most common filetypes and the characteristics assigned to them.

acter delete, be sure to use the logical escape character " to override the special meaning of these characters if they are to be used in a filetype.

Examples:

- A file containing COBOL source code should have a filetype of COBOL.

- A file of Exec commands should have a filetype of EXEC.

- A file containing SCRIPT commands and text to be formatted should have a filetype of SCRIPT.

The Filename (FN)

The filename is used to distinguish one file with a specific filetype and filemode from other files having the *same* filetype and filemode.

The filename can be any combination of letters, numbers and any of the same special characters that can be used in a filetype. No more than eight characters may be used in a filename.

Example:

Suppose you have some data in a file on your A-disk whose filename is XMPL and filetype is DATA and you want to create a new file on your A-disk that has some other data. The new file might have a filetype of DATA, which is the same filetype as that of the existing file, and a filename of NEWXMPL to distinguish it from the existing file.

Exercise:

Examples of legitimate and illegitimate fileids appear below. Which are illegitimate and what is wrong with each?

```
SAMPLE   DATA  A1
$_$_$_$_   COBOL  A1
(SAMPLE)  TEXT  1A
PROFILE  EXEC  A2
BIG  DEAL  FILE
05-09-51  MEMO  A0
ESOTERIC  MICROTRIVIA
+ABC-  PASCAL  D1
SOLOPSIST  DATA  A1
RESUME  SCRIPT  A0
PROFILE  HELP!  D4
COPACETIC  MEMO  99
PROFILE  XEDIT  A9
PROFILE
X.Y.Z
```

4.2 Real Disks and Virtual Disks

On VM/CMS, a real disk is divided into many smaller areas called **minidisks** and also **virtual disks** because they are not the same as an entire real disk. Each and every minidisk belongs to some VM.

When you log onto the system, the disks that are a *permanent* part of your VM are defined in the CP User Directory which specifies how your VM is to be configured. These permanent disks are of two types:

- **Owned minidisks** are those that belong to *your* VM.

- **Shared minidisks** are those that belong to *other* VMs that you are authorized to access.

When you log onto the system, the files that were present on your permanent minidisks when you last logged off are present now. The other permanent disks — those belonging to other VMs — are sometimes referred to as **system disks** because on them reside the system products and facilities available to all system users. These products and facilities may include:

- Language Compilers

- Language Interpreters

- Document Formatting Facilities

- Database Management Facilities

- Statistical Packages

- Graphics Packages

- The CMS Nucleus[2]

- The Disk Resident Commands

- Macro, Text and Subroutine Libraries

- Other Programming Facilities and Utilities

How Virtual Disks are Known to CP and CMS

Minidisks are known to CP and CMS in different ways:

- CP associates a **virtual address (vaddr)** with each minidisk which is a hexadecimal number that identifies the minidisk to CP. (Hexadecimal

---

[2] This is the portion of CMS that resides in the user's virtual storage whenever CMS is running. The CMS nucleus is loaded into virtual storage when the IPL CMS command is executed.

numbers are discussed in the section *Hexadecimal Numbers* at the end of this chapter).

- CMS associates a **mode letter (mode)** with each minidisk which is a letter of the alphabet that identifies the minidisk to CMS.

Every VM has access to at least three disks:

- You have a disk with which CP associates a virtual address of 191 and CMS associates a mode letter of A. This owned minidisk is commonly referred to as your **A-disk**.

- You *may* have a disk with which CP associates a virtual address of 192 and CMS associates a mode letter of D. This owned minidisk is commonly referred to as your **D-disk**.

- You have a disk with which CP associates a virtual address of 190 and CMS associates a mode letter of S. This shared minidisk is commonly referred to as the **S-disk**.

- You have a disk with which CP associates a virtual address of 19E and CMS associates a mode letter of Y. This shared minidisk is commonly referred to as the **Y-disk**.

The disks at virtual addresses 190 and 19E are system disks. They contain the CMS Nucleus, Disk Resident commands for the CMS system and software products that are not part of the VM/CMS system as such.

4.3 Characteristics of CMS Disk Files

A CMS disk file has three important characteristics:

- A Fileid

- A Record Format

- A Logical Record Length

The Record Format (RECFM)

The record format indicates the manner in which records are stored on disk. Files are stored on disk in either of two formats:

- When a file is stored in a **fixed (F)** record length format, all records contain the same number of characters and are, therefore, of the same length. If the last nonblank character on a record occurs before the end of the record, blank characters are inserted between that character and the end of the record.

- When a file is stored in a **variable (V)** record length format, each record can contain a different number of characters so that records can be of different lengths. The length of records can be different because the end of the record occurs after the last nonblank character. Thus, the length of one record may be 1 character, whereas the length of another record may be 133 characters. Files with a variable record format differ from those that are fixed in that each record in a variable record format file is preceded by a number 4 **bytes** (characters) in length to indicate the length of that record. This is done so that any program or utility reading the file can determine how many characters to read in each record. Thus, the number of bytes required to store each record in a file with a variable record format is always four more than the actual number of characters stored on each record.

The Logical Record Length (LRECL)

The logical record length is the maximum number of characters in any record in a file.

- The logical record length of a file with a fixed record format is simply the length of *any* record in that file, since all records in such a file have the same number of character and are, therefore, the same length.

- The logical record length of a file with a variable record format is just the length of the *longest* record in that file.

Characteristics of CMS Disk Files § 83

How Record Length and Record Format are Assigned to a File

A new file is assigned its logical record length and record format based on its filetype. Changing a file's record format and/or record length can sometimes result in a considerable savings of disk space, but, generally speaking, should not be done to a file with a reserved filetype, since the facilities that read these files usually expect a certain record format and record length.

The Amount of Space a Disk File Occupies

The number of bytes of disk space that a file stored in a fixed format occupies is always a product of the number of records in the file and the file's record length.

There is usually, however, no simple formula to compute the number of bytes of disk space that a file stored in a variable format will occupy since the records can vary in length. To determine how much space a variable format file occupies, you must know the length of each record in the file. The amount of space is then the sum of the lengths of all the records *plus* four bytes for each record in the file.

Exercises:

- How many bytes would a file occupy if it contains 100 records and is stored in a fixed format with a record length of 80?

  `(80 x 100) = 8000 bytes`

- How many bytes would a file occupy if it contains 100 records half of which are 40 bytes long, half of which are 80 bytes long and it is stored in a variable record format?

  `(40 x 50) + (80 x 50) + (4 x 100) = 6400 bytes`

Changing the Record Format and/or Record Length

Storing data in fixed length records may improve processing speed but it might also make inefficient use of disk space. Files with filetypes that are not reserved, such as DATA, are always assigned a fixed record format and a record length of 80, which may or may not result in an efficient usage of disk space:

- If file has a record length of 80 but only the first few columns are used on each record, the remaining columns are padded with blank characters, which take up just as much space as nonblank characters. When this is the case, changing the record length to be the length of the longest record in the file will result in the file occupying less disk space.

- If a file has records all of the same length, storing the file with a variable record format will use more disk space than storing it with a fixed record format, since the variable format uses four more bytes per record than does the fixed format.

- If a file has records that differ in their lengths, storing the file with a variable record format will save space proportionate to how widely the records differ in length: the more they differ, the more space is saved. When this is the case, changing the record format to be variable will result in the file occupying less space.

A file's record format and/or record length can be changed in either of two ways:

- Use the RECFM and LRECL options on the COPYFILE command, described in the chapter *Working with Disk Files*.

- Use the RECFM and LRECL functions of the XEDIT SET command, described in the chapter *Customizing the XEDIT Environment*.

4.4 Characteristics of CMS Disks

Minidisks have several important characteristics:

- A Mode Letter
- An Access Mode
- Access Passwords
- A Blocksize
- Storage Capacity

The Mode Letter

The mode letter is a letter of the alphabet that identifies the disk to CMS. Since there are 26 letters in the alphabet, you can access up to 26 disks simultaneously.

The Access Mode

The access mode corresponds to what you can do with a disk when you link to it.[3] The access mode determines whether you can read files from and write files to a disk or whether you can only read files from a disk.

The access mode consists of one or two letters that indicates whether you want to read files from and write files to the disk or just read files from the disk.

- The first letter specifies the **primary** (or preferred) **access mode**. This is the access mode established if no one else is accessing the disk. The primary access modes are:

    R to read from the disk.

    W to write to the disk.

    M for multiple access to write to the disk unless another user has write access to the disk.

- The second letter, if present, specifies the **secondary** (or alternative) **access mode**. This is the access mode established if another user is accessing the disk. If no secondary access mode is specified and another user has access to the disk, no link is made. The optional secondary access modes are:

---

[3] The LINK command, used to link to a disk, is discussed in the chapter *Managing Your Virtual Machine*.

R to read from the disk.

W to write to the disk.

The following access modes are obtained by combining a primary access mode with a secondary access mode:

R   Primary access is read. There is no secondary access. If another user already has access to the disk, no link is made.

W   Primary access is write. There is no secondary access. If another user already has access to the disk, no link is made.

M   Primary access is write. There is no secondary access. If another user has write access to the disk, no link is made.

RR   Primary access is read. Secondary access is read. Even if another user already has access to the disk, a read link is made.

WR   Primary access is write. Secondary access is read. If another user already has access to the disk, a read link is made.

MR   Primary access is write. Secondary access is read. If another user has write access to the disk, a read link is made.

MW   Primary access is write. Secondary access is write. Even if another user has write access to the disk, a write link is made. This link is *always* made. (**Caution:** More than one user should *never* write to the same disk at the same time. If this is done, files will be permanently lost.)

Access modes can be categorized into two groups according to whether you can read *and* write files or *only* read files:

- W, WR, M, MR and MW are all **Read/Write (R/W)** access modes. When a disk is accessed in a R/W mode, you may:

  - Read files from the disk.

  - Write files to the disk.

  - Change files on the disk.

  - Remove files from the disk.

Your A-disk is a R/W disk. In fact, all disks that are a permanent part of your VM, except system disks, are normally accessed as R/W disks.

- R and RR are **Read/Only (R/O)** access modes. When a disk is accessed in a R/O mode, you may *only* read certain files from the disk. All system disks are R/O disks: you can read files from these disks but cannot change an existing file nor write a new file to any of these disks.

Access Passwords

The procedure by which you access a minidisk that belongs to another user is described in the chapter *Managing Your Virtual Machine*. You can restrict others' access to your disks and the files on them by setting up disk access passwords. How to do so is also discussed in the chapter *Managing Your Virtual Machine*. Each disk can have three kinds of access passwords:

- The **read password** allows another user read/only access to a disk.

- The **write password** allows another user read/write access to a disk.

- The **multiple password** allows another user read/write access to a disk *even if* the disk is already being accessed read/write by someone else. (**Caution:** More than one user should **never** write to the same disk at the same time. If this is done, files will be permanently lost.)

To access a minidisk belonging to another user, you must usually know the password corresponding to the access mode you intend to establish. Other than resorting to stealth, you can only determine what the password is by asking the user who owns the disk. On some systems, access to minidisks is controlled by rules rather than passwords. Consult with those who administer your system to determine which is used.

The Blocksize

When CMS stores a file on disk, it combines consecutive records into units of a fixed size. Such a unit of records is called a **block** and the size of the block is called the **blocksize**. The size of the block is the maximum number of characters (bytes) in the block. CMS writes files to disk with a fixed blocksize regardless of whether the files have a fixed or a variable record format. A disk is assigned a blocksize of either 512, 800, 1024, 2048 or 4096 bytes when the disk is set up for your userid.

Exercises:

Suppose a disk's blocksize is 4096 bytes:

- How many blocks would a file occupy if it has 100 records, a record length of 80 and a fixed record format?

- How many blocks would a file occupy if it contains a single record with a single character stored in a variable record format?

The Storage Capacity

The storage capacity refers to the amount of space available for storing files. Storage capacity is measured in cylinders for **Count Key Data (CKD)** devices and in blocks for **Fixed Block Architecture (FBA)** devices. The size of a mini-disk can range from one cylinder (one block for FBA devices) to the entire real disk. The storage capacity of a cylinder depends upon the type of disk.

Exercises:

- A 3380—type disk is a CKD device. If a cylinder is 150 blocks and the blocksize is 4096 bytes, what is the maximum number of bytes in a cylinder?

  (150 x 4096) = 614400 bytes

  If the storage capacity is 2 cylinders, what is the disk's storage capacity in bytes?

  (2 x 614400) = 1228800 bytes

- A 3370—type disk is an FBA device. If the blocksize is 4096 and the storage capacity is 300 blocks, what is the storage capacity in bytes?

  (300 x 4096) = 1228800 bytes

- A file stored in a fixed record format with a record length of 80 contains 100000 records.

  - If the file is stored on a CKD device where a cylinder is 150 blocks and the blocksize is 4096 bytes, how many cylinders are necessary to store the file?

  - If the file is stored on a FBA device where the blocksize is 4096 bytes, how many blocks are necessary to store the file?

4.5 File Directories

Each accessed CMS minidisk has two file directories:

- The **Master File Directory** is a special file stored on disk that contains an entry for every file on that disk. Normally, this directory is updated any time a new file is written to the disk or an existing file is either renamed or removed from the disk.

- The **User File Directory** is another special file created in virtual storage from the master directory whenever you access the disk. It contains an entry for each file you are allowed to access which may be a subset of those in the master directory.

Each directory entry includes:

- The fileid.

- The location of the file on disk.

- The record format used to store the file.

- The logical record length.

- The time and date the file was last written to disk.

- The number of records in the file.

- The number of blocks the file occupies.

4.6 Obtaining Information about Disks

CP and CMS both have QUERY commands which provide the information that each associates with disks to which you have access.

Obtaining the Information CMS Associates with Disks

DISK is an option on the CMS QUERY command that provides the information that CMS associates with disks to which you have access.

Command Format:

> **Query**   DISK   [mode]

where **mode**   is the mode letter that CMS associates with the disk. If the mode is omitted, CMS displays information about all the disks to which you have access. The order in which CMS lists the disks is alphabetical with respect to the mode letter.

Example:

Suppose you want to obtain the information CMS associates with your A-disk:

    QUERY DISK A

The system responds by displaying information resembling this:

```
LABEL  CUU M  STAT  CYL TYPE BLKSIZE   FILES  BLKS USED-(%) BLKS LEFT BLK TOTAL
M-DISK 191 A   R/W    2 3380 4096        125      252-84         48        300
```

The first line of the display consists of labels that describe the information below them. The next line is the information that CMS associates with your A-disk.

- Under LABEL is the name (MDISK) assigned to the disk.

- Under CUU is the virtual address (191) of the disk.

- Under M is the mode letter (A) of the disk.

- Under STAT is the access mode (R/W) of the disk.

- Under CYL is the number of cylinders (2) the disk has.

- Under TYPE is the kind (3380) of disk.

- Under BLKSIZE is the CMS blocksize (4096).

- Under FILES is the number of files (125) on the disk.

- Under BLKS USED is the number of blocks (252) used.

- Under (%) is the percentage of the disk (252/300=84%) used.

- Under BLKS LEFT is the number of blocks (48) unused.

- Under BLK TOTAL is the number of blocks (300) available.

Exercise:

Determine what CMS knows about *all* disks to which you have access:

       QUERY DISK

The system responds by displaying information resembling this:

```
LABEL   CUU M   STAT  CYL TYPE BLKSIZE    FILES  BLKS USED-(%) BLKS LEFT  BLK TOTAL
M-DISK  191 A   R/W     2 3380 4096         125       252-84        48        300
CMSZ    190 S   R/O    58 3380 4096         203      4514-52      4186       8700
CMS19E  19E Y/S R/O   260 3380 4096         971     36721-94      2279      39000
```

Obtaining the Information CP Associates with Disks

DASD is an option on the CP QUERY command that provides the information that CP associates with the disks to which you have access.

Command Format:

| **Query** | **DASD|vaddr** |

where **DASD**   displays information about all your disks. The order in which CP lists the disks is with respect to the size of the virtual address.

      vaddr   displays information about the disk with this virtual address.

Example:

Suppose you want to determine what CP knows about your 191 disk:

       QUERY 191

The system responds by displaying information resembling this:

       DASD 191 3380 CMSA42 R/W   2 CYL

CP does not label the information displayed. Notice that CP displays less information about the disk than CMS. CP knows nothing about blocksize, the number of files on the disk or the percentage of the disk already used. From left to right:

- DASD stands for direct access storage device.

- 191 is the virtual address of the disk.

- 3380 is the type of the disk.

- CMSA42 is the label of the real disk of which the minidisk is a part.

- R/W is the access mode of this disk.

- 2 CYL (2 cylinders) is the amount of space on the disk.

Exercise:

Determine what CP knows about *all* the disks to which you have access:

    QUERY DASD

The system responds by displaying information resembling this:

    DASD 190 3380 CMSA53 R/O   60 CYL
    DASD 191 3380 CMSA42 R/W   2 CYL
    DASD 19E 3380 CMSA42 R/O   260 CYL

Determining Who is Currently Linked to a Disk

LINKS is an option on the CP QUERY command that displays the userids, virtual addresses and access modes of all users currently linked to a specific virtual address.

Command Format:

> **Query**   **Links vaddr**

where **vaddr**   is the virtual address.

Exercise:

Determine who is currently linked to the system disk whose virtual address is 190:

    QUERY LINK 190

4.7 Hexadecimal Numbers

A hexadecimal number is a base 16 number. The relationship between the decimal (base 10) number system with which you are familiar and the hexadecimal (base 16) number system is:

```
Decimal:      0  1  2  3  4  5  6  7  8  9 10 11 12 13 14 15
Hexadecimal: 0  1  2  3  4  5  6  7  8  9  A  B  C  D  E  F
```

```
Decimal:     16 17 18 19 20 21 22 23 24 25 26 27 28 29 30 31
Hexadecimal:10 11 12 13 14 15 16 17 18 19 1A 1B 1C 1D 1E 1F
```

- The numbers 0 through 9 are represented by 0 through 9.

- The numbers 10 through 15 are represented by A, B, C, D, E and F, respectively.

- The numbers 16 through 25 are represented by 11 through 19.

- The numbers 26 through 31 are represented by 1A, 1B, 1C, 1D, 1E and 1F, respectively.

Don't be intimidated by hexadecimal numbers. When using VM/CMS, there is little that you'll have to know about them and you'll never have to convert decimal numbers to hexadecimal or vice versa. Whenever you have to specify a hexadecimal number for a virtual device, you can use any decimal number no greater than three digits that is not already in use. Use the CP QUERY command to determine whether a number is already in use as a virtual address.

Command Format:

Query   **vaddr**

where **vaddr**   is the virtual address.

Part II
Creating and Editing Files with XEDIT

Chapter 5
Becoming Acquainted with XEDIT

Introduction

Much has already been said about disk files and their characteristics. Almost nothing has been said about how files come to exist in the first place. The usual way that a new file is created is with a utility program called an **editor** which provides commands to:

- Put new text into a file.

- Make changes to the text already in the file.

- Determine the status of the editing environment.

- Change the editing environment.

- Display the contents of a file.

- Move around in a file.

Two editors are available on VM/CMS:

- **EDIT** is a **line-oriented editor**, which means that you can only work on a single line at a time and that you do all text editing by entering commands on the command line. EDIT is an older more traditional editor that will not be covered in this text.

- **XEDIT** is a **screen-oriented editor**, which means that you can work on a whole screen of a text at a time. You can move the cursor to *any* part of the input area and either add new text or delete old text. On a terminal that displays 24 lines, you can work on 18 lines of text. When convenient, you can also edit text by entering commands from the command line. Screen-oriented editors are also referred to as **full-screen editors** and **display editors**.

Three other chapters are also concerned with XEDIT:

- *Performing Common Editing Tasks with XEDIT* discusses how to perform the more common editing tasks.

- *Special Topics in XEDIT* is concerned with editing tasks that you may perform infrequently but which are, nevertheless, important and useful.

- *Customizing the XEDIT Environment* discusses how to modify the characteristics of the XEDIT environment so that they better suit your needs and preferences.

5.1 Starting a New File

When you are in CMS, you can start a new file by entering the XEDIT command followed by the fileid of the file to be created.

Command Format:

Xedit	**fn ft [fm]**

where **fn**   is the filename.

ft   is the filetype.

fm   is the filemode. If the filemode is omitted, it becomes A.

Example:

Suppose you must start a file called QUERY MEMO:

        XEDIT QUERY MEMO

Figure 5.1 shows the appearance of the screen in XEDIT when a new file called QUERY MEMO is being created.

```
 QUERY    MEMO    A1   V 80   Trunc=80 Size=0 Line=0 Col=1 Alt=0
 DMSXIN571I Creating New File:




===== * * * Top of File * * *
      |...+....1....+....2....+....3....+....4....+....5....+....6....+....7...
===== * * * End of File * * *




====> _
                                                        X E D I T  1 File
```

Figure 5.1 The appearance of the screen in XEDIT when a new file is being created.

5.2 Saving a File and Ending an Editing Session

When XEDIT creates a file, it does so in virtual storage, which is *temporary*. To make the file *permanent*, you must save it by writing it to disk using either the FILE or SAVE subcommands. The differences between these subcommands and several others are discussed in this section.

- SAVE writes a file to disk and leaves you in the editor.

- FILE writes a file to disk and ends the editing session.

- QUIT ends the editing session only if the file has not been changed.

- QQUIT ends the editing session regardless of whether the file has been changed.

It is **very important** that you frequently write to disk whatever changes you've made to a file. If the computer malfunctions or if the connection between your terminal and the computer is broken, you may lose whatever changes you've made to the file since you last wrote it to disk. The AUTOSAVE function of the SET subcommand, discussed in the chapter *Customizing the XEDIT Environment*, provides a convenient mechanism to automatically write the file to disk after a specific number of changes.

Saving a File and Remaining in XEDIT

SAVE writes the file to disk and leaves you in XEDIT.

Command Format:

SAVE	**[fn [ft [fm]]]**

where	**fn**	is the filename. Substitute an = to write the file to disk with the same filename as the file being edited. If the filename is omitted, it becomes the filename of the file being edited.
	ft	is the filetype. Substitute an = to write the file to disk with the same filetype as the file being edited. If the filetype is omitted, it becomes the filetype of the file being edited.
	fm	is the filemode. Substitute an = to write the file to disk with the same filemode as the file being edited. If the filemode is omitted, it becomes the filemode of the file being edited.

System Messages:

If you change the fileid of the file being edited to one that already exists and enter the SAVE subcommand, XEDIT displays a message to warn you that a file already exists with the same fileid:

> File 'fileid' already exists. Use FFILE/SSAVE.

- To keep the file that already exists, give the file being edited another fileid.

- To replace the file that already exists with the file being edited, use the SSAVE subcommand.

Command Format:

    SSave   [fn [ft [fm]]]

Example:

Suppose you are editing a file called QUERY MEMO A and want to write the file to disk with the same fileid and remain in XEDIT. The following are equivalent:

```
====> SAVE
====> SAVE  =  =  =
====> SAVE  QUERY  MEMO
====> SAVE  QUERY  MEMO  A
```

Ending an Editing Session without Saving the File

QUIT (assigned to PF3) ends an editing session if and only if the file has not been changed since you began editing it or since the last SAVE subcommand. This is useful if you make one or more substantial changes to a file either purposely or inadvertently that should not have been made.

Command Format:

    QUIT

System Messages:

If the file has been changed and you enter the QUIT subcommand, XEDIT displays a message to warn you that the file has been changed:

> File has been changed. Use QQUIT to quit anyway.

- To leave the editor and write to disk the changes you have made, use the FILE subcommand.

- To leave the editor without writing to disk the changes you have made, use the QQUIT subcommand.

Command Format:

>   QQUIT

Saving a File and Ending the Editing Session

FILE writes the file to disk and returns you to CMS. This subcommand is equivalent to doing a SAVE and then a QUIT.

Command Format:

>   FILE   [fn [ft [fm]]]

where **fn**   is the filename. Substitute an = to write the file to disk with the same filename as the file being edited. If the filename is omitted, it becomes the filename of the file being edited.

ft   is the filetype. Substitute an = to write the file to disk with the same filetype as the file being edited. If the filetype is omitted, it becomes the filetype of the file being edited.

fm   is the filemode. Substitute an = to write the file to disk with the same filemode as the file being edited. If the filemode is omitted, it becomes the filemode of the file being edited.

System Messages:

If you change the fileid of the file being edited to one that already exists and enter the FILE subcommand, XEDIT displays a message to warn you that a file with the same fileid already exists:

>   File 'fileid' already exists. Use FFILE/SSAVE.

- To keep the file that already exists, give the file being edited another fileid.

- To replace the file that already exists with the file being edited, use the FFILE subcommand.

Command Format:

>   FFile   [fn [ft [fm]]]

Example:

Suppose you are editing a file called QUERY MEMO A and want to write the file to disk with the same fileid and return to CMS. The following are equivalent:

```
====> FILE
====> FILE  =  =  =
====> FILE  QUERY  MEMO  A
```

5.3 The Areas of the Screen and Their Uses in XEDIT

When you are editing a file with XEDIT, the 24 lines that are normally displayed on the terminal screen are divided into eight areas:

- The File Identification Line

- The Message Line

- The Command Line

- The Status Message Area

- The Prefix Area

- The Scale Line

- The Current Line

- The File Area

Each of these areas has a location and a special function described below. Figure 5.2 shows the locations of each of these areas on the terminal screen. Figure 5.1 displays the screen appearance when a new file is being created.

```
                          File Identification Line
                               Message Line

  Prefix

                   * * * TOP OF FILE * * *
                               Current Line
                               Scale Line
                   * * * END OF FILE * * *


  Area


====> Command Line
                                              Status Area
```

Figure 5.2 The areas of the screen in XEDIT.

The File Identification Line

The file identification line is the topmost line of the screen. From left to right it displays information about the file being edited:

- The filename.

- The filetype.

- The filemode.

- The record format.

- The record length.

- The truncation column.[1]

- The number of lines in the file.

- The line number of the current line.

- The column number of the current column.

- The number of alterations made since the file was last written to disk.

In the case of Figure 5.1:

- QUERY is the filename.

- MEMO is the filetype.

- A1 is the filemode.

- V (variable) is the record format.

- 80 is the record length.

- Trunc = 80 indicates that column 80 is the truncation column.

- Size = 0 indicates that there are 0 lines in the file.

- Line = 0 indicates that line 0 is the current line.

- Col = 1 indicates that column 1 is the current column.

- Alt = 0 indicates that there have been 0 alterations to the file.

---

[1] The **truncation column** is the last column in which text may be entered on a line.

The Message Line

The message line is the second line from the top of the screen. XEDIT uses the message line to display error messages and informational messages resulting from commands that you have entered.

In Figure 5.1, XEDIT displays the message:

```
DMSXIN571I Creating new file:
```

The Command Line

The command line begins with the arrow

```
====>
```

on the second line from the bottom of the screen and continues in the first column of the last line up to, but not into, the status area. This is the area in which you enter commands known as **subcommands**.

In Figure 5.1, notice that the cursor, which appears as an underscore, is positioned in the first column of the command line right after the arrow.

The Status Message Area

The status message area, located in the lower right corner of the screen, indicates whether you are in **edit mode** or **input mode** and how many files you are editing.

In Figure 5.1, the status area indicates that XEDIT is in edit mode with one file.

The Prefix Area

The prefix area is the area filled with equals signs in the left margin of the screen. This is the area in which you enter commands known as **prefix commands**.

The Scale Line

The scale line is the horizontal line displaying column numbers immediately below the middle of the screen.

```
|...+....1....+....2....+....3....+....4....+....5....+....6
```

The vertical bar (|) character on the scale line designates the position of the column pointer.

The Current Line

The position of the current line *on the screen* must be distinguished from the position of the current line *in the file*:

- The position of the current line *on the screen* is the line in the middle of the screen immediately above the scale line.

- The position of the current line *in the file* is the line in the file indicated by the line pointer. The current line's position in the file is shown after Line= on the file identification line. The current line is the line in the file where many subcommands begin to perform their functions.

In Figure 5.1, the current line is line 0, which is the top of the file.

The File Area

The file area is the area between the notices:

```
* * * Top of File * * *
```

and

```
* * * End of File * * *
```

This is the area in which new text is entered. The notices are not part of the file.

In Figure 5.1, the file is empty, so there is nothing in the file area.

Input Areas and Protected Areas

The areas of the screen in which you can enter text are called **input areas**. In XEDIT, the input areas are:

- The File Area — text entered here becomes part of the file when you press the ENTER key.

- The Prefix Area — text entered here is interpreted as a prefix command when you press the ENTER key.

- The Command Line — text entered here is interpreted as a subcommand when you press the ENTER key.

All other areas of the screen in XEDIT are **protected areas**, which means that you cannot enter text in any of them. If you attempt to do so, the keyboard will lock to prohibit you from doing so and the terminal may sound an alarm. If necessary, use the RESET key to unlock the keyboard. Demonstrate this to yourself by moving the cursor into one of these areas and typing something.

5.4 Modes in Which XEDIT Operates

XEDIT operates in either of two modes:

- Edit Mode

- Input Mode

Edit Mode

When you begin editing a file, XEDIT is in edit mode where:

- The current line at the top of the file.

- The cursor is located in the first column of the first line of the command line.

- Columns 1 through 73 are normally displayed. Columns beyond 73 can be displayed using the commands discussed in the section *Shifting the Display Sideways* in the chapter *Special Topics in XEDIT*.

Use edit mode to issue commands from the command line and prefix area to input, examine and/or change the text in the file. Figure 5.1 shows the appearance of the screen in edit mode.

```
 QUERY    MEMO   A1   V 80   Trunc=80 Size=0 Line=0 Col=1 Alt=0
 DMSXMD573I   Input Mode:




* * * Top of File * * *
 |...+....1....+....2....+....3....+....4....+....5....+....6....+....7....+....
 _




====> * * * Input Zone * * *
                                              Input-Mode 1 File
```

Figure 5.3 The appearance of the screen in input mode in XEDIT.

Input Mode

Input mode provides a convenient method to put several consecutive lines of text into a file after the current line.[2] Switch from edit mode to input mode by entering the subcommand:

Input

When XEDIT is in input mode:

- The command line and the prefix area both disappear so you cannot enter subcommands and prefix commands.

- The cursor is located in the first column of the line below the scale line so that new text is placed after the current line.

- Press the ENTER key *once* after typing a line of text to move that line up to the current line and place the cursor in the first column of the line below the scale line again.

- Press the NEW LINE key after typing a line of text to move the cursor to the first column of the next line.

- Press the ENTER key *twice* after typing a line of text to switch XEDIT from input mode to edit mode.

Figure 5.3 shows the appearance of the screen in input mode. Input mode is not the only way to add new lines to a file. Several other commands are discussed in the chapter *Performing Common Editing Tasks with XEDIT*.

Determining Which Mode XEDIT is In

XEDIT uses the status area to display which mode it is in and the number of files being edited.

- When editing one file in edit mode, XEDIT displays the status message:

X E D I T   1 File

- When editing one file in input mode, XEDIT displays the status message:

Input-Mode   1 File

Exercise:

This exercise is designed to familiarize you with how to put text into a file, the

---

[2] *Input mode is not the same as insert mode.*

difference between edit mode and input mode and how to switch between modes.

1. Begin a file called QUERY MEMO by entering the command:

   XEDIT QUERY MEMO

   Your screen should resemble that in Figure 5.1.

2. Switch from edit mode to input mode by entering the INPUT subcommand:

   ====> INPUT

   Your screen should resemble the one in Figure 5.3. Notice that the prefix area and command line have disappeared and that the cursor has moved to the first column of the file area under the current line.

3. While in input mode, type the following line of text and press ENTER:

   who

   Notice that when you press ENTER three things happen:

   a. The line of text moved up to the current line.

   b. The cursor returned to the first column of the file area under the current line.

   c. Some of the information displayed in the file identification line has changed:

      • Size = 1 indicates that the file now contains one line.

      • Line = 1 indicates that line 1 is now the current line.

      • Alt = 1 indicates that you've made one change to the file.

4. While in input mode, type the following line of text, but instead of pressing ENTER, press the NEW LINE key:

   what

   Notice that the line you entered was not moved up to the current line but that the cursor moved the first column of the next line. While the cursor is still in the file area, type the following line and press ENTER:

   when

5. Switch from input mode to edit mode by pressing ENTER twice. Notice that the prefix area and command line have reappeared and that the cursor has moved from the file area to the command line.

6. Move the current line to the top of the file by entering the TOP sub-command on the command line:

    ====> TOP

7. With the current line at the top of the file, switch back to input mode and notice what happens to the lines you've already entered. A line you type into the file now will appear *before* the lines you've already entered. Demonstrate this by switching to input mode, typing the following three lines and switching back to edit mode:

    where
    why
    how

8. Write the file to disk and remain in XEDIT by entering the SAVE sub-command on the command line:

    ====> SAVE

    Notice that the number of changes made to the file, displayed after Alt=, has changed to 0.

9. Write the file to disk and return to CMS by entering the FILE subcommand on the command line:

    ====> FILE

10. When you begin editing a file that already exists, the current line is located at the top of the file. Demonstrate this by returning to the file you were just editing:

    XEDIT QUERY MEMO

    Since input mode adds new lines after the current line, you'll have to move the current line if you want to add lines somewhere other than at the top of the file. Commands to move the current line are discussed in the sections *Locating a Line Target* and *Moving the Current Line*. Suppose you must add lines to the end of the file. The BOTTOM sub-command will move the current line to the end of the file.

    ====> BOTTOM

11. If you've made no changes to the file, you can return to CMS without writing the file to disk either by pressing PF3 or by entering the QUIT subcommand.

    ====> QUIT

Keep the QUERY MEMO file you created here. We'll use it again later.

5.5 The Importance of Case in Entering Text

Normally, the filetype of the file being edited determines whether the letters going into the file are treated as all uppercase or as a mixture of uppercase and lowercase. Table 4.1 lists the treatment of case for the most common filetypes.

- UPPER indicates that all letters going into the file are treated as uppercase.

- MIXED indicates that lowercase letters are not translated to uppercase.

The CASE function of the SET subcommand, discussed in the chapter *Customizing the XEDIT Environment*, can be used to change the treatment of letters going into a file.

Exercise:

This exercise is designed to demonstrate how XEDIT normally uses the filetype to determine how case is treated and how you can use the CASE function to change the normal treatment of case.

In the previous exercise, you created a file called QUERY MEMO. If you examine Table 4.1, you'll see that MEMO is a reserved filetype where the letters going into the file are treated as a mixture of uppercase and lowercase. A filetype of DATA, on the other hand, is not a reserved filetype: all letters going into such a file are treated as uppercase.

1. Begin a file called QUERY DATA by entering the command:

    XEDIT QUERY DATA

2. Switch from edit mode to input mode, using the INPUT subcommand, and enter the following lines of text:

    where
    why
    how

    Notice that each line is translated to uppercase when you press ENTER.

3. Switch from input mode to edit mode and use the CASE function to treat the letters as a mixture of uppercase and lowercase:

    ====> CASE MIXED

4. Switch from edit mode to input mode and enter the following lines of text:

who
what
when

Notice that the lowercase letters are not translated to uppercase.

5. Write the file to disk and return to CMS with the FILE subcommand:

====> FILE

Keep the QUERY DATA file you created here. We'll use it again later.

5.6 Types of XEDIT Commands

XEDIT commands can be distinguished from one another in at least three ways:

- *Where* they are entered.

- *How* they are entered.

- *What* they do.

Accordingly, commands will first be discussed in terms of where and how they are entered, and later, in terms of the functions they perform.

Commands will be described both in general and in particular:

- The general description will provide the command format using the same syntax that was used to describe CP and CMS commands.

- The particular description will provide one or more examples instantiating the use of the command.

Examples will usually demonstrate more than one way to accomplish the same goal either with the same command or with different commands. Examples of subcommands will include the arrow that indicates the beginning of the command line.

====>

Examples of prefix commands will be presented in an abbreviated version of the screen with line numbers in the prefix area instead of equals signs.

```
00000 * * * Top of File * * *
    |...+....1....+....2....+....3....+....4....+....5....
00001 * * * End of File * * *
```

Exercise:

Line numbers displayed in the prefix area become useful when you have to refer to a line by its line number. If you want to have XEDIT automatically display line numbers whenever you begin editing a file:

1. Begin a file called PROFILE XEDIT:

   XEDIT PROFILE XEDIT

2. Enter the subcommand:

   ====> INPUT NUMBER ON

3. Write the file to disk and return to CMS with the FILE subcommand:

Types of XEDIT Commands § 111

====> FILE

The PROFILE XEDIT is a special file that is described in detail in the chapter *Customizing the XEDIT Environment:*.

5.7 Subcommands

A subcommand is a command that you execute in two steps:

1. Type the command on the command line.

2. Press the ENTER key.

Be sure that you enter subcommands on the command line.

- If you enter one in the file area, it becomes part of the file rather than being interpreted as a subcommand.

- If you enter one in the prefix area, it is interpreted as a prefix command and will either result in an error message or produce results other than intended.

Most subcommands can be divided into two categories on the basis of what they work on:

- Subcommands that work on the file being edited. These are discussed in all chapters concerned with XEDIT except *Customizing the XEDIT Environment*.

- Subcommands that work on the editing environment. These are discussed in the chapter *Customizing the XEDIT Environment*.

Some of the More Useful Subcommands

These are some of the subcommands you'll find most useful in editing files:

- INPUT puts text into a file.

- DELETE removes lines from a file.

- CHANGE changes one string of text to another string.

- COPY copies lines to elsewhere in the file.

- MOVE moves lines from their present location to elsewhere in the file.

- DUPLICAT copies lines multiple times.

- LOCATE finds text in a file.

These subcommands and others will be more completely explained in the chapter *Performing Common Editing Tasks with XEDIT*.

Command Syntax and Format

The general format of subcommands is:

cmdname   [operands...]

where **[ ]**   are square brackets indicating that the operand is *op-tional* and need not be specified unless the function the subcommand performs is to be *modified* in the manner specified by the operand.

    cmdname   is a string of one to eight letters in length that is the name of the command to be executed.

    operands   are one or more operands that specify *what* the command is to operate on and *how* the command is to operate. Depending upon the function performed, some subcommands require several operands, while others require none.

    ...   are ellipses to indicate that the command can have more than one operand.[3]

The Importance of Blanks in Entering Subcommands

These rules apply to the use of blanks in XEDIT subcommands:

- At least one space must separate the subcommand name from the first operand *unless* the operand is a number or special character.

- At least one space must separate each of the operands from each other.

Examples:

- These two subcommands are equivalent:

  ```
  ====> ADD  2
  ====> ADD2
  ```

- These two subcommands are equivalent:

  ```
  ====> LOCATE  /how/
  ====> LOCATE/how/
  ```

Entering CP and CMS Commands from XEDIT

CP and CMS commands can both be entered in XEDIT on the command line. You must take special precautions, however, if the CP or CMS command has the same name as an XEDIT subcommand.

---

[3] The brackets, vertical bar and ellipses are only used here to present command syntax. When you actually enter a command, you should *not* use them.

- If a CMS command has the same name as an XEDIT subcommand, precede the CMS command with CMS:

  CMS cmdname

- If a CP command has the same name as an XEDIT subcommand, precede the CP command with CP:

  CP cmdname

Exercise:

HELP is a command recognized by both CMS and XEDIT.

- The XEDIT HELP command displays a menu of XEDIT commands.

- The CMS HELP command displays a menu of available HELP topics.

Enter these commands and notice the difference between them:

====> CMS HELP

====> HELP

- The first HELP command, executed by CMS, displays a menu of HELP topics.

- The second MSG command, executed by XEDIT, displays a menu of XEDIT commands.

5.8 Prefix Commands

A prefix command is a *line-oriented* command that you execute in two steps:

1. Type the command *anywhere* in the prefix area next to the lines it is to manipulate.

2. Press the ENTER key.

Be sure that you enter prefix commands in the prefix area.

- If you enter one in the file area, it becomes part of the file rather than being interpreted as a prefix command.

- If you enter one on the command line, it is interpreted as a subcommand and will either result in an error message or produce results other than intended.

You cannot enter a command in the prefix area if your terminal is in insert mode. If you try to do so, the keyboard will lock to prohibit you and the terminal may sound an alarm. If necessary, use the RESET key to unlock the keyboard. You must get out of insert mode before trying to enter a command in the prefix area.

Some of the More Useful Prefix Commands

These are some of the prefix commands you'll find most useful in editing files:

- I inputs blank lines which you can then fill with text.

- A inputs blank lines which you can then fill with text.

- D removes lines.

- C copies lines to elsewhere in the file.

- M moves lines from their present location to elsewhere in the file.

- " copies a group of lines multiple times.

Command Syntax and Format

All prefix commands can be entered in a format that specifies the exact number of lines to be manipulated.

Command Format:

     nQ or **Qn**

where **Q**   is the prefix command name.

116 § Becoming Acquainted with XEDIT

n is the number of lines to be manipulated. Notice that the number can either precede or follow the command name. If the number of lines is omitted on any prefix command except S (for showing lines), it is assumed to be 1.

Example:

A is a prefix command that adds one or more blank lines immediately after the line where the command is entered. Suppose you must add two blank lines at the top of a file:

```
2A000 * * * Top of File * * *
      |...+....1....+....2....+....3....+....4....+....5....
00001 * * * End of File * * *
```

results in:

```
00000 * * * Top of File * * *
      |...+....1....+....2....+....3....+....4....+....5....
00001 _
00002
00003 * * * End of File * * *
```

An Alternative Format for Most Prefix Commands

An alternative format for all prefix commands except A and I is to specify a **block** of consecutive lines to be manipulated. This format is particularly convenient if you don't know the exact number of lines to be manipulated or if it would simply be inconvenient to determine the number of lines, as might be the case if the lines to be manipulated spanned two or more screens.

1. Place the command name *twice* in the prefix area next to the first of the lines to be manipulated.

   QQ

2. Place the command name *twice* in the prefix area next to the last of the lines to be manipulated.

   QQ

3. Press ENTER.

Example:

D is a prefix command for deleting lines. Suppose you want to delete the last three lines from this file:

```
00000 * * * Top of File * * *
      |...+....1....+....2....+....3....+....4....+....5....
00001 keep this line
00002 keep this line
DD003 delete this line
00004 delete this line
00DD5 delete this line
00006 * * * End of File * * *
```

results in:

```
00000 * * * Top of File * * *
      |...+....1....+....2....+....3....+....4....+....5....
00001 keep this line
00002 keep this line
00003 * * * End of File * * *
```

Specifying the Destination of Lines to be Moved or Copied

The C (for copying lines) and M (for moving lines) prefix commands require you to specify the *destination* of the lines to be copied or moved.

- After you've specified *which* lines are to be copied, XEDIT displays the status message:

  `'C' pending...`

- After you've specified *which* lines are to be moved, XEDIT displays the status message:

  `'M' pending...`

Specify *where* those lines are to be copied or moved in one of two ways:

- Place a **P** in the prefix area next to the line that the lines to be copied or moved are to *precede*.

- Place an **F** in the prefix area next to the line that the lines to be copied or moved are to *follow*.

Example:

Suppose you must move the first line in a file after the second.

```
00000 * * * Top of File * * *
      |...+....1....+....2....+....3....+....4....+....5....
M0001 move this line
00002
OP003 * * * End of File * * *
```

or

```
00000 * * * Top of File * * *
      |...+....1....+....2....+....3....+....4....+....5....
M0001 move this line
0F002
00003 * * * End of File * * *
```

results in:

```
00000 * * * Top of File * * *
      |...+....1....+....2....+....3....+....4....+....5....
00001
00002 move this line
00003 * * * End of File * * *
```

Removing a Command from the Prefix Area

RESET is a subcommand that removes prefix commands that are pending, as in the case of **Cn** or **Mn**, for which you haven't yet specified the destination of the lines. You can also use this subcommand to remove other text from the prefix area, such as a misspelled prefix command or other text you inadvertently put there.

Command Format:

> **RESet**

Beware When Line Numbers are Displayed in the Prefix Area

If line numbers are displayed in the prefix area, use extra care when specifying the number of lines that are to be manipulated, since *the only numbers that are interpreted as part of the prefix command are those that are different from the numbers already in the prefix area.*

Example:

Suppose you must delete two lines beginning with line 2. If you enter D2 as in the following, the 2 is ignored and only a single line is deleted:

```
00000 * * * Top of File * * *
      |...+....1....+....2....+....3....+....4....+....5....
00001 keep this line
000D2 delete this line
00003 delete this line
00004 * * * End of File * * *
```

This avoids the problem:

```
00000 * * * Top of File * * *
      |...+....1....+....2....+....3....+....4....+....5....
00001 keep this line
D2002 delete this line
00003 delete this line
00004 * * * End of File * * *
```

Entering a Prefix Command from the Command Line

LPREFIX is a subcommand that enters a prefix command in the prefix area next to the current line from the command line.

Command Format:

> **LPREFIX**   **command**

where **command**   is a prefix command no longer than five characters that is put in the prefix area next to the current line.

Example:

Suppose you must add two blank lines after the current line:

====> LPREFIX 2A

5.9 Program Function Keys

Normally, you execute a subcommand by typing it on the command line and pressing the ENTER key. Another way is to assign it to a program function key. Once you've assigned a subcommand to a PF key, you can execute it just by pressing the PF key. Thus, a PF key executes a subcommand in a single keystroke.

XEDIT automatically assigns subcommands to PF1 through PF12. The subcommands assigned to these PF keys will be discussed in detail in the next chapter and in the remainder of this chapter in those sections that discuss the functions that these subcommands perform. A brief discussion of the subcommands assigned to PF1 through PF12 follows. (The subcommand name appears in parentheses before the description):[4]

PF1   **(HELP MENU)** Displays a menu of XEDIT commands.

PF2   **(SOS LINEADD)** Adds a blank line immediately below where the cursor is located.

PF3   **(QUIT)** Leaves XEDIT and returns to the environment from which you began editing the file if you have made no changes to the file.

PF4   **(TABKEY)** Moves the cursor to the next tab position.

PF5   **(SCHANGE 6)** Assigns PF6 to execute the SCHANGE subcommand.

PF6   **(?)** Displays the subcommand previously executed on the command line.

PF7   **(BACKWARD)** Scrolls the display backward one full screen.

PF8   **(FORWARD)** Scrolls the display forward one full screen.

PF9   **(=)** Executes the previous subcommand again.

PF10   **(RGTLEFT)** Shifts the display to the right if column 1 is the left-most column displayed. Shifts the display to the left if column 1 is not the left-most column displayed.

PF11   **(SPLTJOIN)** Splits a line where the cursor is located if the cursor is followed by characters other than blanks. Joins two consecutive lines if the cursor is followed only by blanks.

---

[4] On VM/IS systems, the commands assigned to PF keys may be different.

PF12   **(CURSOR HOME)** Moves the cursor from the command line to the file area or from the file area to the the command line, depending on its current position.

Determining Which Subcommands are Assigned to PF Keys

PF is an option on the QUERY subcommand that displays the present assignment of either a single PF key or of PF1 through PF12.

Command Format:

        Query   PF[n]

where **n**   is the number of the PF key whose assignment is to be displayed. If the number is omitted, the assignments of PF1 through PF12 are displayed.

Example:

Suppose you must determine whether PF13 has been assigned a subcommand:

====> QUERY   PF13

Assigning Subcommands to and Removing Them from PF Keys

XEDIT does not assign commands to PF13 through PF24, but you may do so if the type of terminal you are using supports these PF keys. If you wish, you may also assign subcommands to any of the first 12 PF keys, thereby replacing the subcommands initially assigned to them. How to do this is discussed in detail in the chapter *Customizing the XEDIT Environment*.

Exercise:

If you are in input mode and you want to enter the SAVE subcommand, you must normally do three things:

1.   Switch from input mode to edit mode.

2.   Enter the SAVE subcommand.

3.   Switch from edit mode back to input mode.

If the SAVE subcommand were assigned to a PF key, however, you could execute it while remaining in input mode just by pressing the PF key. Suppose you want to assign the SAVE subcommand to PF3:

====> PF3   SAVE

122 § **Becoming Acquainted with XEDIT**

You can automatically assign subcommands to PF keys whenever you begin editing a file by placing the PF assignments in the file called PROFILE XEDIT. How to do so is described in the chapter *Customizing the XEDIT Environment.*

5.10 Using the HELP Facility in XEDIT

HELP (assigned to PF1) is a subcommand that displays:

- A menu of all XEDIT commands.

- Information about a specific XEDIT command.

- Information about the HELP facility itself.

- Information about error messages.

The HELP facility functions in XEDIT just as it does in CMS. Once in a HELP file, use the PF keys as you normally do in a HELP file.

Command Format:

Help	[*MENU*|command|HELP]
where **MENU**	displays a menu of all XEDIT commands.
command	displays information about this command.
HELP	displays information about using the HELP facility.

Exercises:

- Display the menu of all XEDIT commands either by pressing PF1 or with the HELP subcommand:

    ====> HELP

- Display the HELP file for the COPY subcommand:

    ====> HELP COPY

5.11 The Current Line

Subcommands that work on a file by adding new lines, removing existing lines
or changing strings of text begin to do so with the line in the file known as the
current line.

Example:

Suppose you are editing the file called QUERY MEMO and want to make the
line with the word 'how' the current line. Notice that the current line is at the
top of the file.

```
00000 * * * Top of File * * *
      |...+....1....+....2....+....3....+....4....+....5....
00001 where
00002 why
00003 how
00004 who
00005 what
00006 when
00007 * * * End of File * * *
```

LOCATE is a subcommand that moves the current line to the line containing
a specific string of characters:

```
QUERY     MEMO    A1   V 80   Trunc=80 Size=0 Line=0 Col=1 Alt=0




00000 * * * Top of File * * *
      |...+....1....+....2....+....3....+....4....+....5....+....6....+....7...
00001 * * * End of File * * *




====> _
                                              X E D I T   1 File
```

Figure 5.4 The appearance of the screen in XEDIT with line numbers in the
prefix area.

====> LOCATE /how/

results in:

```
00000 * * * Top of File * * *
00001 where
00002 why
00003 how
      |...+....1....+....2....+....3....+....4....+....5....
00004 who
00005 what
00006 when
00007 * * * End of File * * *
```

The Position of the Current Line

The position of the current line **on the screen** must be distinguished from the position of the current line **in the file**:

- The position of the current line **on the screen** is normally the line in the middle of the screen immediately above the scale line. The position of the current line on the screen is normally fixed and does not move.

- The position of the current line **in the file** is the line in the file indicated by the line pointer. The position of the current line in the file changes when the line pointer is moved.

Determining Which Line is the Current Line

The specific line that is the current line is indicated by the **line pointer**. The **line number** of the current line is the position of the current line *relative to the top of the file*. The line number of the current line is the number displayed after Line = in the file identification line at the top of the screen. Thus, in Figure 5.1, the line number of the current line is 0. You can also determine what the line number of the current line is with the subcommand:

Query LINE

If line numbers are displayed in the prefix area, the line number of any line displayed on the screen, including the current line, can easily be determined by examining the number in the prefix area next to the line. For this reason, all examples will display line numbers in the prefix area instead of equal signs. Figure 5.4 shows how the screen appears with line numbers in the prefix area.

Moving the Current Line

Move the position of the current line in a file using the commands discussed in the sections *Locating a Line Target* and *Moving the Current Line.*

5.12 The Current Column

Column-oriented subcommands that delete, insert and replace characters begin to do so with the column known as the current column.

Example:

Suppose you must move the current column to the one containing the letter 'C' in the following file, where column 1 is presently the current column:

```
00000 * * * Top of File * * *
00001 ABCDEFGHIJ
      |...+....1....+....2....+....3....+....4....+....5....
00002 * * * End of File * * *
```

CLOCATE is a subcommand that moves the current column to the one that contains a specific string of characters:

```
====> CLOCATE /C/
```

results in:

```
00000 * * * Top of File * * *
00001 ABCDEFGHIJ
      <.|.+....1....+....2....+....3....+....4....+....5....
00002 * * * End of File * * *
```

Determining Which Column is the Current Column

The specific column on the current line that is the current column is indicated by the **column pointer**. Normally, the current column is the first column of the current line. The **column number** of the current column is the location of the current column on the current line. The location of the current column is indicated on the scale line by the vertical bar (|). The column number of the current column is the number displayed after Col= in the file identification line at the top of the screen. Thus, in Figure 5.1, the column number of the current column is 1. You can also determine what the column number of the current column is with the subcommand:

> Query COLumn

Moving the Current Column

Move the current column using commands that move the column pointer. These commands are discussed in the section *Locating a Column Target.*

5.13 Targets

A target is a specific line or column to be located in a file.

- If the target is a line, the target is a **line target**. Subcommands that use line targets might be described as **line-oriented**.

- If the target is a column, the target is a **column target**. Subcommands that use column targets might be described as **column-oriented**. Since most subcommands are line-oriented, only the column-oriented ones will be designated as such.

Locating a Target

A target is *located* when you enter a subcommand that *searches* for something that identifies the target. One of the most common ways a target can identify a line or column is by a string of characters that occurs in that line or begins in that column.

- If the target is a line target, use one of the subcommands discussed in the section *Locating a Line Target* later in this chapter.

- If the target is a column target, use one of the subcommands discussed in the section *Locating a Column Target* later in this chapter.

The Zone: the Columns within Which XEDIT Searches for Targets

The first and last columns within which a search is conducted is the zone.

- The zone begins at the first tab stop, which is normally column 1. The start of the zone is indicated on the scale line by the < character *unless* the current column and the start of the zone are the same column, in which case the vertical bar appears in that column.

- The zone ends at the truncation column, which depends on a file's filetype. The end of the zone is indicated on the scale line by the > character *unless* the current column and the end of the zone are the same column, in which case the vertical bar appears in that column.

```
....+..<.1....+....2....+....3.|..+....4....+....5....+..>.6
  begin zone                current column              end zone
```

The Range: the Lines within Which XEDIT Searches for Targets

The first and last lines within which a search is conducted is the range.

- The range normally begins at the top of the file.

- The range normally ends at the end of the file.

Controlling the Search for a Target

SET is a subcommand, discussed in detail in the chapter *Customizing the XEDIT Environment*, that has several functions that control:

- Which columns are searched for a target.

- Which lines are searched for a target.

- How targets are defined.

- How target searches are conducted.

- Where searches are conducted.

5.14 Line Targets

Line-oriented subcommands use line targets to:

- Identify the line which is to be made the current line.

- Identify the line where a subcommand is to cease operation.

- Identify the first line that contains a specific string of text.

Locate the line identified by a line target by entering a subcommand that searches for that target. A search for a line target either moves forward or backward in a file:

- A *forward* search for a line target begins with the line *following* the current line and continues line by line toward the end of the file until either the target is found or the end of the file or end of range is reached.

- A *backward* search for a line target begins with the line *preceding* the current line and continues line by line toward the top of the file until either the target is found or the top of the file or top of range is reached.

System Messages:

If the search for a line target is successful, the line pointer is moved to that line, making it the current line. If the search for a line target is unsuccessful, XEDIT displays the message

        Target not found.

and the line pointer is moved to the end of file (or end of range) if the search was in a forward direction or the line pointer is moved to the top of file (or top of range) if the search was in a backward direction.

How to Specify a Line Target

A line target identifies a line in one of four ways:

- An Absolute Line Number identifies a line relative to the top of the file.

- A Relative Line Number identifies a line relative to the current line.

- A Line Name identifies a line in terms of a name assigned to the line.

- A String Expression identifies a line in terms of a string of characters on the line.

Absolute Line Numbers

An absolute line number identifies a line *relative to the top of the file.*

Specify it as a colon followed by the number of lines between it and the top of the file. Since the line number of the top of the file is 0, the absolute line number of a line is simply its line number:

> **:nn**

where   **nn**   is the number of lines between the top of the file and the line to be made the current line.

Examples:

- :9 is the absolute line number of the ninth line from the top of the file.

- :0 is the absolute line number of the top of the file.

Relative Line Numbers

A relative line number identifies a line *relative to the current line.*

How you specify a relative line number depends on whether the line is located before or after the current line.

If a line is positioned *before* the current line, specify its relative line number as a negative number:

> **−nn**

where   **nn**   is the number of lines between the line target and the current line. Substitute an * for **nn**, as in −*, if the target is the top of the file (or top of range).

If a line is positioned *after* the current line, specify its relative line number as a positive number:

> **[+]nn**

where   **nn**   is the number of lines between the line target and the current line. Substitute an * for **nn**, as in +*, if the target is the end of the file (or end of range). Notice that the + is optional.

Examples:

- −1 is the relative line number of the line immediately above the current line.

132   §   Becoming Acquainted with XEDIT

- 1 is the relative line number of the line immediately below the current line.

- If the third line in a five line file is the current line, then the relative line number of the top of the file could be specified as either −3 or −* and the relative line number of the end of the file could be specified as either 3 or *.

String Expressions

A string expression identifies a line in terms of a string of characters on the line.

Specify a simple string expression by preceding and following the character string with a **delimiting character** to indicate the beginning and end of the string:

    /string[/]

where **/**   is a delimiting character that indicates the beginning and end of the text to be found. If the text contains no blanks, the ending delimiter can be omitted. Use the slash (/) as the delimiting character unless a slash is one of the characters in the string to be found. The use of other delimiters will be discussed later in this section.

    string   is the text to be found. The first line on which the string is found is made the current line.

Special characters are used to specify complex string expressions:

- If the character string is on a line located *after* the current line, precede the string expression with an optional plus sign (+) to search *forward* in the file.

    [+] /string/

- If the character string is on a line located *before* the current line, precede the string expression with a minus sign (−) to search *backward* in the file.[5]

    − /string/

---

[5] Notice that the only difference between designating a forward search and a backward search for a string is that a minus sign (−) precedes the first slash in a backward search.

- If the line to be located is one with the first *non-occurrence* of a string, precede the string expression with the logical NOT sign (¬):[6]

  ¬ /string/

- If the line to be located is the first one with **string1** *and* **string2**, separate the two string expressions with the ampersand (**&**) to represent a logical AND:

  /string1/ & /string2/

- If the line to be located is the first one with *either* **string1** *or* **string2**, separate the two string expressions with the vertical bar (**|**) to represent a logical OR:

  /string1/ | /string2/

Examples of simple and complex string expressions are provided in the sections that follow.

String Expressions in Hexadecimal

A character string can also be specified using hexadecimal notation if the HEX function of the SET subcommand, discussed in the chapter *Customizing the XEDIT Environment*, is assigned to be ON. This is useful if one or more characters in the string are not available on your keyboard.

To specify a string expression in hexadecimal:

1. Precede the hexadecimal representation of the string with **X'** (an X followed by a single quote).

2. Follow the hexadecimal representation of the string with **'** (a single quote).

Example:

The hexadecimal representation of the string 123 is F1F2F3. As a string, this becomes X'F1F2F3'. Suppose you must search forward for the string using hex code:

====> HEX ON

====> /X'F1F2F3'

---

[6] On ASCII terminals the character that represents the logical NOT may be the caret.

134 § Becoming Acquainted with XEDIT

Line Names

A line name identifies a line in terms of a name assigned to the line. A line name is a label of one to eight alphanumeric characters that begin with a period:

> .linename

The line name remains associated with the line even if the line number changes either because the line is moved or because other lines are added or deleted.

Assign a name to a line in either of two ways:

- Type the name into the prefix area. A line name typed into the prefix area is limited to four characters.

- Use the POINT function of the SET subcommand to assign a name to the current line.

POINT can also be used to remove a line name.

Command Format:

> **POINT**   .linename   [OFF]

where **.linename**   is a name assigned to the current line.

       OFF   removes **.linename** as the name of the current line.

After a name has been assigned to a line, the name is not actually displayed on the screen. Line names and line numbers can be displayed, however, with the subcommand:

> **Query**   **POINT** [*]

If the * is omitted, only the name of the current line is displayed.

Examples:

- Suppose you must assign the current line a name of FRED. You can either enter .FRED in the prefix area next to the current line or use the command:

```
====> POINT .FRED
```

- Suppose you must remove the line name .FRED from the current line:

```
====> POINT .FRED OFF
```

5.15 Locating a Line Target

These subcommands locate line targets:

- LOCATE searches anywhere in any direction for any kind of line target.

- FIND searches forward for a line that begins with a string.

- NFIND searches forward for a line that does not begin with a string.

- FINDUP searches backward for a line that begins with a string.

- NFINDUP searches backward for a line that does not begin with a string.

The subcommands differ from each other in terms of:

- The *direction* in which they search.

- *Where* they search.

- The *kind* of target for which they search.

- Whether the target *is* or *is not* what is to be found.

Each of the subcommands takes the general form:

> **cmdname   target**

where **cmdname**   is the name of the subcommand.

> **target**   identifies the line to be found.

Searching Anywhere in Any Direction for Any Kind of Line Target

LOCATE is the most versatile and generally useful of the line target location subcommands. It can search anywhere in a file in either a forward or backward direction for any kind of line target.

For convenience, the LOCATE subcommand may be executed by specifying the target without the word LOCATE preceding it whenever the target is an absolute line number, a relative line number, a string expression whose delimiter is a slash (/) or a line name.

Command Format:

> **[Locate]   target**

where **target**   is either an absolute line number, a relative line number, a string expression or a line name.

Exercise:

Suppose you are editing the file called QUERY MEMO and the current line is at the top of the file:

```
00000 * * * Top of File * * *
     |...+....1....+....2....+....3....+....4....+....5....
00001 where
00002 why
00003 how
00004 who
00005 what
00006 when
00007 * * * End of File * * *
```

1. Make the line with 'how' on it the current line. The following are equivalent:

   ```
   ====> 3      (a relative line number)
   ====> :3     (an absolute line number)
   ====> /how   (a string expression)
   ```

2. Suppose now that line 3 is the current line. Make line 2, the line with 'why', the current line. The following are equivalent:

   ```
   ====> -1     (a relative line number)
   ====> :2     (an absolute line number)
   ====> -/why  (a string expression)
   ```

3. Suppose that line 2 is the current line and that you want to locate the first line that does not contain the string 'wh' which would be the line with the word 'how':

   ```
   ====> ¬/wh/
   ```

4. Suppose that line 3 is the current line and that you want to locate the first line that contains the letter 'w' *and* the letter 'h' *and* the letter 'o', which would be the line with the word 'who':

   ```
   ====> /w/ & /h/ & /o/
   ```

5. Suppose that line 1 is the current line and that you want to locate the first line that contains either the word 'why' or the word 'how':

   ```
   ====> /why/ | /how/
   ```

Locating a Line Target   §   137

The Importance of Case in String Expressions

Normally, the case of letters is important in searching for target strings. What this means is that when you are specifying a target string, you must match the case of the letters in the target string to the case of the letters in the string to be found.

- If the string to be found is all uppercase, the target string must be all uppercase.

- If the string to be found is all lowercase, the target string must be all lowercase.

- If the string to be found is a mixture of uppercase and lowercase, the target string must be a corresponding mixture of uppercase and lowercase.

The CASE function of the SET subcommand, discussed in the chapter *Customizing the XEDIT Environment*, can be used to determine whether case is ignored or respected in string expressions.

Exercise:

The file called QUERY DATA that you created earlier should contain some lines that are uppercase and some that are lowercase.

1. Begin editing that file again and notice the difference between searching for a string with a lowercase 'wh' and searching for a string with an uppercase 'WH':

    ====> /wh/

    ====> /WH/

2. Use the CASE function to ignore case in searching for a target string:

    ====> CASE   MIXED   IGNORE

3. Now, notice that searching for a string with a lowercase 'wh' is equivalent to searching for one with an uppercase 'WH'.

Searching for a String Expression That Includes a Slash

If you are searching for a string expression with one or more slashes (/) embedded in it, you must use some character other than the slash to delimit the string to be located.

The characters that *cannot* be used to delimit a target are letters, numbers, special characters that appear in the string to be found and the special characters which already have special significance for the LOCATE subcommand, such as the minus sign (−), the plus sign (+), the logical not sign (¬), the ampersand (&), the vertical bar (|), the asterisk (*) and the period (.).

Example:

Suppose you're at the top of a file and you must find the location of the date 05/09/51. To do so, you could use the comma to delimit the string:

====> LOCATE ,05/09/51,

Locating the Line Where a Subcommand is to Begin

Usually the line where a subcommand is to begin operation is not the current line. Since subcommands commence operation with the current line, you must make that line where the subcommand is to start the current line *before* entering the subcommand. For your convenience, you can specify the line where a subcommand is to begin with a line target on the command line *before* the subcommand. This method of entering a subcommand is equivalent to entering the two subcommands separately:

1. Using a line target to identify the line where the subcommand is to begin.

2. Entering the subcommand.

Exercise:

Suppose you are editing the file called QUERY MEMO and want to remove lines 3 and 4. DELETE is a subcommand that removes the lines beginning with the current line down to a line target. The target line is not removed. Suppose that line 1 is the current line.

```
00000 * * * Top of File * * *
00001 where
      |...+....1....+....2....+....3....+....4....+....5....
00002 why
00003 how
00004 who
00005 what
00006 when
00007 * * * End of File * * *
```

1. Make line 3 the current line. The following are equivalent:

   :3   (an absolute line number)
   2   (a relative line number)
   /how/   (a string expression)

2. Specify a line target on the DELETE subcommand that identifies the line down to which, but not including, the lines are to be deleted. The following are equivalent:

```
====> :3      DELETE 2
====>  2      DELETE 2
====> /how/ DELETE 2
====> :3      DELETE :5
====>  2      DELETE :5
====> /how/ DELETE :5
====> :3      DELETE /what/
====>  2      DELETE /what/
====> /how/ DELETE /what/
```

3. Return to CMS without writing to disk the changes you've made with the QQUIT subcommand:

```
====> QQUIT
```

Searching Forward for a Line That Begins with a String

FIND searches *forward* in a file for the first line that *begins in column 1* with a specific string of text. Use the underscore character (_) in the string to indicate that a blank character is part of the string to be found. Thus, this subcommand cannot be used to search for a string that includes an underscore.

Command Format:

Find   **string**

where **string**   is the text to be located without any delimiters.

Examples:

Suppose a file contains these four lines:

```
00000 * * * Top of File * * *
00001 ABCD
      |...+....1....+....2....+....3....+....4....+....5....
00002 BABC
00003 CBAB
00004 DCBA
00005 * * * End of File * * *
```

• This subcommand would locate line 3 as the line that begins with' C':

```
====> FIND C
```

140 § Becoming Acquainted with XEDIT

- This subcommand would not locate line 1 as the line that begins with 'A', since line 1 is the current line and the search begins on the line following the current line:

  ====> FIND A

Searching Backward for a Line That Begins with a String

FINDUP (**FUp** is a synonym) searches *backward* in a file for the first line that *begins in column 1* with a specific string of text. Use the underscore character (_) in the string to indicate that a blank character is part of the string to be found. Thus, this subcommand cannot be used to search for a string that includes an underscore.

Command Format:

    FINDUp   **string**

where **string**   is the text to be located without any delimiters.

Searching Forward for a Line That Does Not Begin with a String

NFIND searches *forward* in a file for the first line that *does not begin in column 1* with a specific string of text. Use the underscore character (_) in the string to indicate that a blank character is part of the string to be found. Thus, this subcommand cannot be used to search for a string that includes an underscore.

Command Format:

    NFind   **string**

where **string**   is the text not to be located without any delimiters.

Example:

Suppose a file contains these four lines:

```
00000 * * * Top of File * * *
00001 ABCD
      |...+....1....+....2....+....3....+....4....+....5....
00002 BABC
00003 CBAB
00004 DCBA
00005 * * * End of File * * *
```

Locating a Line Target § 141

This subcommand would locate line 3 as the first line that does not begin with 'B':

```
====> NFIND B
```

Searching Backward for a Line That Does Not Begin with a String

NFINDUP (**NFUp** is a synonym) searches *backward* in a file for the first line that *does not begin in column 1* with a specific string of text. Use the underscore character (_) in the string to indicate that a blank character is part of the string to be found. Thus, this subcommand cannot be used to search for a string that includes an underscore.

Command Format:

NFINDUp   **string**

where **string**   is the text not to be located without any delimiters.

5.16 Column Targets

Column-oriented subcommands use column targets to:

- Identify the column that is to be made the current column.

- Identify the column where a specific string of text begins.

- Identify the column where a column-oriented subcommand is to cease operation.

Locate the column identified by a column target by entering a subcommand that searches for that target. A search for a column target either moves forward or backward in the file:

- A *forward* search for a column target begins with the column *following* the current column and continues column by column on each line until either the target is located or the end of the file or end of range is reached.

- A *backward* search for a column target begins with the column *preceding* the current column and continues column by column on each line until either the target is located or the top of the file or top of range is reached.

The STREAM function of the SET subcommand, discussed in the chapter *Customizing the XEDIT Environment*, controls whether the search for a column target is only conducted on the current line or whether the entire file is searched. Normally, the entire file is searched.

If the search for a column target is successful, the column pointer is moved to that column, making it the current column. If a column target is found on the current line, the line pointer is not moved. If a column target is found on a line other than the current line, the line pointer is moved to that line, making that line the current line. Notice that a successful search for a line target *does not* move the column pointer — only the line pointer is moved.

System Messages:

If the search for a column target is unsuccessful, the column pointer is not moved and XEDIT displays the message:

        Target not found.

How to Specify a Column Target

A column target identifies a column in either of three ways:

- An Absolute Column Number identifies a column relative to the beginning of the line.

- A Relative Column Number identifies a column relative to the current column.

- A String Expression identifies a column in terms of a string of characters that begins in that column.

Absolute Column Numbers

An absolute column number identifies a column *relative to the beginning of the line.*

Specify it as a colon followed by the number of columns between it and the beginning of the line. Since the column number of the beginning of the line is 0, a column's absolute column number is simply its column number:

>   :nn

where   **nn**   is the column to be made the current column.

Examples:

- :9 is the absolute column number of column 9.

- :1 is the absolute column number of column 1.

- :0 is the absolute column number of the beginning of the line.

Relative Column Numbers

A relative column number identifies a column *relative to the current column.*

How you specify a relative column number depends on whether the column is positioned before or after the current column.

If a column target is positioned *before* the current column, specify its relative column number as a negative number:

>   −nn

where   **nn**   is the number of columns the target is positioned before the current column. Substitute an * for **nn**, as in −*, to move the column pointer to the column that is one column preceding the beginning of the line or beginning of the zone.

If a column target is positioned *after* the current column, specify its relative column number as a positive number:

>   +nn or nn

where	**nn**	is the number of columns the target is positioned below the current column. Substitute an * for **nn**, as in +*, to move the column pointer to the column that is one column following the end of the line or end of the zone.

Examples:

- −1 is the relative column number of the column immediately before the current column.

- +1 is the relative column number of the column immediately after the current column.

- If column 3 is the current column in a file with 80 column records, then the relative column number of the beginning of the line can be specified as either −3 or −* and the relative column number of the end of the line can be specified as either +78 or *.

String Expressions

A string expression identifies a column in terms of a string of characters that begins in that column.

Specify a column target as a string expression in exactly the same way that you specify a line target as a string expression.

5.17 Locating a Column Target

These subcommands locate column targets:

- CLOCATE searches anywhere in any direction for any kind of column target.

- CFIRST moves the column pointer to the beginning of the zone.

- CLAST moves the column pointer to the end of the zone.

If necessary, use the ZONE function of the SET subcommand, discussed in the chapter *Customizing the XEDIT Environment*, to change the beginning and end of the zone.

Searching for a Column Target

CLOCATE can locate a column target and move the column pointer to any column on a line. It is the most versatile and generally useful of the column target subcommands.

Command Format:

      CLocate   **target**

where **target**   is either an absolute column number, a relative column number or a string expression.

Examples:

Suppose a file contains the following line, where column 1 is presently the current column, and that you must move the current column from its present location to column 3, where the letter 'C' is.

```
00000 * * * Top of File * * *
00001 ABCDE
      |...+....1....+..>.2....+....3....+....4....+....5....
00002 * * * End of File * * *
```

The following are equivalent:

```
====> CL :3   (an absolute column number)
====> CL 2    (a relative column number)
====> CL /C/  (a string expression)
```

Any of these three types of targets would move the column pointer to column 3, as indicated by the vertical bar now in column 3:

```
00000 * * * Top of File * * *
00001 ABCDE
      <.|.+....1....+..>.2....+....3....+....4....+....5....
00002 * * * End of File * * *
```

Moving the Column Pointer to the Beginning of the Zone

CFIRST moves the column pointer to the beginning of the zone.

Command Format:

> **CFirst**

Example:

Suppose that column 3 is the current column, as in the above CLOCATE example. Entering the CFIRST subcommand would move the column pointer to column 1:

```
00000 * * * Top of File * * *
00001 ABCDE
      |...+....1....+..>.2....+....3....+....4....+....5....
00002 * * * End of File * * *
```

Moving the Column Pointer to the End of the Zone

CLAST moves the column pointer to the end of the zone.

Command Format:

> **CLAst**

Example:

Suppose that column 18 is the end of the zone, as in the previous example. Entering the CLAST subcommand would move the column pointer to column 18:

```
00000 * * * Top of File * * *
00001 ABCDE
      <...+....1....+..|.2....+....3....+....4....+....5....
00002 * * * End of File * * *
```

5.18 Moving the Current Line

The line pointer and line number of the current line are changed as you move forward or backward in a file.

- Moving the current line *forward* moves it from its present position toward the end of the file.

- Moving the current line *backward* moves it from its present position toward the top of the file.

Whenever the current line is changed, the lines displayed on the screen also change:

- When the current line is moved forward a specific number of lines, the display is also moved forward the same number of lines.

- When the current line is moved backward a specific number of lines, the display is also moved backward the same number of lines.

The commands discussed in this section are useful for both moving the current line and displaying other parts of a file, but they do not change the file in any way. The subcommands that locate line targets, discussed previously, provide other means to move the current line.

These subcommands move the current line:

- FORWARD scrolls the current line forward one or more screens.

- BACKWARD scrolls the current line backward one or more screens.

- DOWN moves the current line forward one or more lines.

- NEXT moves the current line forward one or more lines.

- UP moves the current line backward one or more lines.

- TOP moves the current line to the top of the file or top of range.

- BOTTOM moves the current line to the end of the file or end of range.

Moving Forward One or More Screens

FORWARD (assigned to **PF8**) scrolls the display forward one or more screens. To *scroll forward* is to display the *next* screen of information. On a 24 line screen, scrolling forward one screen moves the current line forward 18 lines. When the current line is at the end of the file, scrolling forward moves the current line to the top of the file. Using PF8 to scroll forward one screen at a time is a convenient way to browse the contents of a file.

Command Format:

FOrward [n|*1*]

where **n** is the number of screens the file is moved forward. If the number of screens is omitted, the display is scrolled forward one screen.

Moving Backward One or More Screens

BACKWARD (assigned to **PF7**) scrolls the display backward one or more screens. To *scroll backward* is to display the *previous* screen of information. On a 24 line screen, scrolling backward one screen moves the current line backward 18 lines. When the current line is at the top of the file, scrolling backward moves the current line to the end of the file. Using PF7 to scroll backward one screen at a time is a convenient way to browse the contents of a file.

Command Format:

BAckward [n|*1*]

where **n** is the number of screens the file is moved backward. If the number of screens is omitted, the display is scrolled backward one screen.

Moving Forward One or More Lines

DOWN moves the current line forward one or more lines. This subcommand is equivalent to specifying the number of lines the current line is to move forward as a positive relative line number.

Command Format:

Down [n|*1*]

where **n** is the number of lines the current line is moved forward. If the number of lines is omitted, the current line is moved forward one line.

● ● ●

NEXT moves the current line forward one or more lines. This subcommand performs the same function as the DOWN subcommand.

Command Format:

Next [n|*1*]

where **n**   is the number of lines the current line is moved forward. If the number of lines is omitted, it is assumed to be one.

Example:

These subcommands move the current line forward five lines:

```
====> DOWN 5
====> NEXT 5
====> 5
```

Moving Backward One or More Lines

UP moves the current line backward one or more lines. This subcommand is equivalent to specifying the number of lines the current line is to move backward as a negative relative line number.

Command Format:

      Up   **[n|1]**

where **n**   is the number of lines the current line is moved backward. If the number of lines is omitted, the current line is moved up one line.

Example:

These subcommands move the current line backward five lines:

```
====> UP 5
====> -5
```

Moving to the Top of the File

TOP moves the current line to the top of file or top of range. This subcommand is equivalent to specifying the top of the file or top of range as a target.

Command Format:

      TOP

Example:

These subcommands move the current line to the top of the file:

```
====> TOP
====> -*
====> :0
```

150 § Becoming Acquainted with XEDIT

Moving to the Bottom of the File

BOTTOM moves the current line to the end of file or end of range. This sub-command is equivalent to specifying the end of the file or end of range as a target.

Command Format:

Bottom

Example:

These subcommands move the current line to the end of the file:

```
====> BOTTOM
====> *
```

A Prefix Command to Move the Current Line

I is a prefix command that moves the current line.

1. Place a *I* in the prefix area next to the line you want to make the current line.

2. Press the ENTER key.

Example:

Suppose that you want to make line 0, the top of the file, the current line as in this file:

```
/0000 * * * Top of File * * *
00001
      |...+....1....+....2....+....3....+....4....+....5....
00002 * * * End of File * * *
```

results in:

```
00000 * * * Top of File * * *
      |...+....1....+....2....+....3....+....4....+....5....
00001
00002 * * * End of File * * *
```

5.19 Moving the Cursor

The cursor movement keys discussed in the chapter *Becoming Acquainted with VM/CMS* are not XEDIT commands as such, but they can and should be used in XEDIT when it is convenient to do so.

XEDIT also provides several commands to move the cursor in ways that are sometimes more convenient than using the cursor movement keys. The more common commands are discussed in this section. Some more specialized commands are discussed in the chapter *Special Topics in XEDIT*.

These subcommands move the cursor:

- TABKEY moves the cursor to the next tab stop.

- HOME moves the cursor from the command line to the file area or from the file area to the command line, depending on its current position.

Moving the Cursor to the Next Tab Position

TABKEY (assigned to **PF4**) is a function of the **SET** subcommand that moves the cursor to the *next* tab position. Any PF key can be defined to execute this subcommand. To see how this is done, see the PF function on the SET sub-command in the chapter *Customizing the XEDIT Environment*.

The columns to which PF4 moves the cursor depends on the file's filetype. Use the QUERY subcommand to display a file's tab settings:

> **Query TABS**

Use the **TAB** function of the SET subcommand, discussed in the chapter on *Customizing the XEDIT Environment*, to define other *logical* tab stops.

Notice that in XEDIT the cursor is moved in different ways by the TAB FOR-WARD key and the PF4 key:

- The TAB FORWARD key performs a **physical tab** which is set by the system hardware and not under your control. The TAB FORWARD key always moves the cursor to the first column of the next input area.

- The PF4 key performs a **logical tab** which is set by the system software and, therefore, under your control. The PF4 key moves the cursor to the next tab position.

Thus, the TAB FORWARD key moves the cursor from one input area to the next, whereas the PF4 key only moves the cursor to tab positions.

Exercise:

Demonstrate the difference between TAB FORWARD and TABKEY:

- If the cursor is on the command line:

  - TAB FORWARD will move it to the prefix area of the top-most line on the screen.

  - TABKEY will move it to the next tab stop on the current line.

- If the cursor is in the prefix area:

  - TAB FORWARD will move it to the first column of the file area.

  - TABKEY will move it to the first tab stop in the file area.

- If the cursor is in the file area:

  - TAB FORWARD will move it to the prefix area of the next line.

  - TABKEY will move it to the next tab stop in the file area.

Moving the Cursor to and from the File Area

HOME (assigned to **PF12**) is a function of the **CURSOR** subcommand that moves the cursor in either of two ways:

- If the cursor is on the command line, HOME moves the cursor to the last position it occupied in the file area.

- If the cursor is in the file area, HOME moves the cursor to the command line.

This is a faster and more convenient method of moving the cursor from the command line to its previous position in the file area than using any of the cursor movement keys.

Exercise:

Demonstrate this command by moving the cursor to any place in the file area and then pressing the PF12 key. The cursor should return to the command line. Now press the PF12 again. The cursor should return to its previous position in the file area.

5.20 Displaying or Executing the Previous Subcommand

After you execute a subcommand, it is often convenient to be able to display the subcommand again on the command line or to execute the subcommand.

Manually Displaying the Previous Subcommand

? (assigned to **PF6**) displays the previously executed subcommand on the command line. This is useful if the subcommand you now want to execute is a modification of the previous subcommand or if the previous subcommand did not execute due to misspelling or some other kind of mistake:

1. Press PF6 to display the subcommand.

2. Use the edit control keys to make the modification or correct the mistake.

3. Press ENTER to execute the subcommand.

Any PF key can be defined to execute this subcommand. To see how this is done, see the PF function of the SET subcommand in the chapter *Customizing the XEDIT Environment*.

Executing the Previous Subcommand Again

= (assigned to **PF9**) executes the previously executed subcommand again. This subcommand is equivalent to pressing PF6 and then pressing ENTER.

- If the previous command was entered from a PF key, pressing PF9 will execute that command again.

- If the previous command was a prefix command, pressing PF9 will not execute it again.

Any PF key can be defined to execute this subcommand. To see how this is done, see the PF function of the SET subcommand in the chapter *Customizing the XEDIT Environment*.

Example:

Suppose there are many occurrences of a certain string of text in a file and you want to search through the file for a specific occurrence of the string. To search for the first occurrence:

====> /string

To search for the second occurrence, press the PF9 key. Each time the PF9 key is pressed, the LOCATE subcommand previously executed is executed again.

Automatically Displaying the Previous Subcommand

& automatically displays a subcommand on the command line again if & is placed in column 1 of the command line before the subcommand. This command allows you to execute the previous command again by pressing ENTER.

In order to clear the & subcommand, you *must* press the space bar and then the ERASE EOF key. Otherwise, the next time you press ENTER, the & and command will reappear on the command line.

Command Format:

> **& command**

where **&** is placed in column 1 of the command line.

command is the subcommand to be displayed again.

Repeating the Previous Subcommand Line by Line

REPEAT advances the line pointer one line and then executes the previously executed subcommand again and continues to do so up to a target line. If the target precedes the current line, REPEAT begins on the line preceding the current line.

Command Format:

> **REPEat** [target]

where **target** is a line target that identifies the line up to which the command is repeated. The command is not repeated on this line. If the target is omitted, the command is only repeated once.

Example:

Suppose you have a large file and you want to insert the same string of text after each line.

- A brute force approach is to:

    1. Use the INPUT subcommand to insert the text after the first line.

       ====> INPUT text

    2. Advance the current line.

       ====> 1

    3. Repeat steps one and two until the end of the file.

- A much simpler approach is to:

  1. Use the INPUT subcommand to insert the text after the first line.

     ====> INPUT text

  2. Use the REPEAT subcommand to repeat the INPUT subcommand to the end of the file:

     ====> REPEAT *

Chapter 6
Performing Common Editing Tasks with XEDIT

Introduction

Whereas XEDIT provides over 200 commands to accomplish a wide variety of tasks, most of your time with XEDIT will be concerned with the few tasks covered in this chapter.

XEDIT usually provides several ways to perform the same task. Accordingly, each section in this chapter presents different ways of performing the same task. Although it may be unnecessary to read an entire section to learn how to perform a certain type of task, you'll benefit from familiarizing yourself with all of the section and each of the other approaches to the problem since another approach might be more convenient under different circumstances. For example, XEDIT provides several ways to add blank lines that you can then fill with text: a subcommand (ADD), a prefix command (A) and a program function key (PF2). Neither the subcommand, the prefix command or the PF key is better than the other. Each affords its own conveniences under different circumstances.

•   •   •

All examples in this chapter assume that line numbers are displayed in the prefix area. Recall that you can display line numbers with the command:

====> NUMBER ON

6.1 Editing an Existing File

To begin editing an existing file, enter the XEDIT command specifying the fileid of the file to be edited. XEDIT then reads a copy of the file from disk into virtual storage.

When you begin editing an existing file, XEDIT is in edit mode with the current line at the top of the file. If you intend to work on a part of the file other than the top, you will have to move to that part of the file using a command that moves the current line. Commands that move the current line are discussed in the chapter *Becoming Acquainted with XEDIT* in the sections *Moving the Current Line* and *Locating a Line Target*.

Command Format:

	Xedit	**fn** **ft** **[fm]**
where	**fn**	is the filename.
	ft	is the filetype.
	fm	is the filemode. If the filemode is omitted, all disks to which you have access are searched in alphabetical order for a file with the filename and filetype specified.

Example:

Suppose you have a file called QUERY MEMO that you want to resume editing:

```
XEDIT QUERY MEMO
```

6.2 Making Local Changes

There are many ways in which you can delete, insert and replace characters in a file.

- A convenient way to delete a character is to:

  1. Move the cursor under the character.

  2. Press the DELETE key.

- A convenient way to insert a character between two others is to:

  1. Move the cursor under the second of the two characters.

  2. Enter Insert Mode.

  3. Type the character to be inserted.

- A convenient way to replace one character with another is to:

  1. Move the cursor under the character to be replaced.

  2. Type the new character over the one to be replaced, making sure that you are not in insert mode.

The above methods of deleting, inserting and replacing characters are convenient if the number of changes is small. If the change must be made throughout a file or if the characters involved are not available on your keyboard, consider using either the CHANGE subcommand, discussed in the next section, or one of the subcommands discussed in the section *Deleting, Inserting and Replacing Characters* in the chapter *Special Topics in XEDIT*.

6.3 Making Global Changes

CHANGE changes one string of characters to another string of characters beginning with the current line up to a line identified by a line target. As options
you can also specify:

- The number of occurrences to be changed on each line.

- The position of the first occurrence of the string to be changed on each
  line relative to the first occurrence on the line.

- The strings in hexadecimal if the HEX function of the SET subcommand
  is set to ON. (This option is useful if the strings contain characters that
  are not on your keyboard.)

Command Format:

Change	/string1/string2/ [target|*1* [p|*1* [q|*1*]]]

where **/**   is a special character that delimits the character strings.
If the string to be changed or the string to which it is to
be changed contains any **/** characters, use another special character as the delimiter that does not occur in the
string and that does not have special significance in
searches for character strings. The characters that *cannot* be used to delimit a target are letters, numbers,
special characters that appear in the string to be found
and the special characters that already have special significance in target searches such as the minus sign ($-$),
the plus sign ($+$), the logical not sign ($\neg$), the amper-
sand (&), the vertical bar (|) and the asterisk (*).

string1   is the string to be changed.

string2   is the string that replaces **string1**.

target   is a line target that identifies the line up to which the
change is made. This line is not changed. If this target
is omitted, only the current line is changed.

p   is the number of occurrences on each line to be changed.
If the number of occurrences is omitted, only the first
occurrence is changed on each line. Use an * to change
all occurrences on each line.

q   is the position of the first occurrence to be changed relative to the first occurrence of the string on each line. If
the relative position is omitted, the change begins with
the first occurrence.

Examples:

Suppose the first line is the current line in this three line file:

```
00000 * * * Top of File * * *
00001 their is no their their
      |...+....1....+....2....+....3....+....4....+....5....
00002 their is no their their
00003 their is no their their
00004 * * * End of File * * *
```

- Suppose you must change the first occurrence of 'their' on the first line to 'there':

  ====> CHANGE /their/there/

- Suppose you must change all occurrences of 'their' on the first line to 'there':

  ====> CHANGE /their/there/ 1 *

- Suppose you must change all occurrences of 'their' on the first line to 'there' beginning with the second occurrence:

  ====> CHANGE /their/there/ 1 * 2

- Suppose you must change all occurrences of 'their' on all lines to 'there':

  ====> CHANGE /their/there/ * *

- Suppose you must insert some text at the beginning of each line. You can do this by specifying the string to be changed as null:

  ====> :1 CHANGE //text/ *

- Suppose you must change all occurrences of the date 05/09/51 to May 9, 1951. Since the date includes the / character, another string delimiter must be used:

  ====> :1 CHANGE "05/09/51"May 9, 1951" * *

6.4 Adding New Lines

You can add new lines of text *anywhere* in a file between the top of file (or top of range) and end of file (or end of range).

The most convenient way to enter a large number of consecutive lines of text is to use the INPUT subcommand, discussed below. Other commands add one or more blank lines of text that you can then fill with text.

These commands add new lines:

- INPUT, REPLACE and ADD are subcommands.

- I and A are prefix commands.

- LINEADD is a subcommand assigned to PF2.

Subcommands to Add Lines

INPUT either adds a single line of text after the current line or switches XEDIT to input mode.

- To add a single line of text after the current line, enter the INPUT subcommand including the text.

- To switch XEDIT to input mode, enter the INPUT subcommand, omitting any text.

In input mode, the cursor moves to the first column of the line immediately after the current line in the file area so you can enter line after line until you're finished entering text. Figure 5.3 shows the appearance of the screen in input mode. To switch from input mode to edit mode, press the ENTER key twice. Remember that the command line and prefix area disappear in input mode, so that commands cannot be entered in these areas. Only commands assigned to PF keys and PA keys can be executed in input mode.

Command Format:

Input	**[text]**

where **text**   is a line of text to be added after the current line. If the text is omitted, input mode is entered. A single blank is assumed to separate the text operand and the command name. Any blanks after the first are assumed to be part of the text operand.

Example:

Suppose you are editing a new file and want to enter a single line of text without going into input mode:

```
====> INPUT there is no there there
```

results in:

```
00000 * * * Top of File * * *
00001 there is no there there
      |...+....1....+....2....+....3....+....4....+....5....
00002 * * * End of File * * *
```

• • •

REPLACE either replaces the current line with a line of text or deletes the current line and switches XEDIT to input mode.

- To replace the current line with a line of text, enter the REPLACE subcommand, including the text.

- To delete the current line and switch XEDIT to input mode, enter the REPLACE subcommand, omitting any text.

This subcommand is equivalent to entering two subcommands: DELETE and then INPUT.

Command Format:

> **Replace**   **[text]**

where **text**   is a character string that replaces the current line beginning in column 1. If the text is omitted, the current line is deleted and the editor enters input mode placing the cursor in the first column of the first line after the current line. A single blank is assumed to separate the text operand and the command name. Any blanks after the first are assumed to be part of the text operand.

Example:

Suppose you must replace the current line with the text 'there is no there here either' in this file:

```
00000 * * * Top of File * * *
00001 there is no there there
      |...+....1....+....2....+....3....+....4....+....5....
00002 * * * End of File * * *
```

```
====> REPLACE there is no there here either
```

• • •

ADD adds one or more blank lines after the current line and positions the cursor in the first column of the first of the new lines so that you can begin typing text in that line.

Command Format:

>   **Add**   [n|*1*]

where **n**   is the number of blank lines that are added. If the number of lines is omitted, a single blank line is added after the current line.

Example:

Suppose you must add two blank lines at the top of the file but the current line is not at the top of the file:

```
====>  -*   ADD   2
```

results in:

```
00000 * * * Top of File * * *
      |...+....1....+....2....+....3....+....4....+....5....
00001 _
00002
00003 * * * End of File * * *
```

A PF Key to Add Lines

LINEADD (assigned to **PF2**) is a function on the **SOS** subcommand that adds one blank line immediately after the line the cursor is on. After the command is executed, the cursor is positioned in the first column of the new line so you can begin typing text onto the new line. This subcommand is convenient if the cursor is already in the file area on the line directly above where you want to add a blank line.

1. Place the cursor *anywhere* on the line immediately above where you want to add a blank line, including the prefix area next to the line.

2. Press the PF2 key.

Any PF key can be defined to execute this subcommand. To see how this is done, see the PF function on the SET subcommand in the chapter *Customizing the XEDIT Environment*.

Example:

Suppose the cursor is *anywhere* on line 0, the top of the file, and you want to add a line after line 0. Pressing PF2 results in:

```
00000 * * * Top of File * * *
      |...+....1....+....2....+....3....+....4....+....5....
00001 _
00002 * * * End of File * * *
```

Prefix Commands to Add Lines

A is a prefix command that adds one or more blank lines after the line in the prefix area where the command is placed. After the lines have been added, the cursor is positioned in the first column of the first of the new lines.

1. Specify the location and number of blank lines to be added:

   Place **An** or **nA** in the prefix area next to the line after which you want to add **n** blank lines. If the number of lines is omitted, a single blank line is added.

2. Press ENTER.

Example:

Suppose you must add two lines after the top of the file in this file:

```
2A000 * * * Top of File * * *
      |...+....1....+....2....+....3....+....4....+....5....
00001 * * * End of File * * *
```

results in:

```
00000 * * * Top of File * * *
      |...+....1....+....2....+....3....+....4....+....5....
00001 _
00002
00003 * * * End of File * * *
```

● ● ●

I is a prefix command that adds one or more blank lines after the line in the prefix area where the command is placed. After the lines have been added, the cursor is positioned in the first column of the first of the new lines.

1. Specify the location and number of blank lines to be added:

   Place **In** or **nI** in the prefix area next to the line after which you want to add **n** blank lines. If the number of lines is omitted, a single blank line is added.

2. Press ENTER.

6.5 Deleting and Replacing Lines

After you've put text into a file, you may decide that some of the lines are not really necessary and should be removed entirely from the file and other lines should be replaced with other information.

These commands delete lines:

- DELETE is a subcommand.

- D is a prefix command.

- LINEDEL is a subcommand that is only useful when assigned to a PF key.

A Subcommand to Delete Lines

DELETE removes the lines from the current line to a line identified by a line target.

Command Format:

> **DELete**   [target|*1*]

where **target**   is a line target that identifies the line up to which lines are deleted. This line is not deleted.   If the target is omitted, only the current line is deleted.

Examples:

Suppose you must delete lines 2 and 3 from this file:

```
00000 * * * Top of File * * *
00001 this line is not to be deleted
00002 this is the first line to be deleted
00003 this is the second line to be deleted
      |...+....1....+....2....+....3....+....4....+....5....
00004 * * * End of File * * *
```

The following are equivalent:

```
====> DELETE -2
====> DELETE :1
====> DELETE -/not/
====> -2 DELETE 2
====> :2 DELETE :4
```

166 § Performing Common Editing Tasks with XEDIT

A Prefix Command to Delete Lines

D is a prefix command that deletes one or more lines.

1. Specify which lines are to be deleted in one of two ways:

   • If the number of lines to be deleted is known to be **n**, place **Dn** or **nD** in the prefix area next to the first of the lines to be deleted. If the number of lines is omitted, a single line is deleted.

   • If the number of lines to be deleted is unknown, place a **DD** in the prefix area next to the first line to be deleted and a **DD** in the prefix area next to the last line to be deleted.

2. Press ENTER.

Examples:

Suppose you must delete lines 2 and 3 from this file:

```
00000 * * * Top of File * * *
      |...+....1....+....2....+....3....+....4....+....5....
00001 this line is not to be deleted
D2002 this is the first line to be deleted
00003 this is the second line to be deleted
00004 * * * End of File * * *
```

or

```
00000 * * * Top of File * * *
      |...+....1....+....2....+....3....+....4....+....5....
00001 this line is not to be deleted
DD002 this is the first line to be deleted
00DD3 this is the second line to be deleted
00004 * * * End of File * * *
```

results in:

```
00000 * * * Top of File * * *
      |...+....1....+....2....+....3....+....4....+....5....
00001 this line is not to be deleted
00002 * * * End of File * * *
```

A PF Key to Delete Lines

LINEDEL is a function on the **SOS** subcommand that deletes the line that the cursor is on. LINEDEL is only convenient to use if the subcommand is assigned to a PF key. After LINEDEL has been assigned to a PF key, to delete a line:

1. Place the cursor *anywhere* on the line, including the prefix area next to the line.

2. Press the PF key assigned to the subcommand.

LINEDEL can be assigned to any PF key.

Command Format:

>   [SET]   PFn   SOS   LINEDel

where **n**   (immediately after **PF**) is the number of the PF key to be assigned to execute the SOS LINEDEL subcommand when **PFn** is pressed.

Example:

Suppose you must assign LINEDEL to PF13:

====> PF13   SOS   LINEDEL

6.6 Recovering Deleted Lines

Lines deleted by the DELETE or PUTD subcommands or D prefix command are placed in a buffer in the order they are deleted. There is only one such buffer. So, if several files are being edited simultaneously, lines deleted from different files all go into the same buffer.

RECOVER can recover lines that were deleted using the DELETE or PUTD subcommands or D prefix command. When deleted lines are recovered from the buffer, the order in which they are recovered is: last into the buffer — first out of the buffer. Each line recovered is then purged from the buffer. The recovered lines are added to the file after the current line which may not have been their original position. To move the lines to their original position, use one of the commands described in the section on *Moving Lines* later in this chapter.

Command Format:

      RECover   **[n|1]**

where **n**   is the number of lines to be recovered. Use an * to recover all lines. If the number of lines is omitted, a single line is recovered.

Example:

Suppose you've deleted six lines from a file:

1.   This recovers the sixth of the six lines that were deleted:

    ====> RECOVER

2.   This then recovers the fourth and fifth of the deleted lines:

    ====> RECOVER 2

3.   This then recovers the remaining lines in the buffer, which are lines one, two and three:

    ====> RECOVER *

4.   At this point the buffer is empty: all lines that were deleted have been recovered. Consequently, if you enter:

    ====> RECOVER *

    XEDIT displays the message:

    No line(s) recovered.

6.7 Copying Lines

Sometimes the lines in one part of a file are the same as the lines in another part of the file with some modification. When this is the case, it is usually more convenient to make a copy of the original lines and modify them than to enter the lines again as a whole.

These commands copy lines:

- COPY is a subcommand.

- C is a prefix command.

A Subcommand to Copy Lines

COPY copies the lines beginning with the current line up to a line identified by a line target to a location identified by another line target.

Command Format:

COpy	**target1 target2**

where **target1**   is a line target that identifies the line up to which lines are copied. This line is not copied.

target2   is a line target that identifies the line after which the lines are copied.

Examples:

Suppose you must copy the first three lines after the fourth in this file:

```
00000 * * * Top of File * * *
00001 this is the first line to be copied
00002 this is the second line to be copied
00003 this is the third line to be copied
00004 this line is not to be copied
      |...+....1....+....2....+....3....+....4....+....5....
00005 * * * End of File * * *
```

The following are equivalent:

```
====> :1 COPY :4 :4
====> -3 COPY 3 3
====> -/first/ COPY /not/ /not/
====> :1 COPY /not/ 3
```

Notice that:

170 § Performing Common Editing Tasks with XEDIT

- The line where the COPY operation is to begin can be specified as any of these:

    :1   (an absolute line number)

    −3   (a relative line number)

    −/first/   (a string expression)

- The line up to which lines are copied can be specified as any of these:

    :4   (an absolute line number)

    3   (a relative line number)

    /not/   (a string expression)

- The line after which the lines are to be copied can be specified as any of these:

    :4   (an absolute line number)

    3   (a relative line number)

    /not/   (a string expression)

A Prefix Command to Copy Lines

C is a prefix command that copies one or more lines.

1. Specify which lines are to be copied in one of two ways:

   - If the number of lines to be copied is known to be **n**, place **Cn** or **nC** in the prefix area next to the first of the lines to be copied. If the number of lines is omitted, a single line is copied.

   - If the number of lines to be copied is not known, place **CC** in the prefix area next to the first line to be copied and **CC** in the prefix area next to the last line to be copied.

2. Specify the destination of the lines to be copied in one of two ways:

   - Place an **F** in the prefix area next to the line that the lines to be copied are to *follow* (hence, the F).

   - Place a **P** in the prefix area next to the line that the lines to be copied are to *precede* (hence, the P).

3. Press ENTER.

Examples:

Suppose you must copy the first three lines after the fourth in this file:

Copying Lines § 171

```
00000 * * * Top of File * * *
3C001 this is the first line to be copied
00002 this is the second line to be copied
00003 this is the third line to be copied
F0004 this line is not to be copied
      |...+....1....+....2....+....3....+....4....+....5....
00005 * * * End of File * * *
```

or

```
00000 * * * Top of File * * *
3C001 this is the first line to be copied
00002 this is the second line to be copied
00003 this is the third line to be copied
00004 this line is not to be copied
      |...+....1....+....2....+....3....+....4....+....5....
P0005 * * * End of File * * *
```

or

```
00000 * * * Top of File * * *
CC001 this is the first line to be copied
00002 this is the second line to be copied
CC003 this is the third line to be copied
F0004 this line is not to be copied
      |...+....1....+....2....+....3....+....4....+....5....
00005 * * * End of File * * *
```

or

```
00000 * * * Top of File * * *
CC001 this is the first line to be copied
00002 this is the second line to be copied
CC003 this is the third line to be copied
00004 this line is not to be copied
      |...+....1....+....2....+....3....+....4....+....5....
P0005 * * * End of File * * *
```

results in:

```
00000 * * * Top of File * * *
00001 this is the first line to be copied
00002 this is the second line to be copied
00003 this is the third line to be copied
00004 this line is not to be copied
      |...+....1....+....2....+....3....+....4....+....5....
00005 this is the first line to be copied
00006 this is the second line to be copied
00007 this is the third line to be copied
00008 * * * End of File * * *
```

6.8 Duplicating Lines

The COPY subcommand and the C prefix command only create a *single* copy of a sequence of lines. If you require several copies, one of the commands in this section may be more convenient.

These commands copy a sequence of lines any number of times:

- DUPLICAT is a subcommand.
- ″ is a prefix command.

A Subcommand to Duplicate Lines

DUPLICAT duplicates the lines beginning with the current line up to a line identified by a line target a specific number of times immediately after the original lines.

Command Format:

DUPlicat   [n|*1*   [target|*1*]]

where **n**   is the number of times the lines are to be duplicated. If the number of duplicates is omitted, the current line is duplicated once.

target   is a line target that identifies the line up to which lines are duplicated. This line is not duplicated. If the target is omitted, the current line is duplicated **n** times. If the number of duplicates and the target are both omitted, the current line is duplicated once.

Example:

Suppose you must duplicate the first line in a file twice:

```
00000 * * * Top of File * * *
      |...+....1....+....2....+....3....+....4....+....5....
00001 this line is to be duplicated
00002 this line is not to be duplicated
00003 * * * End of File * * *

====> :1 DUP 2 1
```

A Prefix Command to Duplicate Lines

″ is a prefix command that duplicates a line or block of lines any number of times.

174 § Performing Common Editing Tasks with XEDIT

1. Specify which lines are to be duplicated and how many times:

    •   To duplicate a single line **n** times, place **"n** or **n"** in the prefix area next to the line. If the number of duplicates is omitted, it is assumed to be one.

    •   To duplicate a block of lines **n** times, place **""** in the prefix area next to the first line to be duplicated and either **n""** or **""n** in the prefix area next to the last of the lines to be duplicated. If the number of duplicates is omitted, it is assumed to be one.

2. Press ENTER.

Examples:

Suppose you must duplicate the first line in a file twice:

```
00000 * * * Top of File * * *
      |...+....1....+....2....+....3....+....4....+....5....
"2001 this line is to be duplicated
00002 this line is not to be duplicated
00003 * * * End of File * * *
```

results in:

```
00000 * * * Top of File * * *
      |...+....1....+....2....+....3....+....4....+....5....
00001 this line is to be duplicated
00002 this line is to be duplicated
00003 this line is to be duplicated
00004 this line is not to be duplicated
00005 * * * End of File * * *
```

Suppose you must duplicate the first three lines once:

```
00000 * * * Top of File * * *
      |...+....1....+....2....+....3....+....4....+....5....
""001 this is the first line to be duplicated
00002 this is the second line to be duplicated
""003 this is the third line to be duplicated
00004 this line is not to be duplicated
00005 * * * End of File * * *
```

results in:

```
00000 * * * Top of File * * *
      |...+....1....+....2....+....3....+....4....+....5....
00001 this is the first line to be duplicated
00002 this is the second line to be duplicated
00003 this is the third line to be duplicated
00004 this is the first line to be duplicated
00005 this is the second line to be duplicated
00006 this is the third line to be duplicated
00007 this line is not to be duplicated
00008 * * * End of File * * *
```

6.9 Moving Lines

One of the remarkable conveniences of a good text editor is the ability to move blocks of text from one location in a file to another. Being able to move a block of text enables you to change the order of sentences within a paragraph, paragraphs within a section and sections within a chapter.

These commands move lines:

- MOVE is a subcommand.

- M is a prefix command.

A Subcommand to Move Lines

MOVE moves the lines beginning with the current line up to a line identified by a line target to a location identified by another line target.

Command Format:

Move	**target1 target2**

where **target1**   is a line target that identifies the line up to which lines are moved. This line is not moved.

target2   is a line target that identifies the line after which the lines are moved.

Examples:

Suppose you must move the first three lines after the fourth in this file:

```
00000 * * * Top of File * * *
      |...+....1....+....2....+....3....+....4....+....5....
00001 this is the first line to be moved
00002 this is the second line to be moved
00003 this is the third line to be moved
00004 this is the first line not to be moved
00005 this is the second line not to be moved
00006 * * * End of File * * *
```

The following are equivalent:

```
====> :1 MOVE 3 :4
====> :1 MOVE 3 /not/
====> :1 MOVE :4 :4
====> :1 MOVE /not/ /not/
```

A Prefix Command to Move Lines

M is a prefix command that moves one or more lines.

1. Specify which lines are to be moved in one of two ways:

    *   If the number of lines to be moved is known to be **n**, place **Mn** or **nM** in the prefix area next to the first of the lines to be moved. If the number of lines is omitted, a single line is moved.

    *   If the number of lines to be moved is not known, place **MM** in the prefix area next to the first line to be moved and **MM** in the prefix area next to the last line to be moved.

2. Specify the destination of the lines to be moved in one of two ways:

    *   Place an **F** in the prefix area next to the line that the lines to be moved are to *follow* (hence, the F).

    *   Place a **P** in the prefix area next to the line that the lines to be moved are to *precede* (hence, the P).

3. Press ENTER.

Examples:

Suppose you must move the first three lines after the fourth in this file:

```
00000 * * * Top of File * * *
      |...+....1....+....2....+....3....+....4....+....5....
3M001 this is the first line to be moved
00002 this is the second line to be moved
00003 this is the third line to be moved
F0004 this is the first line not to be moved
00005 this is the second line not to be moved
00006 * * * End of File * * *
```

or

```
00000 * * * Top of File * * *
      |...+....1....+....2....+....3....+....4....+....5....
3M001 this is the first line to be moved
00002 this is the second line to be moved
00003 this is the third line to be moved
00004 this is the first line not to be moved
P0005 this is the second line not to be moved
00006 * * * End of File * * *
```

or

```
00000 * * * Top of File * * *
      |...+....1....+....2....+....3....+....4....+....5....
MM001 this is the first line to be moved
00002 this is the second line to be moved
MM003 this is the third line to be moved
00004 this is the first line not to be moved
P0005 this is the second line not to be moved
00006 * * * End of File * * *
```

or

```
00000 * * * Top of File * * *
      |...+....1....+....2....+....3....+....4....+....5....
MM001 this is the first line to be moved
00002 this is the second line to be moved
MM003 this is the third line to be moved
F0004 this is the first line not to be moved
00005 this is the second line not to be moved
00006 * * * End of File * * *
```

results in:

```
00000 * * * Top of File * * *
      |...+....1....+....2....+....3....+....4....+....5....
00001 this is the first line not to be moved
00002 this is the first line to be moved
00003 this is the second line to be moved
00004 this is the third line to be moved
00005 this is the second line not to be moved
00006 * * * End of File * * *
```

6.10 Writing Lines into Another File

PUT writes the lines beginning with the current line up to a line identified by a line target into a file:

- If a fileid is specified, the lines are written to a disk file with that fileid. If the file to which the lines are being written already exists, the lines are written at the end of that file.

- If no fileid is specified, the lines are written to a **buffer** file which is kept in virtual storage and is, therefore, temporary. The contents of the buffer remain available until another execution of the PUT subcommand, which then *replaces* the previous contents. Thus, if you want the lines written by two or more PUTs to *accumulate* in a file, specify a fileid.

Command Format:

PUT	**[target|1] [fn [ft [fm]]]**

where	**target**	is a line target that identifies the line up to which lines are put into the file. This line is not put into the file. If the target is omitted, only the current line is written.
	fn	is the filename of the file the lines are written into. Substitute an = to write the lines to a file with the same filename as the file being edited.
	ft	is the filetype of the file the lines are written into. Substitute an = to write the lines to a file with the same filetype as the file being edited. If the filetype is omitted, it becomes the filetype of the file being edited.
	fm	is the filemode of the file the lines are written into. Substitute an = to write the lines to a file with the same filemode as the file being edited. If the filemode is omitted, it becomes the filemode of the file being edited.

System Messages:

If the file the lines are being written to is new, XEDIT displays the message:

```
DMSXPT571I Creating new file.
```

Examples:

- Suppose you must write all records from the 50th to the end of the file into a new file called NEWFILE DATA:

```
====> :50 PUT * NEWFILE DATA
```

• Suppose you must write the current line to the buffer:

====> PUT

• • •

PUTD writes the lines beginning with the current line up to a line identified by a line target into a file and then *deletes* the lines from the file being edited.

• If a fileid is specified, the lines are written to a disk file with that fileid. If the file to which the lines are being written already exists, the lines are written at the end of that file.

• If no fileid is specified, the lines are written to a **buffer** file which is kept in virtual storage and is, therefore, temporary. The contents of the buffer remain available until another execution of the PUTD subcommand, which then *replaces* the previous contents. Thus, if you want the lines written by two or more PUTDs to *accumulate* in a file, specify a fileid.

Command Format:

PUTD	**[target|1] [fn [ft [fm]]]**
where **target**	is a line target that identifies the line up to which lines are put into the file and then deleted from the file being edited. This line is not put into the file. If the target is omitted, only the current line is written.
fn	is the filename of the file the lines are written into. Substitute an = to write the lines to a file with the same filename as the file being edited.
ft	is the filetype of the file the lines are written into. Substitute an = to write the lines to a file with the same filetype as the file being edited. If the filetype is omitted, it becomes the filetype of the file being edited.
fm	is the filemode of the file the lines are written into. Substitute an = to write the lines to a file with the same filemode as the file being edited. If the filemode is omitted, it becomes the filemode of the file being edited.

System Messages:

If the file the lines are being written to is new, XEDIT displays the message:

DMSXPT571I Creating new file.

Writing Lines into Another File   §   181

6.11 Reading Lines from Another File

GET reads lines from another file into the file being edited and places the lines after the current line.

- If a fileid is specified, one or more lines are read from the file with that fileid.

- If no fileid is specified, all lines written to a temporary file area called the **buffer** by the previous execution of the PUT or PUTD subcommands are read. An execution of the GET command does not affect the contents of the buffer, which means that a file placed in the buffer can be read into the file being edited as many times as you require.

Command Format:

GET	**[fn [ft [fm]]] [firstrec|1 [numrec|*]]**

where	**fn**	is the filename of the file the lines are read from. Substitute an = if the lines are to be read from a file with the same filename as the file being edited.
	ft	is the filetype of the file the lines are read from. Substitute an = if the lines are to be read from a file with the same filetype as the file being edited. If the filetype is omitted, it becomes the filetype of the file being edited.
	fm	is the filemode of the file the lines are read from. Substitute an = if the lines are to be read from a file with the same filemode as the file being edited. If the filemode is omitted, it becomes the filemode of the file being edited.
	firstrec	is the line number of the first record to be read from the file. If the line number is omitted, it is assumed to be the first line of the file.
	numrec	is the number of lines to be read from the file. If the number of records is omitted, all lines from **firstrec** to the end of the file are read in. If **firstrec** and **numrec** are omitted, all lines in the file are read in.

Examples:

- Suppose you must incorporate all of a file called OTHER DATA at the top of the file being edited:

  ====> :0 GET OTHER DATA

- Suppose you must incorporate the first 50 records of a file called OTHER DATA at the top of the file being edited:

182 § Performing Common Editing Tasks with XEDIT

```
====> :0 GET OTHER DATA 1 50
```

- Another way to copy lines from one part of a file to another is to:

  1. Use the PUT subcommand to write the lines to the buffer.

  2. Use the GET subcommand to read those lines from the buffer into the appropriate part of the file.

  Suppose you must copy lines 10 through 20 after line 30:

  1. Write lines 10 through 20 to the buffer:

      ```
      ====>  :10  PUT  :21
      ```

  2. Read the lines in the buffer after line 30:

      ```
      ====>  :30  GET
      ```

- Moving lines from one part of a file to another is equivalent to copying the lines to their new location and then deleting the lines from their original location. Other than using the MOVE subcommand or the M prefix command, another way to move lines from one part of a file to another is to:

  1. Use the PUTD subcommand to write the lines to the buffer and delete the lines from their original location.

  2. Use the GET subcommand to read those lines from the buffer into the appropriate part of the file.

  Suppose you must move lines 10 through 20 after line 30:

  1. Write lines 10 through 20 to the buffer and delete them from their original location:

      ```
      ====>  :10  PUTD  :21
      ```

  2. Read the lines in the buffer after line 30:

      ```
      ====>  :30  GET
      ```

6.12 Changing the Case of Letters

Normally, the filetype of a file controls whether the lowercase letters you put into a file go in as lowercase or whether they are converted to uppercase. This section discusses subcommands to convert letters already in a file from lowercase to uppercase and vice versa. To control whether lowercase letters are converted to uppercase as you put them in, see the section *Controlling the Characteristics of the File Being Edited* in the chapter *Customizing the XEDIT Environment*.

Converting Uppercase to Lowercase

LOWERCAS converts uppercase letters to lowercase beginning with the current line up to a line identified by a line target.

Command Format:

> **LOWercas**   [target|*1*]

where **target**   is a line target that identifies the line up to which lines are converted. This line is not converted. If the target is omitted, only the current line is converted.

Example:

Suppose you must convert uppercase letters to lowercase on all lines in a file:

====> :1   LOWERCAS   *

Converting Lowercase to Uppercase

UPPERCAS converts lowercase letters to uppercase beginning with the current line up to a line identified by a line target.

Command Format:

> **UPPercas**   [target|*1*]

where **target**   is a line target that identifies the line up to which lines are converted. This line is not converted. If the target is omitted, only the current line is converted.

Example:

Suppose you must convert lowercase letters to uppercase on all lines in a file:

====> :1   UPPERCAS   *

6.13 Splitting and Joining Lines

SPLTJOIN (assigned to PF11) either splits one line into two lines or joins two consecutive lines into one line, depending on the position of the cursor.

- If the cursor is positioned before or at the last nonblank character on a line, SPLTJOIN *splits* the line into two lines at the cursor position.

- If the cursor is positioned after the last nonblank on a line, SPLTJOIN *joins* that line with the next line at the cursor position.

When joining two lines, be careful that there are enough columns between the cursor and the end of the top line (or truncation column) to fit the bottom line. If there are not enough columns and the SPILL function of the SET subcommand is set to OFF, any characters beyond the end of the line (or truncation column) will be lost. Otherwise, any characters beyond the end of the line (or truncation column) will *spill* into a new line immediately after the top line.

Example:

Suppose a file contains this one line. (Note the position of the cursor):

```
00000 * * * Top of File * * *
      |...+....1....+....2....+....3....+....4....+....5....
00001 colorless green ideas sleep furiously
00002 * * * End of File * * *
```

To split the one line into two lines beginning with the word 'sleep':

1. Place the cursor in the column where the two lines are to be split, that is, under the letter 's' of the word 'sleep'.

2. Press PF11.

```
00000 * * * Top of File * * *
      |...+....1....+....2....+....3....+....4....+....5....
00001 colorless green ideas _
00002 sleep furiously
00003 * * * End of File * * *
```

To join the two lines that were just split:

1. Move the cursor to the column on the first of the two lines where the second is to join it, that is, in the second blank after the word 'ideas'.

2. Press PF11.

6.14 Sorting Lines

SORT changes the order of the lines between the current line and a line identified by a line target on the basis of the characters that occur within specific columns known as sort fields. Each **sort field** is defined by two columns the first of which is the beginning of the field and the second of which is the end of the field.

If more than one sort field is specified:

- The file is first sorted within the first sort field.

- The file is next sorted within the second sort field.

- The file is finally sorted within the last sort field.

Command Format:

SORT	target [A|D] begcol1 endcol1 [begcol2 endcol2] ...
where **target**	is a line target that identifies the line up to which lines are sorted. This line is not sorted.
A	sorts in ascending EBCDIC order, which puts lowercase letters before uppercase letters and uppercase letters before numbers with letters ordered alphanumerically and numbers ordered according to increasing size.
D	sorts in descending EBCDIC order, which puts numbers before uppercase letters and uppercase letters before lowercase letters with numbers ordered according to decreasing size and letters ordered in reverse alphabetical order.
begcol	is the beginning column of a sort field.
endcol	is the ending column of a sort field.

Example:

Suppose that each line in a file contains, among other things, the name of a city and the state in which the city is located:

```
00000 * * * Top of File * * *
00001 Seattle      WA
00002 Eugene       OR
00003 Berkeley     CA
      |...+....1....+....2....+....3....+....4....+....5....
00004 Phoenix      AZ
00005 Carmel       CA
00006 Bellevue     WA
00007 Portland     OR
00008 Tempe        AZ
00009 * * * End of File * * *
```

Suppose you must sort the file, first by state and second by city within state:

```
====> :1 SORT * 14 15 1 8
```

results in:

```
00000 * * * Top of File * * *
00001 Phoenix      AZ
00002 Tempe        AZ
00003 Berkeley     CA
00004 Carmel       CA
00005 Eugene       OR
00006 Portland     OR
00007 Bellevue     WA
00008 Seattle      WA
      |...+....1....+....2....+....3....+....4....+....5....
00009 * * * End of File * * *
```

Notice that the field that is sorted first begins in column 14 and ends in column 15 and the field that is sorted second begins in column 1 and ends in column 8.

Chapter 7
Special Topics in XEDIT

Introduction

This chapter is concerned with editing tasks that occur less frequently but which are, nonetheless, extremely useful under certain circumstances. They are covered in a separate chapter so that those just learning XEDIT can master the basics and learn how to perform common editing tasks effectively in the chapters *Becoming Acquainted with Xedit* and *Performing Common Editing Tasks with XEDIT* without being burdened with some of the useful, but less common, material presented here.

While the chapter *Customizing the XEDIT Environment* also covers commands and tasks that are infrequently used, that chapter differs from this one in these ways:

- The topics covered in this chapter are a heterogeneous collection of editing commands and tasks.

- The topics covered in *Customizing the XEDIT Environment* have a clear unifying theme: using the functions of the SET subcommand to modify the XEDIT environment to accommodate your needs and preferences.

7.1 Editing Several Files Simultaneously

XEDIT is a subcommand that you can use to edit several files simultaneously. When you are editing one file, you can edit another file by entering the XEDIT subcommand, specifying the fileid of the file to be edited.

When you are editing two or more files, the files form a **ring**. A file's position in the ring depends on the order in which it was brought into the editor and how many other files are being edited. Suppose three files are being edited:

- The first file brought into the editor is positioned before the second file and after the third.

- The second file brought into the editor is positioned before the third file and after the first.

- The third file brought into the editor is positioned before the first file and after the second.

Normally, only one file in the ring is displayed on the screen. If you are currently displaying one file and want to display the next file in the ring, enter the XEDIT subcommand without specifying a fileid. If the last file in the ring is being displayed and you enter the XEDIT subcommand, the first file in the ring will be displayed. If you prefer to display a file in the ring which is not next in the sequence, you can do so by entering the XEDIT subcommand, including the fileid.

Command Format:

    Xedit   **[fn [ft [fm]]]**

where **fn**   is the filename. Substitute an = if the filename is the same as the file being edited. If the filename is omitted, it becomes the filename of the file being edited.

      ft   is the filetype. Substitute an = if the filetype is the same as the file being edited. If the filetype is omitted, it becomes the filetype of the file being edited.

      fm   is the filemode. Substitute an = if the filemode is the same as the file being edited. If the filemode is omitted, it becomes the filemode of the file being edited.

Exercise:

This exercise is intended to show you how to edit and move between three files simultaneously.

1.   In CMS, begin a new file, called FILE1 DATA:

    XEDIT FILE1 DATA

2. In XEDIT, begin another new file called FILE2 DATA:

   ====> XEDIT FILE2 DATA

   Now two files are in XEDIT, but only the contents of the second file are displayed. Notice the message displayed in the status message area:

   X E D I T   2 Files

3. In XEDIT, begin a third file called FILE3 DATA:

   ====> XEDIT FILE3 DATA

   Now three files are in XEDIT but only the contents of the third file are displayed. Notice the message displayed in the status message area:

   X E D I T   3 Files

4. Display the contents of the next, that is, first, file in the ring by entering the XEDIT subcommand, omitting a fileid:

   ====> XEDIT

5. Display the contents of the next, that is, second, file in the ring by entering the XEDIT subcommand, omitting a fileid:

   ====> XEDIT

6. Now that you are displaying the second file, how would you now display the first file?

   ====> XEDIT FILE1 DATA

Displaying Two or More Files Simultaneously

Normally, only one file is displayed on the screen at any one time. The SCREEN function of the SET subcommand, discussed in the chapter *Customizing the XEDIT Environment*, can be used, however, to divide the *physical* screen into several *logical* screens each of which can be used to display a different file, enabling you to display several files simultaneously.

Obtaining Information about the Files in the Ring

RING is an option on the XEDIT QUERY subcommand that displays information about the files in the ring.

Command Format:

   Query   **RING**

Exercise:

Suppose you're editing the three files in the previous exercise and want to know about the files in the ring:

====> QUERY   RING

results in:

```
DMSXQR530I  3  file(s) in storage

FILE1 DATA A1 F 80 Trunc=80 Size=0 Line=0 Col=1 Alt=0
FILE2 DATA A1 F 80 Trunc=80 Size=0 Line=0 Col=1 Alt=0
FILE3 DATA A1 F 80 Trunc=80 Size=0 Line=0 Col=1 Alt=0
```

Leaving XEDIT

CANCEL is a subcommand that leaves the XEDIT environment and returns you to CMS if you have not made *any* change to *any* of the files in the ring. Thus, CANCEL is tantamount to entering QUIT for each of the files. If you've changed any of the files in the ring, you must do one of the following:

- Write the changed file to disk and return to CMS with the FILE sub-command.

- Return to CMS without writing the changed file to disk with the QQUIT subcommand.

Command Format:

   CANCEL

Exercise:

If you are still editing the three files that you began earlier in this section, leave XEDIT and return to CMS without writing the files to disk:

- If you've made no changes to any of the files, use CANCEL.

- If you've made changes to a file, use QQUIT.

7.2 Making Selective Changes

SCHANGE (assigned to **PF5**) locates every occurrence of a string one by one and lets you decide whether to change the string or move to the next occurrence. The subcommand works with either the CHANGE or CLOCATE subcommands, but only when it has been assigned to a PF key.

Whether you use SCHANGE with CHANGE or CLOCATE depends on whether the selective change is always to be the same or sometimes different:

- If the change is always to be the same, use CHANGE.

- If the change is sometimes to be different, use CLOCATE.

Using CHANGE with SCHANGE

SCHANGE works with CHANGE in two steps.

1. Type the CHANGE subcommand on the command line, specifying only **string1** (the string to be changed), **string2** (the string that **string1** is to be changed to) and the string delimiters.

   Change /string1/string2/

   Do not type anything after string2 and do not press the ENTER key. Instead of pressing the ENTER key, press PF5. When the first occurrence of the string is found, the cursor moves to the first character of the string and XEDIT displays the message:

   ```
   String /string1/ found. - PF6 set for selective CHANGE
   ```

2. Either press PF6 to change the string or press PF5 to locate the next occurrence of the string. If PF6 is pressed, the string is changed and XEDIT displays the message:

   ```
   String /string1/ changed to /string2/
   ```

   Continue using PF5 to locate the next occurrence of the string and PF6 to change the string until there are no more occurrences to be changed in which case XEDIT displays the message:

   ```
   Not found on screen.
   ```

   To terminate the SCHANGE subcommand before the last occurrence of the string has been found, press the ENTER key and the cursor will return to the command line.

Example:

Suppose that the word 'no' is to be selectively changed to 'plenty' in this file:

Making Selective Changes § 193

```
00000 * * * Top of File * * *
      |...+....1....+....2....+....3....+....4....+....5....
00001 there is no there there
00002 there is no there there
00003 * * * End of File * * *
```

First, type the CHANGE subcommand on the command line:

====> CHANGE /no/plenty/

Next, instead of pressing ENTER, press PF5. XEDIT moves the column pointer to the column in which 'no' begins and displays the message:

       String /no/ found. - PF6 set for selective CHANGE

```
00000 * * * Top of File * * *
      <...+....|....+....2....+....3....+....4....+....5....
00001 there is no there there
00002 there is no there there
00003 * * * End of File * * *
```

If PF6 is pressed, XEDIT makes the change and displays the message:

       String /no/ changed to /plenty/

```
00000 * * * Top of File * * *
      <...+....|....+....2....+....3....+....4....+....5....
00001 there is plenty there there
00002 there is no there there
00003 * * * End of File * * *
```

To locate the next occurrence of 'no' on line 2, press PF5 again. If that occurrence is to be changed, press PF6. If that occurrence is not to be changed, either press PF5 again to search for the next occurrence of 'no' or press EN-TER to terminate the SCHANGE subcommand and return the cursor to the command line.

Using CLOCATE with SCHANGE

SCHANGE works with CLOCATE in two steps.

1. Type the CLOCATE subcommand on the command line, specifying a string to be located.

    CLocate   target

Then, instead of pressing the ENTER key, press PF5. When the first occurrence of the target is found, the cursor moves to the first character of the target and XEDIT displays the message:

```
Target 'target' found.
```

2. Either type in your correction or press PF5 to locate the next occurrence of the target. Continue using PF5 to locate the target and type in your correction until there are no more occurrences to be changed. PF6 has no effect when CLOCATE is used with SCHANGE.

    To terminate the SCHANGE subcommand before the last occurrence of the string has been found, press the ENTER key and the cursor will return to the command line.

Assigning SCHANGE to a PF Key

SCHANGE can be assigned to any PF key.

Command Format:

SCHANGE   n

where **n**   is the PF number that executes SCHANGE after the string has been located.

7.3 Creating a File with Records Longer Than Normal

The record length that XEDIT normally assigns to a file is based on the file's filetype. Certain filetypes, such as Exec, FORTRAN and SCRIPT, are reserved filetypes and automatically given records of a certain length.. Table 4.1 lists the record lengths of the most common filetypes.

It is usually not wise to modify the record length of a file with a reserved filetype, since the programs that process these files may expect a record length of a certain size.

Files with filetypes that are not reserved are given a record length of 80, which may not be optimal for your purposes. To create a file with a record length longer than 80, you must specify:

1. The virtual storage for each record.

2. The new record length.

3. The new truncation column.

4. The new zone.

How to specify the record length, truncation column and zone is discussed in detail in the chapter *Customizing the XEDIT Environment*. Use the WIDTH option on the XEDIT command to tell XEDIT how much virtual storage to set aside for each record.

Command Format:

Xedit	**fn ft [fm] ([Width nn]**
where **fn**	is the filename.
ft	is the filetype.
fm	is the filemode. If the filemode is omitted, it becomes A.
Width	specifies the number of bytes of storage to be **nn**.

Exercise:

Create a file called HUMONGOS DATA with a record length of 240:

1. Use the WIDTH option on the XEDIT command to tell XEDIT to use 240 bytes of storage for each record:

    ```
    XEDIT HUMONGOS DATA ( WIDTH 240
    ```

2. Once in the editor, notice that the record length displayed next to Lrecl= on the file identification line is still 80, the default. Use the

LRECL function of the SET subcommand to change the record length to 240:

```
====> LRECL 240
```

3. Notice also that the truncation column displayed after Trunc= on the file identification line is still 80, the default. Use the TRUNC function of the SET subcommand to change the truncation column to 240:

```
====> TRUNC 240
```

4. Use the ZONE function of the SET subcommand to change the zone from columns 1 through 80, the default, to columns 1 through 240:

```
====> ZONE 1 240
```

5. Switch to input mode and enter as much text as you can on one line. Notice that even though the record length is 240, only columns 1 through 80 are displayed. You can display other columns, however, using either the VERIFY function of the SET subcommand or one of the commands discussed in the section *Shifting the Display Sideways* in this chapter.

6. Switch from input mode to edit mode and write the file to disk.

Keep the HUMONGOS DATA file you created here. We'll use it later in the section *Shifting the Display Sideways.*

7.4 Displaying and Excluding Selected Lines in a File

Under normal circumstances, all the lines in a file can be displayed. On occasion, however, it may be convenient to display only certain lines in the file, such as those that contain a certain string of characters. This section discusses commands that selectively include or exclude certain lines in a file. See also the section *Controlling the Parts of a File Displayed and Manipulated* in the chapter *Customizing the XEDIT Environment*:

- ALL is a subcommand.

- S and X are prefix commands.

A Subcommand to Display and Exclude Lines

ALL displays only those lines in a file defined by a line target.

- If the target is a (positive) relative line number, every *nth* line is displayed.

- If the target is an absolute line number, only the line identified by that line number is displayed.

- If the target is a line name, only those lines with the line name are displayed.

- If the target is a character string, only those lines that contain the string are displayed.

Command Format:

| **ALL** | **[target]** |

where **target**   is a line target that identifies the lines to be displayed. If the target is omitted, all lines in the file are displayed.

Examples:

Suppose a file contains these lines:

```
00000 * * * Top of File * * *
      |...+....1....+....2....+....3....+....4....+....5....
00001 this is the first line to be excluded
00002 this is the second line to be excluded
00003 this is the first line to be shown
00004 this is the third line to be excluded
00005 this is the second line to be shown
00006 * * * End of File * * *
```

Suppose you want to display only those lines that contain the word 'shown' as in this file:

```
00000 * * * Top of File * * *
      |...+....1....+....2....+....3....+....4....+....5....
00001 ------------------- 2  line(s) not displayed  ------
00003 this is the first line to be shown
00004 ------------------- 1  line(s) not displayed  ------
00005 this is the second line to be shown
00006 * * * End of File * * *
```

- Since every line contains either 'shown' or 'excluded', the following are equivalent:

  ```
  ====> ALL /shown/
  ====> ALL ¬/excluded/
  ```

- Suppose you want to display every 2nd (even-numbered) line:

  ```
  ====> ALL 2
  ```

- Suppose you want to display only the 2nd line:

  ```
  ====> ALL :2
  ```

- Suppose you want to display all lines. Since every line contains either 'shown' or 'excluded', the following are equivalent:

  ```
  ====> ALL
  ====> ALL /excluded/ | /shown/
  ```

Shadow Lines

The lines that report the number of lines not displayed are called shadow lines. The shadow lines are only messages on the screen — they are not part of the file. Use the SHADOW function of the SET subcommand, discussed in the chapter *Customizing the XEDIT Environment*, to remove the shadow lines from the screen.

Example:

Suppose you want to remove the shadow lines in the previous example:

```
====> SHADOW OFF
```

results in:

Displaying and Excluding Selected Lines in a File § 199

```
00000 * * * Top of File * * *
      |...+....1....+....2....+....3....+....4....+....5....
00003 this is the first line to be shown
00005 this is the second line to be shown
00006 * * * End of File * * *
```

A Prefix Command to Exclude Lines

X is a prefix command that excludes one or more lines from the display.

1. Specify which lines are to be excluded in one of two ways:

    • If the number of lines to be excluded is known to be **n**, place **Xn** or **nX** in the prefix area next to the first of the lines to be excluded. If the number of lines is omitted, a single line is excluded.

    • If the number of lines to be excluded is not known, place **XX** in the prefix area next to the first line to be excluded and **XX** in the prefix area next to the last line to be excluded.

2. Press ENTER.

Example:

Suppose you want to exclude lines 1, 2 and 3 from this file:

```
00000 * * * Top of File * * *
      |...+....1....+....2....+....3....+....4....+....5....
3X001 this is the first line to be excluded
00002 this is the second line to be excluded
00003 this is the third line to be excluded
00004 this is the first line to be shown
00005 this is the second line to be shown
00006 * * * End of File * * *
```

results in:

```
00000 * * * Top of File * * *
      |...+....1....+....2....+....3....+....4....+....5....
00001 ------------------- 3 line(s) not displayed ------
00004 this is the first line to be shown
00005 this is the second line to be shown
00006 * * * End of File * * *
```

A Prefix Command to Display Excluded Lines

S is a prefix command that displays lines that were excluded by the X prefix command or ALL subcommand.

1. Specify which lines are to be displayed in either of three ways:

    - To show all excluded lines, place **S** or **S*** in the prefix area next to a shadow line.

    - To show the first **n** excluded lines, place **Sn** or **nS** in the prefix area next to a shadow line.

    - To show the last **n** excluded lines, place **S−n** in the prefix area next to a shadow line.

2. Press ENTER.

Example:

Suppose lines 1, 2 and 3 have been excluded from the display and now you want to display them again:

```
00000 * * * Top of File * * *
      |...+....1....+....2....+....3....+....4....+....5....
3S001 ------------------- 3 line(s) not displayed  ------
00004 this is the first line to be shown
00005 this is the second line to be shown
00006 * * * End of File * * *
```

results in:

```
00000 * * * Top of File * * *
      |...+....1....+....2....+....3....+....4....+....5....
00001 this is the first line to be excluded
00002 this is the second line to be excluded
00003 this is the third line to be excluded
00004 this is the first line to be shown
00005 this is the second line to be shown
00006 * * * End of File * * *
```

Displaying and Excluding Selected Lines in a File § 201

7.5 Shifting the Display Sideways

The commands in this section are useful if the records in a file are longer than the 80 columns displayed on most terminals.

- In edit mode, columns 1 through 73 are normally displayed.

- In input mode, columns 1 through 80 are normally displayed.

Using the commands in this section, *any* 73 columns can be displayed in edit mode and *any* 80 columns can be displayed in input mode.

A distinction should be made between **shifting the display** and **shifting the data**:

- **Shifting the display** changes which columns of data are displayed but does not change the data in the file.

- **Shifting the data** changes which columns the data occupies but does not change which columns are displayed.

Commands that shift the data are covered in the section *Shifting Data Sideways* in this chapter.

These commands shift the display to the side:

- RIGHT shifts the display one or more columns to the right.

- LEFT shifts the display one or more columns to the left.

- RGTLEFT shifts the display to the right or left, depending on its present position.

Shifting the Display to the Right

RIGHT displays the columns that are one or more columns to the right of the first column on the screen.

Command Format:

      RIght   **[n|1]**

where **n**   is the number of columns the display is shifted to the right. If the number of columns is omitted, the display is shifted one column to the right.

Exercise:

This exercise is designed to show you how to shift the display to the right when you are editing a file with more columns than will fit on the terminal screen.

1. Earlier in this chapter you began editing a file called HUMONGOS DATA with a record length of 240 characters. Resume editing that file:

   XEDIT HUMONGOS DATA

2. Previously, you entered text in columns 1 through 79. Now you want to enter text in columns 81 through 159. Shift the display 80 columns to the right:

   ====> RIGHT 80

3. Switch to input mode and enter text in the columns displayed.

4. Display columns 161 through 240 by returning to edit mode and shifting the display *another* 80 columns to the right:

   ====> RIGHT 80

   This exercise is continued in the discussion of the next command, which enables you to shift the display to the left.

Rather than switching from input mode to edit mode to enter the RIGHT sub-command and then switching from edit mode to input mode, you could shift the display in a single keystroke while remaining in input mode if the RIGHT sub-command is assigned to a PF key. How to do so is discussed in the chapter *Customizing the XEDIT Environment*.

Shifting the Display to the Left

LEFT displays the columns that are one or more columns to the left of the first column on the screen.

Command Format:

      LEft   **[n|1]**

where **n**   is the number of columns the display is shifted to the left. If the number of columns is omitted, the display is shifted one column to the left.

Exercise:

This exercise is a continuation of the previous one, in which you learned how to shift the display to the right. Suppose you are editing the file called HUMONGOS DATA and that columns 161 through 233 are displayed in edit mode:

1. Display columns 81 through 153:

   ====> LEFT 80

Shifting the Display Sideways   §   203

2. Display columns 1 through 73 by shifting the display *another* 80 columns to the left:

====> LEFT 80

Rather than switching from input mode to edit mode to enter the LEFT subcommand and then switching from edit mode to input mode, you could shift the
display in a single keystroke while remaining in input mode if the LEFT subcommand is assigned to a PF key. How to do so is discussed in the chapter
Customizing the XEDIT Environment.

A PF Key to Shift the Display

RGTLEFT (assigned to **PF10**) displays columns to the right or left of the present
screen depending on which columns are already displayed.

- If the first, that is, left-most, column displayed is column 1, pressing
  PF10 will display the columns to the right.

- If the first column displayed is not column 1, pressing PF10 will display
  the columns to the left, beginning with column 1.

Second Reading

7.6 Shifting Data Sideways

Suppose you've entered data in columns 1 through 73 in a file with a record length of 80. Now, you must add five columns of data at the beginning of each line. If you try to use insert mode while XEDIT is in edit mode to shift the data, the keyboard will lock to prohibit you from doing so and the terminal may sound an alarm. To circumvent this, you could shift the data using one of the commands in this section.

These commands shift data sideways:

- SHIFT is a subcommand.

- > and < are prefix commands.

Be careful not to shift the data either to the left of the beginning of the zone or to the right of the truncation column. Any data shifted to the left of the beginning of the zone is lost. If data is shifted to the right of the truncation column and the SPILL function of the SET subcommand is set to OFF, any characters at or beyond the truncation column will be lost. Otherwise, any characters that are shifted past the truncation column will *spill* into a new line immediately after the current line.

A Subcommand to Shift the Data to the Right or Left

SHIFT moves the contents of a file from the current line to a line identified by a line target a specified number of columns either to the right or left of its present position.

Don't confuse the SHIFT subcommand with the LEFT, RIGHT and VERIFY subcommands that shift the display but not the data.

Command Format:

SHift	Right|Left [cols|*1*] [target|*1*]	
where **Right**	shifts the data to the right.	
Left	shifts the data to the left.	
col	is the number of columns the data is shifted. If the number of columns is omitted, the lines are shifted one column.	
target	is a line target that identifies the line up to which lines are shifted. This line is not shifted. If the target is omitted, only the current line is shifted.	

Shifting Data Sideways § 205

Example:

Suppose you must shift the first line five columns to the right in this file:

```
00000 * * * Top of File * * *
00001 this line is to be shifted
      |...+....1....+....2....+....3....+....4....+....5....
00002 this line is not to be shifted
00003 * * * End of File * * *
```

```
====> SHIFT RIGHT 5 1
```

A Prefix Command to Shift the Data to the Right

> is a prefix command that shifts the contents of one or more lines to the right. After the lines have been shifted, the cursor is positioned in the first column of the first of the shifted lines. Be careful that you don't shift characters past the truncation column. If you do so and the SPILL function of the SET subcommand is ON, the characters shifted past the truncation column are spilled onto a new line. If the SPILL function is set to OFF, the characters shifted past the truncation column are lost.

1. Specify which lines are to be shifted and how many columns:

   - To shift a single line **n** columns to the right, place **>n** or **n>** in the prefix area next to the line to be shifted. If the number of columns is omitted, the lines are shifted one column.

   - To shift a block of lines **n** columns to the right, place **>>** in the prefix area next to the first line of the block and **>>n** in the prefix area next to the last line. If the number of columns is omitted, the block is shifted one column.

2. Press ENTER.

Examples:

Suppose you must shift the first line five columns to the right in this file:

```
00000 * * * Top of File * * *
      |...+....1....+....2....+....3....+....4....+....5....
5>001 this line is to be shifted
00002 this line is not to be shifted
00003 * * * End of File * * *
```

results in:

206 § Special Topics in XEDIT

```
00000 * * * Top of File * * *
      |...+....1....+....2....+....3....+....4....+....5....
00001 _    this line is to be shifted
00002 this line is not to be shifted
00003 * * * End of File * * *
```

Suppose you must shift the first two lines five columns to the right:

```
00000 * * * Top of File * * *
      |...+....1....+....2....+....3....+....4....+....5....
>>001 this line is to be shifted
>>502 this line is to be shifted
00003 * * * End of File * * *
```

results in:

```
00000 * * * Top of File * * *
      |...+....1....+....2....+....3....+....4....+....5....
00001 _    this line is to be shifted
00002      this line is to be shifted
00003 * * * End of File * * *
```

A Prefix Command to Shift the Data to the Left

< is a prefix command that shifts the contents of one or more lines to the left. Characters shifted to the left of column one are lost, so be careful not to do so.

1. Specify which lines are to be shifted and how many columns:

    •   To shift a single line **n** columns to the left, place <**n** or **n**< in the prefix area next to the line to be shifted. If the number of columns is omitted, the lines are shifted one column.

    •   To shift a block of lines **n** columns to the left, place < < in the prefix area next to the first line of the block and < <**n** in the prefix area next to the last line. If the number of columns is omitted, the block is shifted one column.

2. Press ENTER.

Examples:

Suppose you must shift the contents of the first line five columns to the left:

```
00000 * * * Top of File * * *
      |...+....1....+....2....+....3....+....4....+....5....
5<001      this line is to be shifted
00002 this line is not to be shifted
00003 * * * End of File * * *
```

results in:

```
00000 * * * Top of File * * *
      |...+....1....+....2....+....3....+....4....+....5....
00001 this line is to be shifted
00002 this line is not to be shifted
00003 * * * End of File * * *
```

Suppose you must shift the contents of the first two lines five columns to the left:

```
00000 * * * Top of File * * *
      |...+....1....+....2....+....3....+....4....+....5....
<<001      this line is to be shifted
<<502      this line is to be shifted
00003 * * * End of File * * *
```

results in:

```
00000 * * * Top of File * * *
      |...+....1....+....2....+....3....+....4....+....5....
00001 this line is to be shifted
00002 this line is to be shifted
00003 * * * End of File * * *
```

7.7 Merging Lines

MERGE overlays one block of lines on another block of lines and then deletes the first block from its original location. When one character overlays another character, it replaces the character unless the overlaying character is a blank. The number of lines in the first block must be less than or equal to the number of lines in the second block. This subcommand is especially useful if you have two blocks of lines in a file where:

- The first line of the first block is to be combined with the first line of the second block.

- The second line of the first block is to be combined with the second line of the second block.

- The last line of the first block is to be combined with the last line of the second block.

```
first line of first block
second line of first block
    .
    .
last line of first block

first line of second block
second line of second block
    .
    .
last line of second block
```

When merged, the two blocks of lines might look like this:

```
first line of second block      first line of first block
second line of second block      second line of first block
    .                                .
    .                                .
last line of second block        last line of first block
```

Be sure that there are enough columns between the column where the first sequence of lines is to begin and the truncation column to fit the new text. If the number of columns is insufficient and the SPILL function of the SET subcommand is set to OFF, any characters at or beyond the truncation column will be lost. Otherwise, any characters that are shifted past the truncation column will *spill* into a new line immediately after that line.

Command Format:

> **MErge**   **target1   target2   [col|1]**

where **target1**   is a line target that identifies the line of the first block up to which that is overlayed on the second block. This line is not overlayed.

      target2   is a line target that identifies the first line of the second block where the first block is overlayed on the second block.

      col   is the column in which the first block is overlayed on the second block. If the column is omitted, the first block is overlayed on the second block beginning in column 1.

Examples:

Suppose a file contains these two lines:

```
00000 * * * End of File * * *
00001 A A
00002  BB
      |...+....1....+....2....+....3....+....4....+....5....
00003 * * * End of File * * *
```

Notice that:

- Columns 1 and 3 of line 1 contain blanks.

- Columns 2 and 4 of line 1 contain A's.

- Columns 1 and 2 of line 2 contain blanks.

- Columns 3 and 4 of line 2 contain B's.

====> :1 MERGE 1 :2

results in:

```
00000 * * * End of File * * *
00001 ABA
      |...+....1....+....2....+....3....+....4....+....5....
00002 * * * End of File * * *
```

====> :2 MERGE 1 :1

results in:

210 § Special Topics in XEDIT

```
00000 * * * Top of File * * *
00001 ABB
      |...+....1....+....2....+....3....+....4....+....5....
00002 * * * End of File * * *

====> :2 MERGE 1 :1 5
```

results in:

```
00000 * * * Top of File * * *
00001 A A  BB
      |...+....1....+....2....+....3....+....4....+....5....
00002 * * * End of File * * *
```

7.8 Counting the Number of Times a String Occurs

COUNT reports the number of times a specified character string occurs from the current line to a line identified by a line target.

Command Format:

COUnt	**/string/ [target|*1*]**

where **/** is a special character that delimits the string to be counted. If the string to be counted contains one or more / characters, use another special character as the delimiter that does not occur in the string and that does not have special significance in searches for character strings.

string is the character string whose occurrences are to be counted.

target is a line target that identifies the line up to which lines are searched for the string. This line is not searched. If the target is omitted, only the current line is searched.

System Messages:

The number of occurrences found is displayed in the message area:

```
DMSXCG522I  nn  occurrences
```

Example:

Suppose you have a file that contains dates and you must count the number of times that the date 05/09/51 occurs throughout the file:

```
====> :1 COUNT .05/09/51. *
```

7.9 Moving the Cursor within a File

CURSOR is a subcommand with functions that move the cursor within a file to one of three positions:

- COLUMN moves the cursor to the current column on the current line.

- FILE moves the cursor to any location in the file.

- SCREEN moves the cursor to any location on the screen.

Moving the Cursor to the Current Column on the Current Line

COLUMN is a function of the **CURSOR** subcommand that moves the cursor to the current column on the current line.

Command Format:

CURsor   **Column**

where **Column**   moves the cursor to the current column on the current line.

Example:

Suppose you must move the cursor to the column in a file that begins with a certain string of text:

1. Use CLOCATE to make column where the text begins the current column:

    ====> CLOCATE /text/

2. Use CURSOR COLUMN to move the cursor to the current column:

    ====> CURSOR COLUMN

Moving the Cursor to Any Location in the File

FILE is a function of the **CURSOR** subcommand that moves the cursor to a position in the file that is relative to the beginning of the file.

Command Format:

CURsor   **File   linenum   [colnum|1]**

where **linenum**   is the number of the line relative to the beginning of the file in which the cursor is to be placed.

Moving the Cursor within a File   §   213

> **colnum**   is the number of the column relative to the beginning of the line in which the cursor is to be placed. If the column number is omitted, the cursor is placed in column 1.

Example:

Suppose you must place the cursor in the third column of the first line:

====> CURSOR FILE 1 3

Moving the Cursor to Any Location on the Screen

SCREEN is a function of the **CURSOR** subcommand that moves the cursor to a position on the screen that is relative to the beginning of the logical screen.

Command Format:

> **CURsor**   **Screen   linenum   [colnum|*1*]**

where **linenum**   is the line on the screen where the cursor is to be placed.

> **colnum**   is the column number of the column in which the cursor is to be placed. If the column number is omitted, the cursor is placed in column 1.

Example:

Suppose you must place the cursor in the third column of the current line, which is the 12th line on the screen:

====> CURSOR SCREEN 12 3

7.10 Moving the Cursor between Files

SOS (**S**creen **O**peration **S**imulation) is a subcommand that provides two functions convenient for moving the cursor from screen to screen when you are using the SCREEN function of the SET subcommand, discussed in the chapter *Customizing the XEDIT Environment*, to display two or more files simultaneously.

- TABCMDF moves the cursor forward to the command line of the next screen.

- TABCMDB moves the cursor backward to the command line of the previous screen.

Moving the Cursor Forward to the Next Screen

TABCMDF is a function of the SOS subcommand that moves the cursor forward to the command line of the next screen. This function is most useful when assigned to a PF key within the XEDIT profile, discussed in the chapter *Customizing the XEDIT Environment*.

Command Format:

SOS   **TABCMDF [n|1]**

where **n**   is the number of screens the cursor is moved forward. If the number of screens is omitted, the cursor is moved one screen.

Example:

Suppose you want to assign PF14 to move the cursor to the next screen:

====>   PF14 SOS TABCMDF

Moving the Cursor Backward to the Previous Screen

TABCMDB is a function of the SOS subcommand that moves the cursor backward to the command line of the previous screen. This function is most useful when assigned to a PF key within the XEDIT profile, discussed in the chapter *Customizing the XEDIT Environment*.

Command Format:

SOS   **TABCMDB [n|1]**

where **n**   is the number of previous screens the cursor is moved. If the number of screens is omitted, the cursor is moved one screen.

Example:

Suppose you want to assign PF13 to move the cursor to the previous screen:

```
====>   PF13 SOS TABCMDB
```

7.11 Displaying a File in Hexadecimal

HEXTYPE is a subcommand that displays the characters in a file in both hexadecimal and EBCDIC. This can be useful if the characters in a file are not available on your keyboard. Such characters are nondisplaying characters that normally appear as blank characters and are indistinguishable from each other on the screen. Refer to the NONDISP function of the SET subcommand, discussed in the chapter *Customizing the XEDIT Environment*, for more information about nondisplaying characters.

Command Format:

> HEXType   [target|*1*]

where **target**   is a line target that identifies the line up to which lines are displayed. This line is not displayed. If the target is omitted, only the current line is displayed.

Example:

Suppose a file contains this line:

```
00000 * * * Top of File * * *
00001 12345
      |...+....1....+....2....+....3....+....4....+....5....
00002 * * * End of File * * *
```

====> HEXTYPE

displays this in the message area:

```
      F1F2F3F4 F5404040 40404040 ...
       1 2 3 4  5
```

where F1, F2, F3, F4 and F5 are the hexadecimal codes for the numbers 1 through 5, respectively, and 40 is the hex code for the blank character.

7.12 Deleting, Inserting and Replacing Characters

The subcommands in this section are useful for deleting, inserting and re-placing characters in a file when the number of characters is large or the characters are not available on your keyboard:

- ALTER substitutes one character for another.

- CDELETE deletes characters starting at the current column.

- CINSERT inserts characters after the current column.

- CAPPEND appends characters to the end of the current line.

- CREPLACE replaces characters starting at the current column.

- COVERLAY overlays characters starting at the current column.

- OVERLAY overlays characters starting at either the first tab stop or the first column.

Substituting One Character for Another

ALTER changes one character to another from the current line to a line iden-tified by a line target. As options, you can also specify:

- The number of occurrences to be changed on each line.

- The position of the first occurrence of the character to be changed on each line relative to the first occurrence on the line.

- The characters in hexadecimal. (This option is useful if the character is not on your keyboard).

Command Format:

ALter	char1 char2 [target|*1* [p|*1* [q|*1*]]]
where **char1**	is the character to be changed. Specify it either as a single character or in hexadecimal notation.
char2	is the character to which **char1** is to be changed. Specify it either as a single character or in hexadecimal notation.
target	is a line target that identifies the line up to which the change is made. This line is not changed. If the target is omitted, only the current line is changed.
p	is the number of occurrences on each line to be changed. If the number of occurrences is omitted, only the first occurrence is changed on each line. Use an * to change all occurrences on each line.

q   is the position of the first occurrence to be changed rel-
     ative to the first occurrence of the string on each line. If
     the relative position is omitted, the change begins with
     the very first occurrence.

Example:

Suppose you have a file with a number of characters that normally print as a
bullet (•) which you want to change to the letter 'o'. The bullet cannot be
entered directly from the keyboard. It can be specified, however, using
hexadecimal notation. The hex code for the bullet is AF and the hex code for
the letter 'o' is 96. To change all occurrences of AF to 96 on all lines:

====> :1 ALTER AF   96   * *

If you don't know the hexadecimal representation of the character that is to
be changed, use the HEXTYPE subcommand to display the line in which the
character occurs in both hexadecimal and EBCDIC.

Deleting Characters Starting at the Current Column

CDELETE is a *column-oriented* subcommand that deletes one or more characters on the current line from the current column to a column identified by a
column target. Use the CLOCATE subcommand to position the current column.

Command Format:

CDelete   **[target|*1*]**

where **target**   is a column target that identifies the column up to which
                    characters are deleted. The character in this column is
                    not deleted. If the target is omitted, only the character in
                    the current column is deleted.

Examples:

Suppose that column 3 is the current column in a file containing this line:

```
00000 * * * Top of File * * *
00001 ABCDE
      <.|.+....1....+....2....+....3....+....4....+....5....
00002 * * * End of File * * *
```

• Suppose you must delete all characters from the current column to the
  end of the line, that is, characters 'CDE'. The following are equivalent:

  ====> CDELETE *
  ====> CDELETE 3

Deleting, Inserting and Replacing Characters § 219

```
====> CDELETE :6
====> CDELETE / /
```

- Suppose you must delete all characters from the current column to the beginning of the line, that is, characters 'ABC'. The following are equivalent:

```
====> CDELETE -*
====> CDELETE -3
====> CDELETE :0
```

- Suppose you must delete the letters 'C' and 'D'. The following are equivalent:

```
====> CDELETE :5
====> CDELETE 2
====> CDELETE /E/
```

Inserting Characters after the Current Column

CINSERT is a *column-oriented* subcommand that inserts text into the current line after the current column, shifting to the right any nonblank characters that were previously located after the current column. Use the CLOCATE subcommand to position the current column.

Be careful that the new text you insert does not shift the text that was located to the right of the current column past the truncation column. If you do so and the SPILL function of the SET subcommand is set to OFF, any characters shifted past the truncation column will be lost. Otherwise, any characters that are shifted past the truncation column will *spill* into a new line immediately after the current line.

Command Format:

      CInsert   **text**

where **text**   is a sequence of characters that is inserted. A single blank is assumed to separate the text operand and the command name. Any blanks after the first are assumed to be part of the text operand.

Example:

Suppose that column 3 is the current column and that you must insert the letter 'C' between the letters 'B' and 'D':

220 § Special Topics in XEDIT

```
00000 * * * Top of File * * *
00001 ABDE
      <.|.+....1....+....2....+....3....+....4....+....5....
00002 * * * End of File * * *

====> CINSERT C
```

Appending Characters to the End of the Current Line

CAPPEND is a *column-oriented* subcommand that appends text to the last nonblank character of the current line.

Be careful that the new text you append does not extend beyond the truncation column. If it does and the SPILL function of the SET subcommand is set to OFF, any characters beyond the truncation column will be lost. Otherwise, any characters beyond the truncation column will *spill* into a new line immediately after the current line.

Command Format:

CAppend   **[text]**

where **text**   is a sequence of characters that is appended. A single blank is assumed to separate the text operand and the command name. Any blanks after the first are assumed to be part of the text operand. If the text is omitted, the column pointer is moved to the column following the last nonblank character.

Example:

Suppose that current line contains the letters 'ABC' and you must append the letters 'DE':

```
00000 * * * Top of File * * *
00001 ABC
      |...+....1....+....2....+....3....+....4....+....5....
00002 * * * End of File * * *

====> CAPPEND DE
```

results in:

```
00000 * * * Top of File * * *
00001 ABCDE
      |...+....1....+....2....+....3....+....4....+....5....
00002 * * * End of File * * *
```

Deleting, Inserting and Replacing Characters § 221

Overlaying Characters

When one character overlays another, the replacement is selective:

- A blank character used in the text operand leaves the corresponding character in the file unchanged.

- An underscore character (_) in the text operand changes the corresponding character in the file to a blank character. (Thus, subcommands that overlay characters cannot be used to put an underscore character in a line.)

- Any other character in the text operand replaces the corresponding character in the file.

• • •

COVERLAY is a *column-oriented* subcommand that selectively replaces characters with other characters on the current line beginning at the current column. Use the CLOCATE subcommand to position the current column.

Command Format:

> **COVerlay**   **text**

where **text**   is a sequence of characters that replaces characters on the current line beginning with the current column. A single blank is assumed to separate the text operand and the command name. Any blanks after the first are assumed to be part of the text operand.

Examples:

Suppose that column 10 is the current column in a file containing this line:

```
00000 * * * Top of File * * *
00001          12345
      <...+....|....+....2....+....3....+....4....+....5....
00002 * * * End of File * * *
```

- Suppose you must change '12345' to 'AB DE':

  ====> COVERLAY AB_DE

- Suppose you must change '12345' to 'AB3DE':

  ====> COVERLAY AB DE

• • •

OVERLAY selectively replaces characters on the current line with other characters, just as the COVERLAY subcommand does. This subcommand differs from COVERLAY in where it begins replacement on the line:

- If the IMAGE function of the SET subcommand is set to OFF, replacement begins at the first column of the current line.

- If IMAGE is set to ON, replacement begins at the first tab stop.

The setting of the IMAGE function is based on a file's filetype.

Command Format:

      Overlay   **text**

where **text**   is a sequence of characters that replaces the corresponding characters on the current line. A single blank is assumed to separate the text operand and the command name. Any blanks after the first are assumed to be part of the text operand.

Replacing Characters Starting with the Current Column

CREPLACE is *column-oriented* subcommand that replaces the characters on the current line beginning at the current column, one for one, with another string of characters. A blank character in the text operand replaces the corresponding character in the file with a blank, and an underscore character in the text operand replaces the corresponding character in the file with an underscore. Use the CLOCATE subcommand to position the current column.

Be sure that there are enough columns between the current column and the truncation column to fit the new text. If the number of columns is insufficient and the SPILL function of the SET subcommand is set to OFF, any characters at or beyond the truncation column will be lost. Otherwise, any characters that are shifted past the truncation column will *spill* into a new line immediately after the current line.

Command Format:

      CReplace   **text**

where **text**   is a character string that replaces the characters on the current line beginning with the current column. A single blank is assumed to separate the text operand and the command name. Any blanks after the first are assumed to be part of the text operand.

Examples:

Suppose that column 10 is the current column in a file containing this line:

Deleting, Inserting and Replacing Characters § 223

```
00000 * * * Top of File * * *
00001          12345
      <...+....|....+....2....+....3....+....4....+....5....
00002 * * * End of File * * *
```

- Suppose you must change '12345' to 'AB DE':

  ====> CREPLACE AB DE

- Suppose you must change '12345' to 'AB_DE' replacing '3' with an underscore:

  ====> CREPLACE AB_DE

7.13 XEDIT Macros: Creating New XEDIT Commands

While XEDIT has more than 200 commands to perform a wide variety of editing and utility functions, you will often find yourself confronted with an editing task for which there is no *single* command to perform the task. The task might involve:

- Any sequence of commands executed more than once.

- Any sequence of commands executed repetitively.

- Any sequence of commands executed as part of another procedure.

- Any sequence of commands in which the arguments that commands take change from one execution to another.

Such problems are usually well handled by an XEDIT **macro**, which is a file containing a *sequence* of commands to be executed. The commands can be:

- XEDIT commands to perform editing functions.

- REXX commands to control the sequence in which commands are executed and the overall flow of the program.

- CMS commands to work with files and perform tasks on your VM.

Macros becomes especially useful when you have the same task to perform over and over again, since a macro can be constructed in which the sequence of editing commands to be repeated are embedded within REXX commands that control when and how often the editing commands are executed.

The PROFILE XEDIT, discussed in the chapter *Customizing the XEDIT Environment*, is an example of an XEDIT macro. This macro is special in that it is executed whenever you begin editing a file.

This text does not discuss the writing of XEDIT macros as such. That topic is covered in another text, *VM/CMS: A Guide to Programming and Applications*.

Creating an XEDIT Macro

You create an XEDIT macro using a text editor such as XEDIT. An XEDIT macro can have any CMS filename, but it *must* have a filetype of XEDIT.

Running an XEDIT Macro

Under normal circumstances, you run an XEDIT macro just as you execute a subcommand:

1. Type the macro's filename on the command line followed by any arguments to be passed to the macro.

2. Press ENTER.

XEDIT Macros: Creating New XEDIT Commands § 225

Chapter 8
Customizing the XEDIT Environment

Introduction

When you begin editing a file with XEDIT, the characteristics of the editing environment are established based on the filetype of the file being edited and the default assignments of the functions of the XEDIT subcommand SET. These characteristics include:

- How targets are defined.

- How target searches are conducted.

- Where target searches are conducted.

- Which parts of the screen are displayed.

- Where the parts of the screen are displayed.

- What the characteristics of the file being edited are.

- How commands are interpreted and executed.

- Which parts of a file are displayed and acted upon.

The functions of the SET subcommand provide means to control these characteristics. Each of the SET functions have assignments initially set by XEDIT to create the *default* editing environment. You can, however, use the SET functions to *customize* the editing environment so that it better suits your needs and preferences. You can change the assignment of a SET function at any time during an editing session.

Example:

NUMBER is a function that determines whether line numbers are displayed in the prefix area. The NUMBER function has two alternative assignments: ON and OFF.

- When NUMBER is set to ON, line numbers are displayed in the prefix area.

- When NUMBER is set to OFF, equal signs are displayed in the prefix area.

Normally, NUMBER is set to OFF. Suppose you want to replace the equal signs with line numbers:

====> SET NUMBER ON

The more useful SET functions are presented in this chapter in terms of the characteristics of the editing environment that they control. The final section discusses a procedure by which you can automatically modify the XEDIT environment whenever you begin editing a file. Use the HELP facility to obtain a complete list of the functions and what they do:

```
HELP XEDIT SET
```

8.1 Obtaining the Current Assignment of a SET Function

QUERY is a subcommand that displays the current assignment of a specific function.

Command Format:

> **Query**   **function**

where **function**   is the function whose assignment is to be displayed.

Example:

Suppose you want to determine the present assignment of the NUMBER function:

====> QUERY NUMBER

                          ●   ●   ●

STATUS is a subcommand that either displays the assignments of *all* the SET functions or creates an XEDIT macro that contains the current assignments of *all* the SET functions.

Command Format:

> **STATUS**   **[fn]**

where **fn**   is the filename of the file that contains the current assignments of the SET functions. The filetype is XEDIT and the filemode is A. If the filename is omitted, the assignments of the SET functions are displayed on the terminal.

8.2 Changing the Assignment of a SET Function

Only one function may be changed in each execution of the SET subcommand. For convenience, you may execute any of the SET functions, except MACRO, without preceding the function name with the word SET. The SET subcommand takes the general form:

[SET] **function assignment**

where **function** is the function to be changed.

assignment is the assignment made to the function.

Example:

Suppose you want to display line numbers in the prefix area. The following are equivalent:

```
====> NUMBER ON
====> SET NUMBER ON
```

Displaying the Assignment of a Function on the Command Line

MODIFY is a subcommand that provides a convenient method of changing one of the SET functions. If you enter the MODIFY subcommand with a SET function, XEDIT displays the SET subcommand with that function and its current assignment on the command line so that you can change the assignment by typing over it and then pressing ENTER.

Command Format:

MODify **function**

where **function** is the function to be displayed.

Example:

Suppose you want to display the assignment of the NUMBER function:

```
====> MODIFY NUMBER
```

XEDIT displays the command in the command input area:

```
====> SET NUMBER OFF
```

You can then move the cursor to the word OFF and replace it with the word ON and press the ENTER key.

8.3 Controlling Target Definition and Searches

Understanding this section requires a prior understanding of:

- What targets are and how they are specified.

- What a search is and how one is conducted.

These concepts are discussed in the sections on *Targets*, *Locating a Line Target* and *Locating a Column Target* in the chapter *Becoming Acquainted with XEDIT*.

Using a Wildcard in a String Expression

ARBCHAR defines a single character to represent that part of a character string to be located and/or changed which can vary from one string to another and is, therefore, arbitrary. The use of an arbitrary character is convenient if the character string to be located and/or changed is not always the same. Normally, the $ character is defined to represent the arbitrary string, but the arbitrary string function is turned off.

The ARBCHAR function separates the *definition* of a character to represent an arbitrary string from the *implementation* of the arbitrary string function. What this means is that a character defined to represent the arbitrary string will do so only if the arbitrary string function is engaged.

The character you choose to represent an arbitrary string should be one that is not already present in the file. Otherwise, you may find it difficult to locate targets and change text that contain the character.

Command Format:

ARBchar	OFF|ON [$|char]

where	**ON**	engages the arbitrary character string function.
	OFF	disengages the arbitrary character string function.
	char	is the character defined to represent the arbitrary string. If the character is omitted, the $ character represents the arbitrary string.

Example:

Suppose you must change 'this' to 'that' and 'that' to 'this' regardless of what text appears between 'this' and 'that' in this file:

```
00000 * * * Top of File * * *
00001 this and that
      |...+....1....+....2....+....3....+....4....+....5....
00002 this or that
00003 this but not that
00004 * * * End of File * * *
```

1. Use the ARBCHAR function to turn on the arbitrary character function. Since the $ character is already defined to be the arbitrary character, the following are equivalent:

   ```
   ====> ARB ON
   ====> ARB ON $
   ```

2. Use the $ character in the CHANGE command to represent whatever text happens to occur between 'this' and 'that':

   ```
   ====> CHANGE /this$that/that$this/ *
   ```

   results in:

```
00000 * * * Top of File * * *
00001 that and this
      |...+....1....+....2....+....3....+....4....+....5....
00002 that or this
00003 that but not this
00004 * * * End of File * * *
```

Thus, the $ represents *whatever string occurs between* 'this' and 'that':

- On line 1, $ represented 'and'.

- On line 2, $ represented 'or'.

- On line 3, $ represented 'but not'.

The Importance of Case in a String Expression

CASE controls whether letters put into a file are treated as all uppercase or a mixture of uppercase and lowercase. It also determines whether the case of letters is important in searching for target strings. Normally, the setting of the CASE function is based on the filetype.

The CASE function does not convert the letters that are already in a file from uppercase to lowercase or lowercase to uppercase.

- Use the LOWERCAS subcommand to convert uppercase characters already in a file to lowercase.

232 § Customizing the XEDIT Environment

• Use the UPPERCAS subcommand to convert lowercase characters already in a file to uppercase.

Command Format:

CASE Uppercas|Mixed [Respect|Ignore]

where **Uppercas** converts lowercase letters to uppercase.

Mixed does not convert lowercase letters to uppercase.

Respect respects the case of a letter in a string expression.

Ignore ignores the case of a letter in a string expression.

Example:

Suppose that sometimes a word occurs in all uppercase, sometimes in all lowercase and sometimes in a mixture of uppercase and lowercase as in this file:

```
00000 * * * Top of File * * *
      |...+....1....+....2....+....3....+....4....+....5....
00001 SOME
00002 Some
00003 some
00004 * * * End of File * * *
```

• To find the first occurrence of 'Some', a mixture of uppercase and lowercase:

1. Use the CASE function to specify that the case of letters in a target is important.

    ====> CASE MIXED RESPECT

2. Search for the string.

    ====> /Some/

• To find any occurrence of 'some', regardless of the case of the letters:

1. Use the CASE function to specify that the case of letters in a target is not important.

    ====> CASE MIXED IGNORE

2. Search for the string. Since case is ignored, the following are equivalent:

Controlling Target Definition and Searches § 233

```
====> /some/
====> /Some/
====> /SOME/
```

Specifying Targets and Text Operands in Hexadecimal

HEX allows you to specify targets and text operands to subcommands in hexadecimal notation. This function is useful if you must locate or change a character that is not represented on your keyboard. Normally, targets and text operands cannot be specified in hexadecimal.

Command Format:

HEX	**OFF|ON**

where	**OFF**	prohibits you from entering target strings and text operands in hexadecimal.
	ON	enables you to enter target strings and text operands in hexadecimal.

Example:

Suppose you have a file with a number of characters that normally print as a bullet (•) which you want to change to the letter 'o'. The bullet cannot be entered directly from the keyboard. It can be specified, however, using hexadecimal notation. The hex code for the bullet is AF and the hex code for the letter 'o' is 96. To specify a character in hex code:

1. Turn on the HEX function:

   ```
   ====> HEX ON
   ```

2. Change all occurrences of AF to 96 on all lines:

   ```
   ====> :1 CHANGE /X'AF'/X'96'/ * *
   ```

If HEX is set to OFF, the CHANGE subcommand would not change the bullet to the letter 'o', it would change the character string X'AF' to the character string X'96'.

Defining the Range

RANGE defines the top and bottom lines within which the line pointer can move. Once a new range has been defined, subcommands only operate within that range. The RANGE function is useful when you must limit the lines within which a subcommand is to operate. Normally, the top of the file is the top of the range and the end of file is the end of the range.

Command Format:

       RANge   **target1 target2**

where **target1**   is a line target that identifies the line that is the top of the range.

       target2   is a line target that identifies the line that is the end of the range.

System Messages:

- If the top of the range is different from the actual top of the file, the message

  ```
  * * * Top of File * * *
  ```

  changes to

  ```
  * * * Top of Range (Line=topline) * * *
  ```

  where *topline* is the actual line number of the top of the range.

- If the end of the range is different from the actual end of the file, the message

  ```
  * * * End of File * * *
  ```

  changes to

  ```
  * * * End of Range (Line=endline) * * *
  ```

  where *endline* is the actual line number of the end of the range.

Exercises:

- How could you limit the search for a character string to lines 100 through 200?

  ```
  ====> RANGE :100 :201
  ```

  ```
  ====> /string
  ```

- How could you restore the RANGE to the top and end of file?

  ```
  ====> RANGE -* *
  ```

Controlling Target Definition and Searches   § 235

Controlling Which Lines Can Be Searched and Manipulated

SCOPE controls which lines XEDIT can manipulate and search for targets. This function is used in conjunction with the SELECT and DISPLAY functions, described in the section *Controlling the Lines Displayed and Manipulated*. Normally, the SCOPE function is set to search for targets and manipulate text only on the lines that are displayed.

Command Format:

> **SCOPE**   **Display|All**

where **Display**   limits the lines that can be searched and manipulated to those in the range defined by the DISPLAY function.

> **All**   permits all lines in the file to be searched and manipulated.

Holding the Current Line When a Search is Unsuccessful

STAY determines whether the current line is moved when a target search is unsuccessful or when subcommands such as CHANGE that use targets as operands are executed. Normally, the current line is moved. Movement of the current line when a search is unsuccessful may be inconvenient if you must return to that line in the file from which the search was initiated.

Command Format:

> **STAY**   **OFF|ON**

where **OFF**   moves the current line when a target search is unsuccessful or when subcommands such as CHANGE that use targets as operands are executed.

> **ON**   holds the current line when a target search is unsuccessful or when subcommands such as CHANGE that use targets as operands are executed.

Example:

Suppose you want to hold the current line in the event of an unsuccessful search:

====> STAY ON

Controlling Where Column-Oriented Searches are Conducted

STREAM controls whether the search for a character string is to be conducted through the entire file or just the current line when the target is the object of either the CLOCATE or CDELETE subcommands. Normally, the search for a character string is conducted through the entire file.

Command Format:

       STReam   **ON|OFF**

where **OFF**   limits a search to the current line.

      ON   permits a search that is unsuccessful on the current line to continue to the end of the file if the search is in a forward direction or to the top of the file if the search is in a backward direction.

The Importance of Blanks in a String Expression

VARBLANK controls whether the number of blank characters is important in the search for a target. Normally, the number of blanks is important.

Command Format:

       VARblank   **OFF|ON**

where **OFF**   makes the number of blank characters in a target important in a search for that target.

      ON   makes the number of blank characters in a target unimportant in a search for that target.

Example:

Suppose a file contains this line:

```
00000 * * * Top of File * * *
      |...+....1....+....2....+....3....+....4....+....5....
00001 horse      feathers
00002 * * * End of File * * *
```

If VARBLANK is set to OFF, the following would not locate the string, since the number of blanks between 'horse' and 'feathers' is not the same in the file and in the string to be located.

```
====> /horse feathers/
```

Controlling Target Definition and Searches § **237**

If VARBLANK was set to ON, however, the string would be located.

Searching for a String Expression That Spans Lines

SPAN determines whether a character string must reside on a single line or may span two or more lines. Normally, a character string must reside on a single line to be found. This function is useful if a character string is sometimes continued from one line to the next. Finding a string that spans two or more lines is most easily done when the VARBLANK and SPAN functions are both set to ON.

Command Format:

SPAN   ON|OFF [*Blank*|Noblank [n|2]]

where **ON**   permits a target string to reside on more than one line.

OFF   restricts a target string to a single line.

Noblank   places no blank character between consecutive lines when a search is conducted for a target string that spans more than one line. Normally, one blank character is placed between consecutive lines.

n   is the number of lines that the target string may span. If the number of lines is omitted, it is assumed to be two and the string to be located may occupy two consecutive lines. Use an * to search to the end of file or end of range.

Example:

Suppose a file contains these two lines:

```
00000 * * * Top of File * * *
      |...+....1....+....2....+....3....+....4....+....5....
00001 horse
00002 feathers
00003 * * * End of File * * *
```

If VARBLANK and SPAN are both set to ON, this subcommand would locate the string:

```
====> /horse feathers/
```

If either VARBLANK or SPAN were set to OFF, however, the string would not be located.

238 § Customizing the XEDIT Environment

Controlling Where an Unsuccessful Search Ends

WRAP controls where an unsuccessful search ends:

- An unsuccessful forward search either terminates at the end of the file (or end of the range) or continues up to the line preceding the current line. Normally, an unsuccessful forward search terminates at the end of the file.

- An unsuccessful backward search either terminates at the top of the file (or top of the range) or continues up to the line following the current line. Normally, an unsuccessful backward search terminates at the top of the file.

Command Format:

WRap   **OFF|ON**

where **ON**   continues an unsuccessful search.

OFF   terminates an unsuccessful search at the end or top of the file.

Defining the Zone

ZONE defines the first and last columns on each line that are searched for a character string.

- The start of the zone is indicated on the scale line by the < character *unless* the current column and the start of the zone are the same column, in which case the vertical bar appears in that column.

- The end of the zone is indicated on the scale line by the > character *unless* the current column and the end of the zone are the same column, in which case the vertical bar appears in that column.

Normally, the start of the zone is the first tab stop and the end of the zone is the truncation column. ZONE is useful for restricting substitutions to certain columns.

Command Format:

Zone   **startcol endcol**

where **startcol**   is the column number of the start of the zone.

endcol   is the column number of the end of the zone.

Exercises:

- How would you change all occurrences of one string to another string on all lines but only between columns 20 and 30, inclusive?

  1. Set the zone to be between columns 20 and 30:

     ====> ZONE 20 30

  2. Change the one string to the other:

     ====> :1 CHANGE /one string/other string/ * *

- Suppose you have a file where column 1 of each line contains either a zero or a one. How could you determine the number of zeros and ones in column 1 throughout the file? Recall that the COUNT subcommand will determine the number of times that a string occurs in a file.

  1. Restrict the search that COUNT conducts to column 1 with ZONE:

     ====> ZONE 1 1

  2. Count the number of zeros from the beginning to the end of the file:

     ====> :1 COUNT /0/ *

  The number of ones will be the difference between the number of lines in the file (displayed after Size= in the file identification line) and the number of zeros.

- XEDIT provides several commands to remove lines from a file. There is, however, no single command to remove the data from certain columns. How would you remove whatever data is present in columns 73 through 80 throughout a file?

  1. Use ARBCHAR to turn on the arbitrary character. (It is normally defined to be $).

     ====> ARBCHAR ON

  2. Use ZONE to restrict the columns that can be searched to 73 through 80.

     ====> ZONE 73 80

  3. Use the CHANGE subcommand to remove whatever data is present in the zone.

     ====> :1 CHANGE /$// *

•   How could you display all the lines in a file that contain a specific string of characters but only when that string occurs between columns 25 and 40?

1.   Use ZONE to restrict the columns to be searched to 25 through 40.

   ====> ZONE 25 40

2.   Use ALL to display the lines that contain the string.

   ====> ALL /string/

8.4 Controlling Screen Layout

Understanding this section requires a prior understanding of the location and function of the various areas of the screen in XEDIT. These concepts are discussed in the section *The Areas of the Screen and Their Uses in XEDIT* in the chapter *Becoming Acquainted with XEDIT*.

This section is concerned with *which* parts of the screen are displayed in XEDIT and *where* they are displayed. In order to change the position of a part of the screen, you must know how to refer to that position. The first part of this section discusses how to do so. Throughout this section, the lines on the screen will be discussed in terms of their position relative to these reference points:

- The Top of the Screen

- The Middle of the Screen

- The Bottom of the Screen

The number of lines on the screen is assumed to be 24.

How to Specify the Location of a Line on the Screen

Specify a line's position relative to the top of the screen as the number of lines between it and the top of the screen preceded by a plus sign:

> **+n**

Specify a line's position relative to the bottom of the screen as the number of lines between it and the bottom of the screen preceded by a minus sign:

> **−n**

If a line is located below the middle of the screen (line 12), specify its position relative to the middle of the screen as the number of lines between it and the middle of the screen preceded by a plus sign and the letter M:

> **M+n**

If a line is located above the middle of the screen (line 12), specify its position relative to the middle of the screen as the number of lines between it and the middle of the screen preceded by a minus sign and the letter M:

> **M−n**

Examples:

- The top of the screen is indicated by any of these:

```
+ 1
M-11
-24
```

- The middle of the screen is indicated by any of these:

```
+12
M
-13
```

- The bottom of the screen is indicated by any of these:

```
+24
- 1
M+12
```

Defining the Location of the Command Line

CMDLINE controls where the command line is displayed. Normally, the command line occupies the last two lines on the screen.

Command Format:

	CMDline	**Bottom|Top|On|OFf**
where	**Bottom**	defines the last line on the the screen as the command line.
	Top	defines the second line from the top of the screen as the command line. Normally, the message line occupies the second line from the top of the screen, so if you move the command line to this position you should also move the message line elsewhere on the screen. Otherwise, you'll have to clear the command line by pressing the ENTER key each time a message is displayed. The command to move the message line is discussed next in this section.
	On	defines the last two lines on the screen as the command line.
	OFf	removes the command line. If the command line is removed from the screen, subcommands can no longer be entered from it. Do not remove the command line from the screen unless you provide some other means for either displaying it again or leaving the editor, such as using a PF key.

Controlling Screen Layout § 243

Defining the Location of the Message Line

MSGLINE controls the location of the message line and the number of lines that a message may occupy. Normally, the message line occupies one line at the second line from the top of the screen.

Command Format:

       MSGLine   ON|OFF M+n|M−n|+n|−n [p|*1* [Overlay]]

where **ON**   permits messages to be displayed on the message line.

      OFF   turns off the message line. If the message line is turned off, messages from XEDIT are sent to CMS and the screen is cleared.

      M+n   displays the message line **n** lines below the middle of the screen.

      M−n   displays the message line **n** lines above the middle of the screen.

      +n   displays the message line **n** lines below the top of the screen.

      −n   displays the message line **n** lines above the bottom of the screen.

      p   is the maximum number of lines to be used to display messages. If the number of lines is omitted, it is assumed to be one.

      Overlay   does not reserve a blank line for the message line.

Example:

Suppose you want to display the message line on the third line from the bottom of the screen, as it is in FILELIST, PEEK and RDRLIST:

```
====> MSGLINE  ON  -3  3
```

Defining the Location of the Current Line

CURLINE controls the position of the current line on the screen. Normally, the current line is located in the middle of the screen.

If you move the current line, you might also want to move the scale line. The command to move the scale is discussed next in this section.

244 § Customizing the XEDIT Environment

Command Format:

CURLine   ON M+n|M−n|+n|−n

where **M+n**   displays the current line **n** lines below the middle of the screen.

   M−n   displays the current line **n** lines above the middle of the screen.

   +n   displays the current line **n** lines below the top of the screen.

   −n   displays the current line **n** lines above the bottom of the screen.

Example:

Suppose you want to display the current line at the third line below the top of the screen as it is in FILELIST, PEEK and RDRLIST:

====> CURLINE ON 3

Defining the Location of the Scale Line

SCALE controls the location of the scale line. Normally, the scale line is displayed one line below the middle of the screen.

Command Format:

SCAle   ON|OFF [M+n|M−n|+n|−n]

where **ON**   displays the scale line.

   OFF   turns off the scale line.

   M+n   displays the scale line **n** lines below the middle of the screen.

   M−n   displays the scale line **n** lines above the middle of the screen.

   +n   displays the scale line **n** lines below the top of the screen.

   −n   displays the scale line **n** lines above the bottom of the screen.

Example:

Suppose you've displayed the current line on the third line below the top of the screen. Now, you want to display the scale immediately below it:

====> SCALE ON 4

Displaying the Location of Nondisplaying Characters

NONDISP defines some character to represent all nondisplaying characters. Nondisplaying characters are characters that normally appear on the screen as blank characters, but they are not blanks. They are simply characters that have no counterpart on the keyboard and that are normally indistinguishable from blanks. This function is useful if you must be able to locate nondisplaying characters or to distinguish them from blanks.

The character you choose to represent the nondisplaying characters should be one that is not already present in the file. Otherwise, you will not be able to distinguish a normal occurrence of that character from a nondisplaying character.

Notice that the NONDISP function only indicates the *location* of a nondisplaying character; it does not indicate *which* nondisplaying character is present at the location. To determine which nondisplaying character is present, use the HEXTYPE subcommand to display the line that contains the character in both hexadecimal and EBCDIC.

Command Format:

> **NONDisp** [char]

where **char** is the character that is to represent any nondisplaying characters. If the character is omitted, a blank is used to represent any nondisplaying character.

Example:

Suppose you want to assign the logical not character to represent nondisplaying characters:

====> NONDISP ¬

Defining the Contents of the Prefix Area

NUMBER specifies whether line numbers or equal signs are displayed in the prefix area. Normally, equal signs are displayed in the prefix area. Line numbers in the prefix area will simplify your use of commands that use line numbers as targets.

Command Format:

      NUMber   **OFF|ON**

where **OFF**   displays equal signs in the prefix area.

        ON   displays line numbers in the prefix area.

Defining the Location of the Prefix Area

PREFIX controls the location of the prefix area. Normally, the prefix area is located on the left side of the screen.

Command Format:

      PREfix   **ON|OFF** **[Left|Right]**

where **ON**   displays the prefix area.

      OFF   removes the prefix area.

      Right   locates the prefix area on the right side of the screen. Normally, the prefix area is located on the left side of the screen.

```
FILE1   DATA   A1   F   80   Trunc=80        FILE2   DATA   A1   F  80 Trunc=80




00000 * * * Top of File * * *                00000 * * * Top of File * * *
      |...+....1....+....2....+....3...             |...+....1....+....2....+....3...
00001 * * * End of File * * *                00001 * * * End of File * * *




====> _                                      ====>
```

Figure 8.1 The physical screen in XEDIT divided into two vertically arranged logical screens.

Displaying Two or More Files Simultaneously

SCREEN divides the *physical screen* into two or more *logical screens* so you can simultaneously display and edit either two or more *different* files or two or more different parts of the *same* file. Editing two or more different files simultaneously is discussed in the section *Editing Several Files Simultaneously* in the chapter *Special Topics in XEDIT*. SCREEN also enables you to specify the shape and size of each logical screen. There are three different command formats:

- One format divides the physical screen into two or more logical screens of the *same* size that are either horizontally or vertically arranged.

- One format divides the physical screen into two or more logical screens of *different* sizes that are either horizontally or vertically arranged.

- One format divides the physical screen into two or more logical screens of *different* sizes that are *both* horizontally or vertically arranged.

Two options on the SOS subcommand provide a convenient way to move the cursor from screen to screen when two or more files are displayed:

- TABCMDF moves the cursor forward to the command line of the next screen.

- TABCMDB moves the cursor backward to the command line of the previous screen.

These options are discussed in the section *Moving the Cursor between Files* in the chapter *Special Topics in XEDIT*.

● ● ●

One format divides the physical screen into logical screens of the same size. On a physical screen with 24 lines and 80 columns, the maximum number of equally sized screens is four.

Command Format:

> **SCReen**   n [*Horizontal*|**Vertical**]

where **n**   is the number of logical screens into which the physical screen is to be divided. Specify the number of logical screens such that all horizontal screens are at least 5 lines long and all vertical screens are at least 20 columns wide.

> **Horizontal**   arranges the screens one on top of the other.

Vertical   arranges the screens side by side.

Examples:

Suppose you are editing two files, FILE1 DATA and FILE2 DATA.

- To display both files side by side on equally sized screens, as in Figure 8.1:

  ====> SCREEN 2 V

- To display both files one on top of the other on equally sized screens, as in Figure 8.2:

  ====> SCREEN 2 H

• • •

One format allows logical screens of different sizes. Specify as many logical screens as you like so long as each horizontal screen is at least 5 lines long and each vertical screen is at least 20 columns wide.

Command Format:

SCReen   **Size|Width s1 [s2]** ...

```
FILE1   DATA     A1  F 80  Trunc=80 Size=0 Line=0 Col=1 Alt=0


00000 * * * Top of File * * *
      |...+....1....+....2....+....3....+....4....+....5....+....6....+....7...
00001 * * * End of File * * *


====> _
                                                  X E D I T   2 Files
FILE2   DATA     A1  F 80  Trunc=80 Size=0 Line=0 Col=1 Alt=0


00000 * * * Top of File * * *
      |...+....1....+....2....+....3....+....4....+....5....+....6....+....7...
00001 * * * End of File * * *


====>
                                                  X E D I T   2 Files
```

Figure 8.2 The physical screen divided into two horizontally arranged logical screens.

where **Size**   arranges the screens horizontally.

Width   arranges the screens vertically.

s1   is the number of lines in the first screen if the screens are horizontal. If the screens are vertical, **s1** is the number of columns in the first screen.

s2   is the number of lines in the second screen if the screens are horizontal. If the screens are vertical, **s2** is the number of columns in the second screen.

Examples:

Suppose you are editing two files, FILE1 DATA and FILE2 DATA.

- To display both files side by side on equally sized screens, as in Figure 8.1:

  ====> SCREEN W 40 40

- To display both files one on top of the other on equally sized screens, as in Figure 8.2:

  ====> SCREEN S 12 12

                    • • •

One format allows both horizontal and vertical screens of different sizes. Specify as many logical screens as you like so long as all horizontal screens are at least 5 lines long and all vertical screens are at least 20 columns wide.

Command Format:

SCReen   **Define   s1 w1 l1 c1   [s2 w2 l2 c2] ...**

where **s1**   is the number of lines in the first screen.

w1   is the number of columns in the first screen.

l1   is the line number of the upper left corner of the logical screen on the physical screen.

c1   is the column number of the upper left corner of the logical screen on the physical screen.

Examples:

Suppose you are editing two files, FILE1 DATA and FILE2 DATA.

250 § Customizing the XEDIT Environment

- To display both files side by side on equally sized screens, as in Figure 8.1:

  ====> SCREEN D 24 40 1 1 24 40 1 41

- To display both files one on top of the other on equally sized screens, as in Figure 8.2:

  ====> SCREEN D 12 80 1 1 12 80 13 1

- Suppose you are editing four files and want to divide the physical screen into four logical screens, as in Figure 8.3:

  ====> SCREEN D 12 40 1 1 12 40 1 41 12 40 13 1 12 40 13 41

Defining the Contents of New Lines

MASK controls what text is displayed in a new line added to a file by any of these commands:

- The PF2 key.

- The ADD, INPUT and REPLACE subcommands.

- The A and I prefix commands.

```
FILE1   DATA  A1  F  80  Trunc=80       FILE2   DATA  A1  F 80 Trunc=80


00000 * * * Top of File * * *           00000 * * * Top of File * * *
    |...+....1....+....2....+....3...        |...+....1....+....2....+....3...
00001 * * * End of File * * *           00001 * * * End of File * * *


====> _                                 ====>
FILE3   DATA  A1  F  80  Trunc=80       FILE4   DATA  A1  F 80 Trunc=80


00000 * * * Top of File * * *           00000 * * * Top of File * * *
    |...+....1....+....2....+....3...        |...+....1....+....2....+....3...
00001 * * * End of File * * *           00001 * * * End of File * * *


====>                                   ====>
```

Figure 8.3 The physical screen in XEDIT divided into four rectangularly arranged logical screens.

Normally, a new line is filled with blanks. A mask is useful in several ways. It can serve as a template for inputting text or you can use it like a preprinted form. In both cases, the mask displays the same text on each line, which you can then change from line to line. If you use a mask in this way for data entry, consider using the TABS function, described later, to move the cursor from one input field to the next. Since the mask is part of the file, you can replace any part of the mask just by typing text over it.

Command Format:

MASK	**Immed [text]|Define|Modify**
where **Immed**	uses **text** as the mask. If the text is omitted, the mask becomes blank.
Define	displays the scale line in the command line so that you can type the mask over the scale line. If you leave the scale line unchanged, the new mask will be the scale line. The scale is especially useful if certain parts of the mask must begin in certain columns. The mask is limited to 133 characters, since this is maximum length of the command line.
Modify	displays the current mask in the command line so that you can change it by typing in any modifications.

Reserving a Line on the Screen

RESERVED reserves a line on the screen, preventing the editor from using the line, and allows you to display specified information on the line.

Command Format:

RESERved	**M+n|M−n|+n|−n High|Nohigh [text]**
where **M+n**	reserves the line **n** lines below the middle of the screen.
M−n	reserves the line **n** lines above the middle of the screen.
+n	reserves the line **n** lines below the top of the screen.
−n	reserves the line **n** lines above the bottom of the screen.
High	highlights the text in the reserved line.
Nohigh	displays the text in the reserved line at normal intensity.
text	is the text, if any, that is displayed on the reserved line.

Example:

Suppose you want to display the functions performed by the PF keys in the two lines immediately above the command line. To display the functions performed by the first six PF keys in the first of these two lines, which is the fourth line from the bottom of the screen:

```
====> RESERVED -4 H PF1=HELP PF2=LINEADD PF3=QUIT PF4=TAB PF5=SCHANGE PF6=?
```

To display the functions performed by the last six PF keys in the second of these two lines, which is the third line from the bottom of the screen:

```
====> RESERVED -3 H PF7=BACKWARD PF8=FORWARD PF9= = PF10=RGTLEFT PF11=SPLTJOIN
```

•   •   •

RESERVED is also used to *unreserve* a line and return it to its original status.

Command Format:

> **RESER**ved   **M + n|M − n| + n| − n   Off**

Example:

Suppose you want to return the lines reserved in the previous example to their original status:

```
====> RESERVED -3 OFF
```

```
====> RESERVED -4 OFF
```

Displaying the Locations of Tab Stops in the File Area

TABLINE controls whether a line is displayed that has a T in every column defined to be a tab stop.

Command Format:

> **TAB**line   **OFF|ON   [M + n|M − n| + n| − n]**

where **ON**   displays the tab line.

OFF   turns off the tab line.

M + n   displays the tab line **n** lines below the middle of the screen.

M − n   displays the tab line **n** lines above the middle of the screen.

+n displays the tab line **n** lines below the top of the screen.

−n displays the tab line **n** lines above the bottom of the screen.

Example:

XEDIT normally defines the tab stops for a file with a filetype of SCRIPT to be at every fifth column. Suppose you want to display a tabline in the line immediately above the current line. The following are equivalent:

```
====> TABLINE ON M-1
====> TABLINE ON 11
```

results in:

```
         T   T   T    T    T    T    T    T    T    T    T
00000 * * * Top of File * * *
         |...+....1....+....2....+....3....+....4....+....5....
00001 * * * End of File * * *
```

Handling the Top of File and End of File Notices

TOFEOF controls whether the Top of File (or Top of Range) and End of File (or End of Range) notices are displayed.

Command Format:

TOFEOF **ON|OFF**

where **ON** displays the notices.

OFF removes the notices.

Example:

Suppose you want to removes the notices:

```
====> TOFEOF OFF
```

results in:

```
00000
         |...+....1....+....2....+....3....+....4....+....5....
00001
```

254 § Customizing the XEDIT Environment

Handling Shadow Lines

SHADOW controls whether shadow lines which indicate the number of lines excluded from a display are themselves excluded from the display. Normally, shadow lines are displayed.

Command Format:

> **SHADow**   **ON|OFF**

where **ON**   displays shadow lines.

> **OFF**   removes shadow lines from the display.

Displaying Selected Columns

VERIFY controls which columns of a file are displayed on the screen and whether the lines changed by subcommands are displayed in the message area. Up to 28 different areas can be displayed. This function is especially useful when you are editing a file with a record length longer than the 80 characters that can normally fit on most terminal screens because you can use VERIFY to display any part(s) of the line that you want. Other ways to control which columns are displayed are discussed in the section on *Shifting the Display Sideways* in the chapter *Special Topics in XEDIT*.

Command Format:

> **Verify**   **[*OFF*|ON] [Hex] begcol endcol [begcol [endcol]] ...**

where **ON**   displays lines that are changed. Normally, lines changed are not displayed.

> **Hex**   displays the contents of the file in hexadecimal.

> **begcol**   is the first column of an area to be displayed.

> **endcol**   is the last column of an area to be displayed.

Examples:

- Suppose you are editing a file with a record length of 130 and want to display only the first 10 columns and the last 10 columns:

  ====> V 1 10 120 130

- VERIFY is also convenient when you are in edit mode with a file whose records extend beyond column 73, since XEDIT normally spills the data in columns 74 and beyond onto the next line, giving the file a disheveled appearance. You can tidy the screen's appearance by only

displaying 73 columns at a time. Suppose you want to display the first
73 columns:

====> V 1 73

8.5 Controlling Characteristics of the File Being Edited

Understanding this section requires a prior understanding of:

- Filenames, Filetypes and Filemodes

- Logical Record Length and Record Formats

- The Truncation Column

These concepts are discussed in the sections *The CMS File Identifier* and *Characteristics of CMS Disk Files* in the chapter *CMS Disks and CMS Disk Files*.

The Importance of Case for Letters Going into a File

CASE controls whether letters being put into a file are to be treated as all uppercase or a mixture of uppercase and lowercase. Normally, the assignment of the CASE function is based on the filetype.

Command Format:

> **CASE**   **Uppercas|Mixed   [Respect|Ignore]**

where **Uppercas**   converts lowercase letters to uppercase.

Mixed   does not convert lowercase letters to uppercase.

Respect   respects the case of a letter in target searches.

Ignore   ignores the case of a letter in target searches.

Example:

Suppose you are putting text into a file that you've given a filetype of DATA. The default setting of the CASE function for a file with a filetype of DATA is UPPERCAS. Thus, all lowercase text would be translated to uppercase. If you want to be able to enter lowercase and have the text remain lowercase, you would have to use:

```
====> CASE MIXED
```

Changing the Filemode

FMODE changes the filemode of the file being edited. This function is useful if the original filemode was that of a disk to which you cannot write, either because the disk is full or because you only have read access to the disk. The filemode you specify must be that of a disk to which you have write access.

Command Format:

>　**FMode**　　　**fm**

where　**fm**　　　is the new filemode.

Changing the Filename

FNAME changes the filename of the file being edited. This function is useful if a file already exists with the same fileid and you don't want to replace that file with the file being edited.

Command Format:

>　**FName**　　　**fn**

where　**fn**　　　is the new filename.

Changing the Filetype

FTYPE changes the filetype of the file being edited. This function is useful if a file already exists with the same fileid and you don't want to replace that file with the file being edited.

Command Format:

>　**FType**　　　**ft**

where　**ft**　　　is the new filetype.

Changing the Record Length

LRECL changes the logical record length. Normally, the setting of this function is based on the filetype. The record length you assign cannot be greater than the value assigned to the WIDTH option on the XEDIT command. Using this function can save disk space when the last nonblank characters in a file with a fixed record format occur well before the last column on a record.

Command Format:

>　**LRecl**　　　**n**

where　**n**　　　is the new logical record length.

Example:

Consider a file with a fixed record format and a record length of 80 which contains 1000 records. The number of bytes in this file is (80 x 1000) = 80000.

258　§　Customizing the XEDIT Environment

Now, suppose that data is only recorded in the first 10 columns of each record. Thus, blanks are used to pad the file from column 11 to column 80 which means that 70000 bytes in the file are blanks and really not necessary. By changing the record length to 10, the number of bytes in the file becomes (10 x 1000) = 10000, which is a considerable reduction in size.

Changing the Record Format

RECFM changes the file's record format. Normally, the setting of this function is based on the filetype.

Command Format:

RECFm   F|V

where **F**   assigns the file a fixed record format.

V   assigns the file a variable record format.

Examples:

- When the length of the records in a file varies from record to record, that file will occupy *less* disk space when stored in a variable record format than when stored in a fixed record format.

  Consider a 100 line file where half of the records contain nonblank characters up through column 80 and half of the records contain non-blank characters up through column 10.

  - Under a fixed record format, the file would occupy (100 x 80) = 8000 bytes.

  - Under a variable record format, the file would occupy (80 x 50) + (10 x 50) + (4 x 100) = 4900 bytes.

- When the length of the records in a file are all the same, that file will occupy *more* disk space when stored in a variable record format than when stored in a fixed record format.

  Consider a 100 line file where all records contain nonblank characters up through column 80.

  - Under a fixed format, this file would occupy (100 x 80) = 8000 bytes.

  - Under a variable format, the file would occupy (100 x 80) + (100 x 4) = 8400 bytes.

Controlling Characteristics of the File Being Edited   §   259

Defining the Truncation Column

TRUNC specifies the last column in which text may be entered or changed. Initially, the setting of this function is based on the filetype. This function can be useful if you want to protect an area of the file by not allowing data to be entered past a certain column.

Command Format:

> **TRunc**   **n**

where **n**   is the new truncation column.

Example:

Suppose you have a file with text already entered and now have to edit the text only in columns 1 through 40. To prevent any data from being entered past column 40:

====> TRUNC 40

8.6 Controlling Command Interpretation and Execution

Understanding this section requires a prior understanding of:

- Computing Environments

- Line Editing Symbols

- Program Function Keys

- Program Attention Keys

These concepts are discussed in the chapter *Becoming Acquainted with VM/CMS*.

Automatically Saving a File

AUTOSAVE determines whether a file is automatically saved after a specific number of changes. Normally, a file is not automatically saved.

When this function is in effect:

- The file is saved in a file whose filetype is AUTOSAVE and whose filename is of the form **nnnppppp** where **nnn** is the number of times XEDIT has been invoked and **ppppp** is the current autosave number. Autosave numbers begin at 00001 and are incremented by one if another autosave file with that autosave number already exists.

- If the system crashes, you can recover all changes up to the last autosave by erasing the original file and renaming the autosave file.

- A SAVE or FILE subcommand will erase the corresponding autosave file, whereas a QUIT subcommand will not. If you make an erroneous change and the change has not yet been autosaved, use the QUIT subcommand to leave the editor, erase the original file and rename the autosave file.

Command Format:

      AUTOsave   n|OFF [mode|A]

where **n**   is the number of changes after which the file is saved.

      OFF   does not automatically save the file.

      mode   is the mode letter of the disk to which the file is written. If the mode letter is omitted, the file is written to the A-disk.

Example:

Suppose you want to save a file automatically after every fifth change:

====>   AUTOSAVE   5

Defining Tab Stops

TABS specifies which columns are tab stops. XEDIT normally defines the tab stops for a file based on its filetype. Table 4.1, in the chapter *CMS Disks and CMS Disk Files*, lists the tab stops of most common filetypes.

- Files with reserved filetypes, such as FORTRAN, are assigned special tab stops to make it easier to enter text in specific columns.

- Files with filetypes that are not reserved are assigned tab stops at every fifth column beginning in column 1.

TABS is useful when you are putting data into a file and certain information must always begin in a specific column.

Up to 28 columns may be defined. Tab stops can only be defined from left to right. Thus, the column defined to be the second tab stop must be to the right of the column defined to be the first, the column defined to be the third tab stop must be to the right of the column defined to be the second, and so forth.

Command Format:

TABS	**tabset1** [**tabset2** [**tabset3**]] ...

where **tabset1**   is the column number of the first tab stop.

tabset2   is the column number of the second tab stop.

tabset3   is the column number of the third tab stop.

Example:

Suppose you are entering three fields of information on each line in a file and that the first field begins in column 1, the second field in column 15 and the third field in column 30.

1. Define the beginning of each field to be a tab stop:

    ====> TABS 1 15 30

2. Enter the first field of information and press PF4 to tab over to column 15.

3. Enter the second field of information and press PF4 to tab over to column 30.

4. Enter the third field of information and press PF4 to tab over to column 1 of the next line.

5. Repeat steps 2 − 4 until you have filled the input area.

Forcing XEDIT to Execute a Subcommand

COMMAND is a subcommand that forces XEDIT to execute a subcommand without checking first for a synonym or macro with the same name. This command is useful if you want to force XEDIT to execute a subcommand with the same name as an XEDIT macro or synonym.

Command Format:

COMMAND [command]

where **command** is the command to be executed by XEDIT. If the command is omitted, COMMAND has no effect.

Forcing XEDIT to Execute an XEDIT Macro

MACRO is a subcommand that forces XEDIT to execute an XEDIT macro. This command is useful if you want to force XEDIT to execute a macro with the same name as an XEDIT subcommand.

Command Format:

MACRO command

where **command** is the command to be executed by XEDIT. If the command is omitted, MACRO has no effect.

Forcing CMS to Execute a Command

CMS is a subcommand that either sends a command to CMS to be executed or causes XEDIT to enter CMS subset mode. This subcommand is useful if you want to force CMS to execute a command with the same name as an XEDIT subcommand or macro.

Command Format:

CMS [command]

where **command** is the command to be executed by CMS. If the command is omitted, you enter the CMS subset. Use the RETURN command to return to XEDIT from the CMS subset.

Controlling Command Interpretation and Execution § 263

Example:

HELP is an XEDIT subcommand that displays information about XEDIT commands. HELP is also a CMS command that displays information about CP and CMS commands. To invoke the CMS HELP facility from XEDIT, you must precede HELP with CMS:

====> CMS HELP

Forcing CP to Execute a Command

CP is a command that either sends a command to CP to be executed or causes XEDIT to enter the CP environment. This command is useful if you want to force CP to execute a command with the same name as an XEDIT subcommand or macro.

Command Format:

>   **CP**   [command]

where **command**   is the command to be executed by CP. If the command is omitted, you enter the CP environment. Use the CP BEGIN command to return to XEDIT from the CP environment.

Example:

MSG is an XEDIT command that displays a message in the message area of the screen. MSG is also a CP command that sends a message to another user. To use the CP MSG command from XEDIT, you must precede MSG with CP:

====> CP MSG AFRIEND blah blah blah

Controlling Whether Unrecognized Commands are Sent to CMS

IMPCMSCP controls whether commands not recognized by XEDIT are passed on to CMS and then to CP if not recognized by CMS. Normally, commands not recognized by XEDIT are passed to CMS.

Command Format:

>   **IMPcmscp   ON|OFF**

where **ON**   passes unrecognized commands to CMS.

>   **OFF**   does not pass unrecognized commands to CMS.

264 § Customizing the XEDIT Environment

Defining a Logical Line End

LINEND defines some character to represent a logical line end. A logical line end enables you to enter more than one command on the same command line by separating each command from the next by a character defined to represent the logical line end. Normally, the # character is set to represent the logical line end.

Command Format:

| **LINENd** | **ON\|OFF [#\|char]** |

where **ON**   turns on the logical line end function.

OFF   turns off the logical line end function.

char   is the character defined to function as the logical line end. If the character is omitted, the # character becomes the logical line end.

Examples:

- Suppose you are going to use the CHANGE subcommand to make a global substitution of one string for another beginning with line 1 and you want line 1 to be the current line after the substitution is made:

  ====> :1 CHANGE /caterpillars/butterflies/ * # :1

  is equivalent to the following two commands:

  ====> :1 CHANGE /caterpillars/butterflies/ *

  ====> :1

- You can assign two or more subcommands to be executed sequentially to a single PF key or PA key:

  1. Turn off the LINEND function:

     ====> LINEND OFF

  2. Assign the commands to the PF or PA key, separating each command from the next with a logical line end:

     ====> PF1 SAVE#INPUT

  3. Turn the LINEND function back on:

     ====> LINEND ON

Assigning Commands to and Removing Them from PF Keys

PF assigns a subcommand to or removes a subcommand from a program function key. PF1 through PF12 are initially set by XEDIT, but you can assign a subcommand to any of these PF keys at any time. PF13 through PF24 are not automatically set by XEDIT and may be defined if PF13 through PF24 are available on your type of terminal. Program function keys are discussed in more detail in the chapter *Becoming Acquainted with XEDIT*.

Command Format:

> **PFn** [*BEFORE*|AFTER|ONLY|IGNORE] [command|TABKEY|COPYKEY]

where **n**   (immediately after **PF**) is a number between 1 and 24 specifying the number of the PF key.

BEFORE   performs the function assigned to the PF key before any command on the command line is executed.

AFTER   performs the function assigned to the PF key after any command on the command line is executed.

ONLY   performs only the function assigned to the PF key and ignores any command on the command line.

IGNORE   ignores the function assigned to the PF key when a command is on the command line.

command   is any command to be executed when the PF key is pressed. If the command is omitted, any command previous command assigned to the PF key is removed.

TABKEY   moves the cursor to the next tab stop when the PF key is pressed.

COPYKEY   sends a copy of the present screen to the printer when the PF key is pressed.

Examples:

- Suppose you want to assign the INPUT subcommand to PF13:

====> SET PF13 INPUT

Thereafter, when you press PF13, XEDIT switches to input mode.

- Suppose you then want to remove the INPUT subcommand from PF13:

====> SET PF13

- You can display a subcommand on the command line without executing it using the CMSG subcommand. This is similar to using the DELAY option on the CP SET command.

```
====> SET PF13 CMSG INPUT
```

Assigning Commands to and Removing Them from PA Keys

PA assigns a subcommand to or removes a subcommand from a program attention key. PA1 through PA3 are initially set by XEDIT, but you can assign a subcommand to any of these PA keys at any time.

The normal settings of the PA keys in XEDIT are:

PA1   **(CP)** Enters the CP environment, terminating any program that was running.

PA2   **(NULLKEY)** Changes blank characters to null characters on the line where the cursor is located.

PA3   **(?)** Displays the previous subcommand on the command line.

Program attention keys are discussed in more detail in the chapter *Becoming Acquainted with VM/CMS*.

Command Format:

PAn   **[*BEFORE*|AFTER|ONLY|IGNORE] [command|TABKEY]**

where **n**   (immediately after **PA**) is a number between 1 and 3 specifying the number of the PA key.

BEFORE   performs the function assigned to the PA key before any subcommand on the command line is executed.

AFTER   performs the function assigned to the PA key after any subcommand on the command line is executed.

ONLY   performs only the function assigned to the PA key and ignores any subcommand on the command line.

IGNORE   ignores the function assigned to the PA key when a subcommand is on the command line.

command   is any command to be executed when the PA key is pressed. If the command is omitted, any command previously assigned to the PA key is removed.

TABKEY   moves the cursor to the next tab stop when the PA key
            is pressed.

Examples:

- Suppose you want to assign the INPUT subcommand to PA1:

  ====> SET PA1 INPUT

  Thereafter, whenever PA1 is pressed, XEDIT switches to input mode.

- Suppose you then want to remove the INPUT subcommand from PA1:

  ====> SET PA1

Defining Synonyms for Prefix Commands

PREFIX defines a synonym for a prefix command.

Command Format:

PREfix   Synonym   newname   oldname

where **newname**   is the synonym to be used for the prefix command. The
                     synonym can be up to five characters.

      oldname   is the prefix command for which **newname** is a synonym.

Examples:

- Suppose you want to make R a synonym for the D prefix command,
  which deletes lines:

  ====> PREFIX SYNONYM R D

- Suppose you also want to be able to use RR to specify the first and last
  lines of a block of lines to be deleted. RR must be made a synonym for
  DD:

  ====> PREFIX SYNONYM RR DD

Defining Synonyms for Subcommands and Macros

SYNONYM defines synonyms for subcommands and macros and specifies
whether XEDIT looks for synonyms. Normally, XEDIT looks for synonyms.

• • •

One format indicates whether XEDIT should look for synonyms.

Command Format:

SYNonym   ON|OFF

where **ON**   looks for synonyms.

OFF   does not look for synonyms.

•   •   •

One format defines a synonym.

Command Format:

SYNonym   newname [n] oldname

where **newname**   is the synonym to be used for the command.

oldname   is the name of the command for which **newname** is to be recognized as a synonym.

n   is the minimum number of characters that must be specified in order for the synonym to be recognized. If the number of characters is omitted, the complete synonym name must be specified.

Example:

Suppose you want to make SWITCH a synonym for CHANGE with 'SW' being the minimum number of characters that must be specified:

====> SYNONYM SWITCH 2 CHANGE

Changing the Search Order for Subcommands and Macros

MACRO controls the order in which the editor searches for subcommands and macros. XEDIT macros are discussed in the chapter *Special Topics in XEDIT*. Normally, the editor looks for XEDIT subcommands before it looks for macros. This function is useful if you have an XEDIT macro with the same name as an XEDIT subcommand because this function determines which of the two is executed. The SET subcommand must precede the MACRO function to distinguish it from the MACRO subcommand.

Command Format:

SET   MACRO ON|OFF

where **ON**   begins a search with XEDIT macros and finishes with XEDIT commands.

OFF   begins a search with XEDIT commands and finishes with XEDIT macros.

Example:

Suppose you have an XEDIT macro called MOVE.

- If MACRO is set to OFF, the XEDIT MOVE command is executed — not the macro.

- IF MACRO is set to ON, the macro is executed — not the XEDIT MOVE command.

8.7 Controlling the Lines Displayed and Manipulated

Under normal circumstances, the lines in a file are grouped *physically* as a sequence from the first line to the last line. The second line follows the first, the third follows the second, and so forth to the last line. Furthermore, when the editor displays lines and manipulates them, it does so in the order they occur in the file.

This section describes functions that can be used to group lines *logically* that do not physically occur together so that they can be displayed and manipulated independently of the other lines in the file. Lines are logically grouped together by assigning them to the same **selection level**, represented by a positive integer. Normally, all lines in a file have a selection level of 0. The ALL subcommand and the X and S prefix commands provided other means to display lines selectively.

Assigning Lines to a Selection Level

SELECT assigns a selection level to the lines from the current line to a line identified by a line target. A **selection level** is a logical grouping of lines that can then be manipulated together.

Command Format:

> SELect   [+|−]n   [target|*1*]

where **n**   is the selection level assigned.

> • If **n** is preceded by +, **n** is added to the current selection level of the lines.

> • If **n** is preceded by −, **n** is subtracted from the current selection level of the lines.

> **target**   is a line target that identifies the line up to which the selection level is assigned. This target line is not assigned to the selection level. If the target is omitted, only the current line is assigned to the selection level.

Examples:

Suppose you have a file with 30 lines.

> • Suppose you want to assign a selection level of 1 to the first 10 lines:

> ====>   :1 SELECT 1 10

> • Suppose you want to assign a selection level of 2 to lines 11 through 20:

====> :11 SELECT 2 10

- Suppose you want to assign a selection level of 3 to lines 21 through 30.

====> :21 SELECT 3 10

- Suppose you now wanted to subdivide the first 10 lines and the last 10 lines such that lines 1 through 5 have a selection level of 0 and lines 26 through 30 have a selection level of 4.

This would subtract 1 from the current selection level of 1, making the new selection level 0:

====> :1 SELECT -1 5

This would add 1 to the current selection level of 3, making the new selection level 4:

====> :26 SELECT +1 5

In summary:

- Lines 1 through 5 have a selection level of 0.

- Lines 6 through 10 have a selection level of 1.

- Lines 11 through 20 have a selection level of 2.

- Lines 21 through 25 have a selection level of 3.

- Lines 26 through 30 have a selection level of 4.

Displaying Only Lines in Certain Selection Levels

DISPLAY controls which lines are displayed by only including only those with specified selection levels. Normally, lines with a selection level of 0 are displayed.

Command Format:

| | DISPlay | slevel1 [slevel2] |

where **slevel1** is a positive number representing the selection level of lines to be displayed.

slevel2 is an optional positive number greater than or equal to **slevel1** representing another selection level of lines to be displayed. If **slevel2** is omitted, only lines with a selection level of **slevel1** are displayed. If **slevel2** is specified, all lines with selection levels between **slevel1** and **slevel2**

inclusive are displayed. To display all selection levels greater than or equal to **slevel1**, specify **slevel2** as an asterisk (*).

Examples:

Consider the previous example of the SELECT subcommand.

- Suppose you want to display the lines with a selection level of 1:

```
====> DISPLAY 1
```

- Suppose you want to display the lines with selection levels between 1 and 4, inclusive:

```
====> DISPLAY 1 4
```

- Suppose you want to display all selection levels of 0 and greater:

```
====> DISPLAY 0 *
```

Controlling Which Lines Can Be Searched and Manipulated

SCOPE controls which lines the editor can manipulate and search for targets. Normally, only those lines in the display can be searched for targets and manipulated.

Command Format:

SCOPE	**Display|All**
where **Display**	limits the lines that can be manipulated to those lines in the range defined by the DISPLAY function.
All	permits all lines in the file to be manipulated.

Example:

The ALL subcommand enables you to display only those lines that contain a certain string of text:

```
====>  ALL /text/
```

If the SCOPE function is set to DISPLAY, you can use the PUT subcommand to create a new file that contains only those lines that are displayed:

```
====>  :0  PUT  *  NEWFN  NEWFT
```

8.8 Preserving and Restoring Assignments of SET Functions

PRESERVE is a subcommand that saves the assignments of selected SET functions until you want to restore them. This subcommand is useful if you are going to change the assignments of several SET functions for a while and then want to restore the changed assignments to their original state. Not all SET functions can be preserved.

The SET functions preserved include:

```
ARBCHAR   AUTOSAVE  CASE      CMDLINE   COLOR     COLPTR
CURLINE   DISPLAY   ESCAPE    FMODE     FNAME     FTYPE
HEX       IMAGE     IMPCMSCP  LINEND    LRECL     MACRO
MASK      MSGMODE   NUMBER    PREFIX    RECFM     SCALE
SCOPE     SHADOW    SPAN      SPILL     STAY      STREAM
SYNONYM   TABLINE   TABS      TOFEOF    TRUNC     VARBLANK
VERIFY    WRAP      ZONE      =
```

Command Format:

PREServe

•   •   •

RESTORE is a subcommand that restores the SET functions to the assignments they had when the PRESERVE command was executed.

Command Format:

RESTore

8.9 Automatically Customizing the XEDIT Environment

Any modification of the XEDIT environment made by changing the assignments of SET functions only remains in effect for the duration of an editing session. The next time you begin editing a file, the editing environment that is established is the *default* environment, where the SET functions are given *default* assignments.

```
/* Assign filetype and filemode to the variables ftype.1 and fmode.1 */
'extract /ftype /fmode'
/* Display line numbers in the prefix area */
'set number on'
/* Engage '$' to be the arbitrary character */
'set arbchar on $'
/* Display '¬' in place of nondisplaying characters */
'set nondisp ¬'
/* Hold the line pointer when a target search is unsuccessful */
'set stay on'
/* Remove the tof and eof notices */
'set tofeof off'
/* Remove shadow lines */
'set shadow off'
/* Assign PF13 to move the cursor to the previous command line */
'set pf13 sos tabcmdb'
/* Assign PF14 to move the cursor to the next command line */
'set pf14 sos tabcmdf'
/* Assign file characteristics based upon filetype */
if ftype.1 = 'MEMO' then signal mode0
if ftype.1 = 'SCRIPT' then signal mode0
if ftype.1 = 'EXEC' then signal casemxd
if ftype.1 = 'FORTRAN' then signal casemxd
if ftype.1 = 'XEDIT' then signal casemxd
if ftype.1 = 'LISTING' then signal listing
if ftype.1 = 'C' then signal c
if ftype.1 = 'TEX' then signal c
exit
/* Set the case to be mixed */
casemxd:
'case mixed ignore'
exit
/* Set the mode number to '0' */
mode0:
fmode = substr(value(fmode.1),1,1)||'0'
'set fmode' fmode
exit
/* Remove the prefix area and change the case to be mixed */
listing:
'prefix off'
'case mixed ignore'
'verify 1 80'
c:
'set recfm v'#'case mixed respect'
'set input 4a e0'
exit
```

Figure 8.4 An example of a PROFILE XEDIT.

XEDIT provides a convenient mechanism by which the editing environment is always customized in ways that you specify whenever you begin editing a file. You can do this by putting the commands that customize the environment into a file with a filename of PROFILE and a filetype of XEDIT. This file is an example of a type of file called an **XEDIT Macro**, discussed in the chapter *Special Topics in XEDIT*. The XEDIT profile is special in that this macro is automatically executed by XEDIT whenever you begin editing a file. Thus, you can always enter an editing environment that suits your needs and preferences.

Figure 8.4 provides an example of a PROFILE XEDIT written in REXX. A line beginning with /* and ending with */ is a comment describing the command on the line following it. Most of the subcommands being executed are familiar SET functions and should require no explanation. EXTRACT is a subcommand that obtains information about the file being edited and the XEDIT environment and assigns that information to variables that can be used in a macro.

• • •

PROFILE is an option on the XEDIT command that allows you to specify the filename of an XEDIT macro to be used instead of the PROFILE XEDIT.

NOPROFILE is an option on the XEDIT command that suppresses execution of the PROFILE XEDIT and allows you to begin editing a file in the default XEDIT environment.

Command Format:

Xedit	**fileid ([NOPROFile] [PROFile fn]**

| where **fn** | is the filename of a file whose filetype is XEDIT that is to be used instead of the PROFILE XEDIT. |

Part III
Working with Disk Files

Chapter 9
Working with Disk Files

Introduction

While most of the time you are using VM/CMS you'll be using XEDIT to create new files and edit old ones, you will also spend considerable time engaged in these activities with files:

- RENAME changes a file's filename and/or filetype.

- COPYFILE copies all or part of file.

- COPYFILE appends two or more files.

- COPYFILE splits one file into two.

- ERASE removes files from a disk.

- TYPE displays a file.

- COMPARE determines whether two files are identical.

- SORT sorts the records in a file into another order.

- PRINT sends a file to your virtual printer.

- PUNCH sends a file to your virtual punch.

9.1 Wildcards: Asterisks and Equals Signs in Fileids

Several CMS commands that deal with disk files (COPYFILE, ERASE, FILELIST, LISTFILE, and RENAME) permit you to substitute an asterisk for the filename and/or the filetype and/or the filemode.

- Substitute an * for the filename to use *all* filenames with the specified filetype and filemode.

- Substitute an * for the filetype to use *all* filetypes with the specified filename and filemode.

- Substitute an * for the filemode to use *all* filemodes with the specified filename and filetype.

An asterisk used in this fashion is sometimes called a **wildcard**.

Example:

Suppose you want to erase all files on the A-disk with a filename of MYPROG regardless of their filetype:

```
ERASE MYPROG *
```

Specifying the Fileids of Output Files

When an * is used to indicate all filenames or all filetypes in the input fileid of the COPYFILE or RENAME commands, an equals sign (=) may be used in the output fileid to indicate the same filenames or filetypes of the input fileid.

Example:

Suppose you've accessed another user's disk as a D-disk and you want to copy all files on that D-disk onto your A-disk and give those files the same filenames and filetypes on the A-disk that they had on the D-disk:

```
COPY * * D = = A
```

- The first = indicates that when the files are copied to the A-disk, they are to be given the same filenames they had on the D-disk.

- The second = indicates that when the files are copied to the A-disk, they are to be given the same filetypes they had on the D-disk.

9.2 Renaming Files

RENAME changes the filenames and/or the filetypes of files on any disk to which you have read/write access. This command will not change the filemode, since changing the filemode is equivalent to copying the file to another disk. Use the COPYFILE command to copy a file to another disk.

Command Format:

Rename	**fileid1 fileid2 ([*NOType*|Type] [*UPdirt*|NOUPdirt]**

where **fileid1**   is the old fileid to be changed. The filename, filetype and filemode must all be specified.

- Use an * for the filename to rename *all* files with the specified filetype and filemode.

- Use an * for the filetype to rename *all* files with the specified filename and filemode.

- Use an * for the filemode to rename *all* files with the specified filename and filemode.

fileid2   is the new fileid to be given to the file. The filename and filetype must be specified. If the filemode is omitted, it is assumed to be A.

- If an * was used for the filenames in **fileid1**, use an = for the filenames in **fileid2** to give the files the same filenames they had before.

- If an * was used for the filetypes in **fileid1**, use an = for the filetypes in **fileid2** to give the files the same filetypes they had before.

- If an * was used for the filemodes in **fileid1**, use an = for the filemodes in **fileid2** to give the files the same filemodes they had before.

Type   displays the new fileids of those files that are renamed, but only when an * is used for the filenames and/or filetypes of the files to be renamed. Normally, the new fileids are not displayed.

NOUPdirt   does not update the master file directory upon completion of the command. Only the user file directory is updated. Normally, the master file directory is updated upon completion of the command. This option will save system resources if you are going to use the RENAME command many times. However, be careful to execute some command that does update the master file directory before you leave the system. Otherwise, none of the files will be renamed.

Examples:

- Suppose you have a file called PRECIOUS DATA A and want to change the filename to SPECIOUS. The following are equivalent:

```
RENAME PRECIOUS DATA A SPECIOUS DATA A
RENAME PRECIOUS DATA A SPECIOUS = =
```

- Suppose you have several files with a filetype of MEMO and want to change that filetype to be DATA for all files:

```
RENAME  * MEMO A  = DATA =
```

9.3 Copying Files

COPYFILE is one of the most useful and versatile CMS commands. The basic command, used without options, does either of two things:

- Make an exact copy of a file, placing the copy on the same disk as the original with a *different fileid.*

- Make an exact copy of a file, placing the copy on a *different disk* than the original with any fileid that doesn't exist on that disk.

Used with the appropriate option, COPYFILE can also be used to:

- Replace an existing file with the copy being produced.

- Change the record format and record length.

- Remove trailing blanks.

- Reduce the amount of disk space a file occupies.

- Append or concatenate two or more files.

- Copy only certain records and/or columns.

- Overlay one file with another.

- Translate characters.

Command Format:

COPYfile	**infileid1 [infileid2 ...] [outfileid] (options**

where **infileid1** is the fileid of the first file to be copied. The filename, filetype and filemode must all be specified.

- Use an * for the filename to copy *all* files with the specified filetype and filemode.

- Use an * for the filetype to copy *all* files with the specified filename and filemode.

- Use an * for the filemode to copy *all* files with the specified filename and filemode.

infileid2 is the fileid of an optional second file to be copied. If specified, this fileid *must* include the filename, filetype and filemode.

outfileid is the fileid of the new file to be created. If this fileid is omitted, it is assumed to be the fileid of the file being copied. If this fileid is specified, it must include the filename, filetype and filemode.

- If an * was used for the filenames in **infileid1** or **infileid2**, use an = for the filenames in **outfileid** to give the files the same filenames they had before.

- If an * was used for the filetypes in **infileid1** or **infileid2**, use an = for the filetypes in **outfileid** to give the files the same filetypes they had before.

options   are discussed below.

Options Concerning the Replacement of an Existing File

[*NEWFile*|REPlace]

where **REPlace**   replaces an existing file with the same fileid as the file being created with the new file. Normally, COPYFILE determines whether the fileid of the output file already exists. If so, COPYFILE displays an error message indicating that this is the case and suggests the REPLACE option if you want to replace the existing file with the one to be output.

Options to Change a File's Record Format and Record Length

[RECfm F|V] [LRecl nn] [*NOTRunc*|TRunc]

where **RECfm**   changes the record format to fixed length if **F** is specified or to variable length if **V** is specified.

LRecl   changes the record length to be **nn**. If **nn** is shorter than the old record length, be aware that any nonblank characters beyond column **nn** will be truncated in the new file.

TRunc   removes trailing blanks from files that are converted from fixed to variable record format. Normally, trailing blanks are not removed when a file is converted from a fixed to variable record format.

Examples:

- Suppose you have a file called XMPL DATA with a fixed record format that you want to convert to a variable format and remove trailing blanks:

      COPY XMPL DATA A (RECFM V TRUNC

- Suppose you have a file called XMPL DATA with a record length of 80 and want to increase the record length to 240:

      COPY XMPL DATA A (LRECL 240

Options to Reduce the Disk Space a File Occupies

[PAck|UNPack]

where **PAck**   compresses the records in a file so that they occupy less disk space.[1]

UNPack   restores a file that has been compressed by the PACK option to its original condition.

Options to Append or Concatenate Two or More Files

[APpend] [SIngle]

where **APpend**   appends the contents of the input files (**infileid1 infileid2 ...**) to the end of the output file (**outfileid**).

SIngle   writes multiple input files (**infileid1 infileid2 ...**) to a single output file (**outfileid**).

Examples:

* Suppose you have one file called FILE1 DATA A and another called FILE2 DATA A and want to concatenate them into a new file called FILE12 DATA A:

```
COPY  FILE1 DATA A  FILE2 DATA A  FILE12 DATA A
```

* Suppose you have a file called MASTER DATA A to which you want to append a file called UPDATE DATA A:

```
COPY  UPDATE DATA A  MASTER DATA A  (  APPEND
```

* Suppose you have several files with a filetype of DATA that you want to combine into single file called ALL DATA A:

```
COPY  * DATA A  ALL DATA A  (  SINGLE
```

Options to Copy Only Certain Records and/or Columns

[FRom begrec] [FOR numrec]
[FRLabel frstring] [TOLabel tostring]
[SPecs]

---

[1] Do not edit or otherwise change a packed file. If you do, the UNPACK option may not be able to restore the file to its original condition.

where **FRom**	designates the first record to be copied as the one whose record number is **begrec**. If this option is omitted, copying begins at the first record.
FOR	designates the last record to be copied by specifying **numrec** as the number of records to be copied. If this option is omitted, copying ends at the last record in the file.
FRLabel	designates the first record to be copied as the one that begins with the character string **frstring**. The character string can be up to eight nonblank characters. If this option is omitted, copying begins at the first record.
TOLabel	designates the last record to be copied as the one just before the record that begins with the character string **tostring**. The character string can be up to eight non-blank characters. If this option is omitted, copying ends at the last record in the file.
SPecs	indicates that you are going to enter a specification list defining either which columns are to be copied and/or which characters are to be translated.

Example:

Suppose you have a file called HUMPTY DATA A and want to create a new file called DUMPTY DATA A that contains only records 101 through 200 of HUMPTY DATA. Suppose you also know that record 101 begins with the character 'X' and record 201 begins with the character 'Y'. The following are equivalent:

```
COPY HUMPTY DATA A DUMPTY = = ( FROM 101 FOR 99
COPY HUMPTY DATA A DUMPTY = = ( FRLABEL X TOLABEL Y
COPY HUMPTY DATA A DUMPTY = = ( FROM 101 TOLABEL Y
COPY HUMPTY DATA A DUMPTY = = ( FRLABEL X FOR 99
```

Options to Overlay One File with Another

[OVly]

where **OVly**	overlays the characters in an existing file with the characters in an input file. When one character overlays another, it replaces the other character unless the overlaying character is a blank.

Options to Translate Characters

[EBcdic] [UPcase] [LOwcase] [TRAns]

where **EBcdic** converts a BCD (Binary Coded Decimal) file to an EBCDIC file. Six character conversions are made: < to), & to +, % to (, # to =, @ to ' and ' to :.

     UPcase converts all lowercase letters to uppercase.

     LOwcase converts all uppercase letters to lowercase.

     TRAns indicates that you will enter a list of the translations to be made.

Entering a Specification List

A specification list actually defines the new file column by column. Columns omitted from the specification list are filled with blanks. The SPECS option is convenient when you want to copy only certain columns in a file, rearrange the columns in a file or insert new characters into the same columns on each record.

System Messages:

When you use the SPECS option, the system requests the specification list by displaying the message:

    Enter specification list:

A specification list consists of one or more operands in the these formats:

    begcol – endcol outcol
    /string/   outcol
    Hxxyy   outcol

where **begcol** is a column in the input file where copying is to begin.

     endcol is a column in the input file where copying is to end.

     string is any string of characters delimited by any other special character that does not occur in the character string. You may use a / if that character does not occur in the character string.

     H is followed by an even number of hexadecimal digits. **xx** is the hexadecimal code for one character. **yy** is the hexadecimal code for another character.

     outcol is a column in the output file where copying is to begin.

A specification list can be continued on the next line if you use two plus signs (+ +) at the end of the present line as a continuation indicator.

Copying Files § 285

Example:

Suppose you have a file called HUMPTY DATA A and want to create a new file called DUMPTY DATA A with these characteristics:

- Columns 1 through 10 of HUMPTY DATA are to become columns 11 through 20 of DUMPTY DATA.

- Columns 11 through 20 of HUMPTY DATA are to become columns 1 through 10 of DUMPTY DATA.

- Column 21 in DUMPTY DATA is to begin with the string $+ + + + +$.

Use the SPECS option to have the system prompt you for the columns to be copied:

```
COPY  HUMPTY DATA A  DUMPTY = = ( SPECS
```

When prompted for the specification list, enter:

```
1-10 11  11-20 1  /+++++/ 21
```

Entering a Translation List

Specific characters in an input file can be converted to other characters in an output file.

System Messages:

When you use the TRANS option, the system requests the translation list by displaying the message:

```
Enter translation list:
```

A translation list consists of one or more pairs of characters:

inchar1 outchar1 [inchar2 outchar2]...

where **inchar**   is a character to be translated. Specify it as either as an EBCDIC character or in hexadecimal as a pair of digits.

where **outchar**   is the character to which **inchar** is to be translated. Specify it as either as an EBCDIC character or in hexadecimal as a pair of digits.

A translation list can be continued on the next line if you use two plus signs $(+ +)$ at the end of the present line as a continuation indicator.

286 § Working with Disk Files

Example:

Suppose you want to translate the < character to the > character and the blank character to the _ character. The hexadecimal code for the blank character is X′40′. When prompted for the translation list:

        < >   40 _

9.4 Removing Disk Files

There are four commands for removing files from disks to which you have read/write access:

- ERASE removes one or more files but will not remove all files on the same disk in a single execution. This command is discussed in this section.

- DISCARD removes one file at a time from the display produced by FILELIST. This command is only valid in FILELIST.

- ERASE is an option on the ACCESS command that removes *all* files on a disk being accessed. The ACCESS command is discussed in the chapter *Managing Your Virtual Machine*.

- FORMAT initializes a disk and removes *all* files on it. This command is discussed in the chapter *Managing Your Virtual Machine*.

A standard practice on most VM/CMS systems is to copy to tape those disk files that are new and those that have been changed. The primary reason for this backup procedure is to enable you to recover disk files in case of a disk hardware failure. A secondary reason is to enable you to recover files that you might mistakenly remove. If you remove a disk file that you later recognize to have been of value, contact those who support your system and ask how the file might be recovered.

● ● ●

ERASE removes files from a disk to which you have read/write access.

Command Format:

ERASE	**fn ft [fm] (** *[Notype|*Type**]**
where **fn**	is the filename of the file(s) to be erased. Substitute an * to erase *all* files with the specified filetype and filemode.
ft	is the filetype of the file(s) to be erased. Substitute an * to erase *all* files with the specified filename and filemode.
fm	is the filemode of the file(s) to be erased. Use an * to erase *all* files with the specified filename and filetype. If the filemode is omitted, it is assumed to be A. An * cannot be used for the filemode if an * was also used for the filename and an * was used for the filetype. If an * is used for the filenames and an * is used for the filetypes, you *must* specify both a filemode letter and number.
Type	displays the new fileids of those files that are erased but only when an * is used for the filenames and/or filetypes

288 § **Working with Disk Files**

of the files to be erased. Normally, the fileids are not displayed.

Examples:

- Suppose you have a file called SPECIOUS DATA A that you want to remove:

  ERASE SPECIOUS DATA

- Suppose you must remove all files on your A-disk that have a filetype of DATA:

  ERASE * DATA

- Suppose you must remove all files on your A-disk that have a mode number of five:

  ERASE * * A5

9.5 Displaying a Disk File

There are several facilities on VM/CMS for displaying the contents of a file:

- XEDIT, the full-screen editor, is especially convenient if you must:

  - Move backward and forward in the file.

  - Search the file for character strings.

  - Identify the precise line and column where some text is located.

  - Display two or more files simultaneously.

  - Display only certain lines and/or columns.

  - Display columns beyond column 80.

  The size of the files you can display with XEDIT is limited, however, by your virtual storage capacity. XEDIT is discussed in detail in four other chapters.

- BROWSE is a full screen facility that provides many of the commands available in XEDIT for moving backward and forward in a file and for searching for text, although it does not allow you change a file in any way. BROWSE is especially convenient for displaying files that are too large for XEDIT because they exceed the virtual storage capacity. Unfortunately, BROWSE is not a standard CMS product and is not available on all systems. Consult with those who support your system to determine whether it is available. If it is available, use the HELP facility to learn how to use it.

- TYPE displays all or part of a file on your terminal. It is, however, very limited when compared with XEDIT and BROWSE.

Displaying a File with TYPE

TYPE displays all or part of a file on your terminal. TYPE, however, is very limited compared with XEDIT and BROWSE. TYPE only displays one file at a time, only moves forward in a file and does not allow you to search for text.

Command Format:

> **Type fileid [begrec [endrec]] ([HEX] [COL begcol [endcol]] [MEMber [n]]**

where **fileid**   is the fileid of the file to be displayed. The filename and filetype must be specified. If the filemode is omitted, it is assumed to be A. Substitute an * to search all accessed disks in alphabetical order for a file with the specified filename and filetype.

begrec   is the record number of the first record to be displayed. If this is omitted, the first record displayed is the first in the file.

endrec   is the record number of the last record to be displayed. If this is omitted, the last record displayed is the last in the file.

HEX   displays the file in hexadecimal.

COL   displays only the columns beginning with **begcol** and ending with **endcol**.

MEMber   displays the member of a library whose filename is **n**. To display all members of the library, use an * for **n**. The library should be in a MACLIB or TXTLIB format which is discussed in the text *VM/CMS: A Guide to Programming and Applications*. Substitute an * to display all members of a library.

9.6 Comparing Two Files

COMPARE determines whether two files are identical. The two files are compared record by record from the first record to the last record.

Command Format:

       COMpare   **fileid1 fileid2 ([COL begcol endcol]**

where **fileid1**   is the fileid of one file. The filename, filetype and filemode must all be specified.

     fileid2   is the fileid of another file. The filename, filetype and filemode must all be specified.

- Use an = for the filename if it is the same as the first file.

- Use an = for the filetype if it is the same as the first file.

- Use an = for the filemode if it is the same as the first file.

     COL   only compares the files beginning with column **begcol** and ending with column **endcol**. If this option is omitted, all columns are compared.

System Messages:

After you enter the COMPARE command, the system displays the message:

    `Comparing 'fileid1' with 'fileid2'`

- If the two files are not identical, those records that differ are displayed and the system displays the message:

    `Files do not compare.`

- If one file has fewer records than the other, the system displays the message:

    `Premature EOF on file 'fileid'`

- If the two files are identical, no lines are displayed.

Example:

Suppose you want to determine whether a file called QUERY MEMO A contains the same information as another file called QUERY DATA A:

```
COMPARE QUERY MEMO A QUERY DATA A
```

9.7 Sorting the Records in a File into Another Order

SORT rearranges the order of all the records in a file on the basis of what characters are present in certain columns known as sort fields and puts them into a new file. The file must have a fixed record format. If it does not have a fixed record format, use the RECFM option on the COPYFILE command to convert it.

The records are arranged in ascending EBCDIC order which puts the records in this order:

1. Lowercase letters ordered alphabetically (a, b, c, ...z).

2. Uppercase letters ordered alphabetically (A, B, C, ...Z).

3. Numbers ordered by magnitude (0, 1 ,2, ...9).

A **sort field** is defined by two columns, the first of which is the beginning of the field and the second of which is the end of the field:

begcol1 endcol1   begcol2 endcol2 ... begcoln endcoln

If more than one sort field is specified:

- The file is first sorted within the first sort field.

- The file is next sorted within the second sort field.

- The file is finally sorted within the last sort field.

There may be other utilities on your system for sorting files that operate more efficiently and offer more versatility than the CMS SORT utility. Check with those that support your system to determine whether one is available.

Command Format:

SORT   fileid1 fileid2

where **fileid1**   is the fileid of the file to be sorted. The filename, filetype and filemode must all be specified.

fileid2   is the fileid of the sorted file. The filename, filetype and filemode must all be specified. This fileid cannot be the same as that of the file to be sorted. (**Caution:** If a file with this fileid already exists, it is replaced.)

- Use an = for the filename if it is the same as that of the first file.

- Use an = for the filetype if it is the same as that of the first file.

- Use an = for the filemode if it is the same as that of the first file.

System Messages:

After you enter the SORT command, SORT requests the sort fields:

    `DMSSRT604R Enter sort fields:`

Example:

Suppose you want to sort a file, first on the data in columns one through eight, and second on the data in column 9. The sort fields would be 1 8 9 9.

9.8 Sending a File to the Virtual Printer

A wide variety of printing devices are available for VM/CMS systems. Consult with those who support your system to determine:

- What kinds of printers are available.

- How to use the printers.

- What commands are needed.

- Where to pick up printed output.

- How printed output is filed.

Sending a File to a Line Printer

PRINT sends a file to your virtual printer. Normally, your virtual printer is directed to a real line printer. A line printer is so called because it prints a line at a time. Output sent to the printer may be filed by an identifier known as your **distribution code**. Use the CP QUERY command to determine what your distribution code is.

A file destined for a printer often has the first column of each line reserved for a **carriage control character** that controls vertical spacing, such as how many lines are skipped between records and when to start printing on a new page. It isn't necessary that you know which characters produce which kind of vertical spacing. It is important, however, that you know whether a file has carriage control characters. Most programs that create such files give them a filetype of LISTING, which is normally recognized by the PRINT command to be the filetype of a file containing carriage control characters.

- If a file has a filetype of LISTING and the first column of the file *does not* contain carriage control characters, use the NOCC option on PRINT to indicate that the first character on each line is not to be used for carriage control.

- If a file does not have a filetype of LISTING and the first column of the file *does* contain carriage control characters, use the CC option on PRINT to indicate that the first character on each line is to be used for carriage control.

Command Format:

PRint fileid ([*NOCC*|CC] [LInecoun *55*|nn] [UPCASE] [HEX] [OVersize]

where **fileid**   is the fileid of the file to be printed. The filename and filetype must be specified. If the filemode is omitted, it is assumed to be A. Use an * for the filemode to search all accessed disks in alphabetical order for a file with the specified filename and filetype.

CC   interprets the first character of each line as a carriage control character. This option is assumed if the filetype is LISTING or LIST3800.

NOCC   does not interpret the first character of each line as a carriage control character.

LInecoun   specifies the maximum number of lines that are to be printed on each page to be **nn**, which may be any whole number from 0 through 144. If **nn** is set to 0, there are no page ejects. This option is ignored if the CC option is in effect. If this option is not specified, 55 lines are printed on each page.[2]

UPCASE   prints all letters in uppercase.

HEX   prints all characters in hexadecimal. If this option is used, the CC and UPCASE options are ignored if also used.

OVersize[3]   prints a file with records wider than the carriage size of the virtual printer. Records wider than the carriage size are truncated to the carriage size.

---

[2] The total number of lines printed on a page is **nn** plus 3. The three extra lines are for the heading: one heading line and two blank lines.

[3] This option is not available in releases of CMS before Release 5.

9.9 Sending a File to the Virtual Punch

There was a time when cards, keypunches and card readers played an important role in computing:

- The keypunch was used to create programs and data files on card decks.

- The card deck was a primary storage medium for programs and data files.

- The card reader was a primary device for inputting files to a computer system.

- The card punch was a primary device for outputting files from a computer system.

Times have changed. Cards became obsolete with the advent of interactive systems in which programs and data are entered online and stored in disk files. There is still a need, however, for some way to input files to a computer system and some way to output files from a computer system. VM/CMS uses the concept of a *virtual* reader and a *virtual* punch for these purposes:

- Your virtual reader is used to get files into your virtual machine.

- Your virtual punch is used to send files to other virtual machines.

Three commands send files to your virtual punch:

- PUNCH sends files with either a fixed or variable record format, but records longer than 80 are excluded.

- DISK DUMP sends files with any record length and any record format.

- SENDFILE sends files with any record length and any record format. This command is discussed in the chapter *Communicating with Other Computer Users*.

Using PUNCH

PUNCH sends a file to your virtual punch. Both fixed and variable record format files can be punched, but records longer than 80 are excluded. If the length of a record is less than 80, the record is padded with blanks out to column 80. Use the DISK DUMP command to punch a file with a record length greater than 80. Output sent to the real card punch will probably be filed by your distribution code. Use the CP QUERY command to determine what your distribution code is.

Command Format:

> **PUnch**   fileid ([*Header*|NOHeader] [MEMber name]

where **fileid**   is the fileid of the file to be punched. The filename and filetype must be specified. If the filemode is omitted, it is assumed to be A. Use an * for the filemode to search all accessed disks in alphabetical order for a file with the specified filename and filetype.

> **NOHeader**   does not include a header card. Normally, a header card is included in front of the punched file and includes:

- The fileid of the file punched.

- The label of the disk from which the file was read.

- The time and date the file was last written to disk.

> **MEMber**   specifies **name** as the filename of a member of a MACLIB or TXTLIB, discussed in the text *VM/CMS: A Guide to Programming and Applications*, to be punched. Use an * for the member name if all members of a macro or text library are to be punched.

Using DISK DUMP

DISK DUMP sends a file to your virtual punch in a special format. Both fixed and variable record format files with any record length can be punched.

Command Format:

> **DISK**   DUMP fileid

where **fileid**   is the fileid of the file to be punched. The filename and filetype must be specified. If the filemode is omitted, it is assumed to be A. Use an * for the filemode to search all accessed disks in alphabetical order for a file with the specified filename and filetype.

Chapter 10
Managing Disk Files

Introduction

As you accumulate more and more files, you will need to have some facility for keeping track of them. VM/CMS provides two such facilities for file management:

- LISTFILE produces a simple list of files and their characteristics.

- FILELIST produces a full-screen display of a list of files that you can then work on in the display.

10.1 Using FILELIST to Display and Manipulate Lists of Files

FILELIST is a *full screen* facility that displays a list of disk files and their characteristics. FILELIST is an environment created by XEDIT to facilitate the management and use of disk files. When you enter the FILELIST command, XEDIT creates a file whose filename is your userid and whose filetype is FILELIST. Once in the FILELIST environment, you have all the capabilities of XEDIT at your disposal to manipulate the display of files by entering commands from the command line. FILELIST is particularly convenient to work with files for two reasons:

- FILELIST allows you to use certain abbreviations for fileids that save you from having to type out the complete fileid.

- Program function keys are assigned to execute useful commands.

Command Format:

FILEList	**[fn|* [ft|* [fm|A]]] ([Append] [PROFile fn]**

where **fn**   is the filename(s) of the file(s) to be displayed. If the filename is omitted, all filenames are used.

- Use an * to match any arbitrary combination of characters.

- Use an % to match any arbitrary single letter.

ft   is the filetype(s) of the file(s) to be displayed. If the filetype is omitted, all filetypes are used.

- Use an * to match any arbitrary combination of characters.

- Use an % to match any arbitrary single letter.

fm   is the filemode(s) of the file(s) to be displayed. Substitute an * if all filemodes are to be used. If the filemode is omitted, only files on the A-disk are used.

Append   appends another list of files to be displayed to the present list. This option only works if used from within the FILELIST environment.

PROFile   uses the XEDIT macro with the filename **fn** to establish the FILELIST environment. If this option is omitted, the file PROFFLST XEDIT is used to set up the default FILELIST environment.

How to Specify Which Files are to be Listed

When you specify the list of files to be displayed, FILELIST permits you to specify part of a filename and/or filetype with an asterisk (*) or a percent (%) sign:

- An * matches any combination of characters.

- A % matches any single character.

Examples:

- Suppose you want to display a list of all files on your A-disk. The following are equivalent:

  ```
  FILELIST
  FILELIST   *   *
  FILELIST   *   *   A
  ```

- Suppose you want to display a list of all files on your A-disk having a filename of PROFILE. The following are equivalent:

  ```
  FILELIST   PROFILE
  FILELIST   PROFILE   *
  FILELIST   PROFILE   *   A
  ```

- Suppose you want to display a list of all files on your A-disk that begin with the letters 'PROF'. The following are equivalent:

```
 CHASE      FILELIST A0   V 109   Trunc=109 Size=9 Line=1 Col=1 Alt=0
 Cmd    Filename Filetype Fm Format Lrecl    Records    Blocks    Date      Time
        ALL        NOTEBOOK A0 V       132       228         1 11/21/88 15:36:46
        CHASE      NETLOG   A0 V       106        42         1 11/21/88 15:36:46
        CHASE      NAMES    A1 V       165        51         1  4/07/88  9:11:25
        PROFILE    XEDIT    A1 V        71        57         1  2/12/88 10:24:11
        PROFFLST XEDIT      A1 V        91       107         1  1/11/88 23:01:55
        PROFPEEK XEDIT      A1 V        79       111         1  1/11/88 12:14:44
        PROFRLST XEDIT      A1 V        85       119         1  1/11/88 02:22:28
        PROFILE    EXEC     A2 F        80        23         1 12/12/87 14:21:42
        CHASE      SYNONYM  A1 F        80        37         1 12/12/87 12:30:12




 1= Help      2= Refresh  3= Quit    4= Sort(type)  5= Sort(date)  6= Sort(size)
 7= Backward  8= Forward  9= FL /n   10=            11= XEDIT       12= Cursor

 ====>
                                                   X E D I T   1 File
```

Figure 10.1 A sample FILELIST display.

```
FILELIST  PROF*
FILELIST  PROF*   *
FILELIST  PROF*   *   A
```

- Suppose you want to display a list of all files on your A-disk having filenames consisting of a single character. The following are equivalent:

```
FILELIST  %
FILELIST  %   *
FILELIST  %   *   A
```

The Areas of the Screen and Their Uses in FILELIST

When you enter the FILELIST command, the fileids are displayed in the format shown in Figure 10.1. Notice that the files are ordered by the time and date they were last written to disk, with the most recent file listed first.

- Under **Cmd** is the Command Area.

- Under **Filename**, **Filetype** and **Fm** is the fileid of each file.

- Under **Format** is the record format of each file.

- Under **Lrecl** is the record length of each file.

- Under **Records** are the number of records in each file.

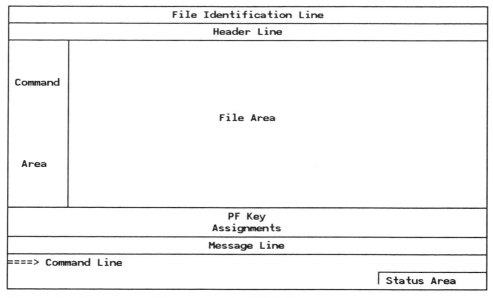

Figure 10.2 The areas of the screen in FILELIST.

- Under **Blocks** are the number of blocks each file occupies.

- Under **Date** is the month, day and year each file was last written to disk.

- Under **Time** is the time of day each file was last written to disk.

Figure 10.2 shows the areas of the screen in FILELIST.

- The **File Identification Line** displays information about the *userid FILELIST* file.

- The **Header Line** labels the areas in the file area below.

- The **Command Area** is where you enter commands to work with files.

- The **File Area** displays fileids and information about the files.

- The **PF Key Assignments** displays the commands assigned to PF keys.

- The **Message Line** displays messages issued in response to your commands.

- The **Command Line** is where you enter XEDIT commands to manipulate the display and CMS and CP commands to perform other tasks.

Working with Files in FILELIST

Once you enter the FILELIST command to display a list of files, you can work with a file in the display:

1. Position the cursor in the command area next to the file to be used.

2. Type the command that uses the file in the desired way, specifying one of these abbreviations:

    /   represents the whole fileid.

    /n   represents the filename.

    /t   represents the filetype.

    /m   represents the filemode.

    /o   executes a command omitting all parts of the fileid.

    Any combination of **n**, **t**, and **m** up to seven characters can also be used:

    /nt   represents the filename followed by the filetype.

    /tn   represents the filetype followed by the filename.

Using FILELIST to Display and Manipulate Lists of Files § **305**

/tm   represents the filetype followed by the filemode.

/ntm   is equivalent to /.

If the command is longer than the command area, continue typing the command into the file area over the fileid. **You cannot enter a command in the command area if your terminal is in insert mode. If you try to do so, the keyboard will lock to prohibit you and the terminal may sound an alarm.** If necessary, use the RESET key to unlock the keyboard.

3. Press the ENTER key to execute the command.

4. When you've finished working with the files and want to leave FILELIST, press PF3.

Examples:

- Suppose you've just entered FILELIST and want to edit the file at the top of the list. Since the cursor is positioned next to the file and PF11 is assigned to XEDIT, pressing PF11 is equivalent to entering the XEDIT command next to the file and pressing ENTER.

  To edit any file in the FILELIST display:

  1. Position the cursor in the command area next to the file.

  2. Press PF11.

- Suppose you want to make a copy of a file, giving it a filetype of BACKUP with a filename and filemode the same as the original:

  1. Position the cursor in the command area next to the file.

  2. Type the COPYFILE command using a / to represent the fileid:

     COPY / = BACKUP =

  3. Press ENTER.

- Many application programs on CMS require the command files they process to have a filetype that is the same as the name of the command that invokes the program. SCRIPT, a document formatting language, is such a program. Suppose you've put your resume into a file with SCRIPT control words to format it. The file has a filename of RESUME and a filetype of SCRIPT. The usual way of running the program from CMS and displaying the results on the screen would be to enter:

  SCRIPT RESUME

  Running the program from FILELIST, however, is much simpler:

  1. Position the cursor in the command area next to the file.

2. Run the program with either of these:

```
/tn
SCRIPT /n
```

3. Press ENTER.

- If the command you are entering uses a single fileid as input and does not output a second fileid, you don't have to specify a fileid: FILELIST automatically uses the fileid on the same line as the cursor. Suppose you want to print a file called QUERY MEMO:

  1. Position the cursor in the command area next to the file.

  2. Type the PRINT command. The following are equivalent:

```
PRINT
PRINT  /
```

  3. Press ENTER.

Program Function Keys in FILELIST

Another attractive feature of FILELIST is that program function keys are auto-matically assigned to execute some commonly used commands. These are the commands assigned to the program function keys in FILELIST. (The com-mand name appears in parentheses followed by a brief description of what the command does):

PF1	**(Help)** Invokes the HELP facility to display information about FILELIST.
PF2	**(Refresh)** Updates the display to include files created since you entered FILELIST, remove discarded files and clean up FILELIST's responses to your commands.
PF3	**(Quit)** Exits from FILELIST.
PF4	**(Sort)** Sorts the files in the display first by filetype and then by filename.
PF5	**(Sort)** Sorts the files in the display first by date and then by time of day with the newest files first.
PF6	**(Sort)** Sorts the files in the display by their size, the largest being first.
PF7	**(Backward)** Scrolls the display backward one screen.
PF8	**(Forward)** Scrolls the display forward one screen.

PF9   **(FL /n)** Displays a list of all files with the filename of the file that the cursor is next to. This command is only valid if the cursor is in the file area.

PF10   Unassigned.

PF11   **(Xedit)** Places the file next to the cursor in XEDIT.

PF12   **(Cursor)** If the cursor is in the file area, move the cursor to the command line. If the cursor is on the command line, move the cursor to its previous position in the file area.

Notice that the commands assigned to the PF keys are also displayed below the file area.

How FILELIST Responds to Your Commands

FILELIST responds to the commands you enter in the command area by displaying one of these symbols:

*   indicates that the command was successfully executed.

*n   indicates that the command was not successfully executed and that the return code was **n**.

*?   indicates that the command was an unknown CP or CMS command.

Displaying or Executing the Previous Command

FILELIST also allows you to execute the command previously executed or to display the command previously executed again in the command area without executing it.

= executes the command previously executed using the file in the display next to which the = sign is placed.

1. After executing a command that you want to execute again, place = in the command area next to the file to be used when the command is executed again. If you want to execute the command using several different files, place = in the command area next to each of the files.

2. Press ENTER.

? displays the command previously executed in the command area next to any file in the display but does not execute it. This is useful if the previous command did not execute due to an error, because now you can display the command again, edit the mistake using the edit control keys and then press

ENTER. It's also useful if the command you now want to execute is a minor variation on the previous command.

1. After executing a command that you want to display again, place **?** in the command area next to the file where you want the command displayed again. If you want to display the command in the command area next to several different files, place **?** next to each of the files.

2. Press ENTER.

Moving the Cursor in FILELIST

The TAB FORWARD, TAB BACKWARD and PF12 keys provide convenient ways to move the cursor in FILELIST.

- If the cursor is on the command line:

  - TAB FORWARD moves the cursor to the first file in the file area.

  - TAB BACKWARD moves the cursor to the last file in the file area.

  - PF12 moves the cursor to its previous location in the file area.

- If the cursor is in the file area:

  - TAB FORWARD moves the cursor to the next file in the file area.

  - TAB BACKWARD moves the cursor to the previous file in the file area.

  - PF12 moves the cursor back to the command line.

The Command Line in FILELIST

The command line is the second line from the bottom of the screen. It begins with the arrow:

====>

Use the command line to:

- Execute XEDIT commands to manipulate the display by:

  - Move the display up or down a specific number of lines.

  - Scroll the display up or down a specific number of screens.

  - Locate a specific file or position in the list, such as bottom or top.

- Execute CP and CMS commands.

Exercises:

Begin this exercise by using FILELIST to display a list of the files on your A-disk:

> FILELIST

1. Use PF12 to move the cursor from the command area to the command line.

2. Move the display up one line:

   > ====> UP   1

3. Move the display down one line:

   > ====> DOWN   1

4. Search forward in the list for a file with a filename of PROFILE:

   > ====> /PROFILE

5. Search backward in the list for a file with a filetype of MEMO:

   > ====> -/MEMO

6. Send a message to yourself using the CP MSG command. (Since XEDIT also has an MSG command, remember to precede MSG with CP):

   > ====> CP   MSG   *   blah   blah   blah

7. Begin a new file called XMPL MEMO while in FILELIST:

   > ====> XEDIT XMPL MEMO

8. Put some text into the file and write the file to disk.

9. Press PF2 to update the list of files. Notice that the file called XMPL MEMO is now included in the list.

The Order of Files in the Display

When FILELIST displays a list of files, it normally displays the files in the order that they were last written to disk, with the newest file at the top of the list, the second newest file next and the oldest file listed last. This ordering is usually convenient, since the files you work with most are the ones most recently written to disk.

These are commands you can enter on the command line to sort the list of files:

SNAME sorts the list alphabetically by filename, filetype and filemode.

STYPE sorts the list alphabetically by filetype, filename and filemode.

SMODE sorts the list alphabetically by filemode, filename and filetype.

SLREC sorts the list by logical record length and size (number of blocks) from largest to smallest.

SSIZE sorts the list by size (number of blocks) and number of records from largest to smallest.

SDATE sorts the list by year, month, day and time from most recent to last.

You can also use the SORT subcommand to order the files by any field in the file area by specifying which columns begin and end each sort field. Suppose you want to display the scale line and columns numbers:

====> SCALE   ON

Examples:

• PF4, which sorts the files in the display by filetype, is equivalent to:

====> :1   SORT   *   16   23

• Suppose you want to sort the files displayed by filename. Filenames are displayed in columns 7 through 14:

====> :1   SORT   *   7   14

Writing the FILELIST Display to a Disk File

In FILELIST, as in XEDIT, the FILE subcommand writes a file being edited to disk and returns you to CMS. If you enter the FILE subcommand in FILELIST, XEDIT writes the FILELIST display to a disk file with a filename that is your userid and a filetype of FILELIST.

10.2 Using LISTFILE to Display a List of Files

LISTFILE displays a list of files on your terminal but, unlike FILELIST, does not allow you to work with the files. Its primary usefulness is its ability to place the information normally displayed on your terminal in one of three files:

- A CMS EXEC file.

- A file being edited.

- A buffer file placed in the program stack[1] for use by an Exec or other program.

Command Format:

Listfile	[fn|* [ft|* [fm|*A]]] (options
where **fn**	is the filename of the files. If the filename is omitted, all filenames are used.

- Use an * to match any arbitrary combination of characters.

- Use an % to match any arbitrary single letter.

ft	is the filetype of the files. If the filetype is omitted, all filetypes are used.

- Use an * to match any arbitrary combination of characters.

- Use an % to match any arbitrary single letter.

fm	is the filemode of the files. Substitute an * to use all filemodes. If the filemode is omitted, it is assumed to be A.
options	are discussed below.

Options to Control What Information is Displayed

[Header|*NOHeader*] [FName|FType|*FMode*] [FOrmat] [Date] [Blocks]

where **Header**	displays a line that labels the information displayed. Normally, the information is not labeled.

---

[1] The **program stack** is a temporary storage area used to pass information to certain CMS and Exec commands that are discussed in the text *VM/CMS: A Guide to Programming and Applications*.

FName   displays only the filenames.

FType   displays filetypes and filenames.

FMode   displays filemodes in addition to the filenames and filetypes.

FOrmat   displays the record formats and record lengths in addition to the filenames, filetypes and filemodes.

Date   displays the date each file was last written to disk and the number of blocks each file occupies in addition to all the information displayed by the **FORMAT** option.

Blocks   displays the total number of blocks occupied by *all* files listed. The number is displayed as a separate line at the end of the list. If the **STACK** option is used, the number of blocks is displayed but not stacked.

Exercise:

Use LISTFILE with and without the DATE option to compare the information displayed.

Options to Place the LISTFILE Information in a CMS EXEC File

[Exec [Trace] [ARGS] [APpend]]

where **Exec**   creates a file with a filename of CMS, a filetype of EXEC and a filemode of A. In addition to the output displayed on the screen, each entry in the file is preceded by two EXEC2 arguments &1 and &2.

Trace   writes the EXEC2 argument &TRACE OFF as the first record of the CMS EXEC file. When the CMS EXEC file is executed, this argument suppresses the display of the statements in the file on the terminal. Notice that the EXEC option must be specified before this parameter.

ARGS   places the EXEC2 arguments &3 &4 ... &15 after each fileid in the CMS EXEC file. Notice that the EXEC option must be specified before this parameter.

APpend   appends a new CMS EXEC file to an existing CMS EXEC file if it exists. If this option is omitted, an existing CMS EXEC file is replaced with a new one. Notice that the EXEC option must be specified before this parameter.

Using the EXEC option to create a CMS EXEC file is useful if you must perform the same operation on a large number of files.

Examples:

- Suppose you must print all files on your A-disk with a filetype of MEMO. The PRINT command doesn't allow the use of wildcards: only a single fileid can be specified on each execution of the command.

  1. Create a CMS EXEC file that lists all files with a filetype of MEMO:

  ```
  LISTFILE  *  MEMO  (  EXEC
  ```

  2. To print the files, run the CMS EXEC:

  ```
  CMS  PRINT
  ```

  The word PRINT will be substituted for the EXEC variable &1. Nothing is substituted for &2 so it becomes blank.

Options to Place the LISTFILE Information in the Program Stack

[STACK [*FIFO*|LIFO]]

where **STACK**   places the LISTFILE information in the program stack.

LIFO   stacks the information last in − first out (LIFO). Normally, the information is stacked first in − first out (FIFO). Notice that the **STACK** option must be specified before this parameter.

Options to Place the LISTFILE Information in a File Being Edited

[XEDIT]

where **XEDIT**   places the information in the XEDIT file being edited after the current line. If you are editing a *ring* of files, the information is placed in the file currently being displayed. The file must either have a variable record format or a fixed record format and a record length of at least 108.

How to Specify Which Files are to be Listed

When specifying a list of files, LISTFILE permits you to specify part of a filename and/or filetype with an asterisk (*) or a percent (%) sign:

- An * matches any combination of characters.

- A % matches any single character.

Examples:

- Suppose you want to display a list of all files on your A-disk. The following are equivalent:

```
LISTFILE
LISTFILE  *  *
LISTFILE  *  *  A
```

- Suppose you want to display a list of all files on your A-disk having a filename of PROFILE. The following are equivalent:

```
LISTFILE  PROFILE
LISTFILE  PROFILE  *
LISTFILE  PROFILE  *  A
```

- Suppose you want to display a list of all files on your A-disk that begin with the letters 'PROF'. The following are equivalent:

```
LISTFILE  PROF*
LISTFILE  PROF*  *
LISTFILE  PROF*  *  A
```

- Suppose you want to display a list of all files on your A-disk having filenames consisting of a single character. The following are equivalent:

```
LISTFILE  %
LISTFILE  %  *
LISTFILE  %  *  A
```

Part IV
Communicating with Other Computer Users

Chapter 11
Communicating with Other Computer Users

Introduction

VM/CMS provides three forms of communication between users on your computer system and users on other systems to which yours is connected:

- A **note** is a communication similar in format to that of a letter. It normally includes the date and headers to identify the sender, the primary recipients, complimentary copy recipients and the subject.

  - Use the **NOTE** command to send a note.

- A **file** is any collection of information stored on disk. It might include data, text, a program or any other information to be shared with another computer user.

  - Use the **SENDFILE** command to send files to users on your system and other IBM operating systems to which yours is connected.

  - Use the **NOTE** command to send files to users on systems to which yours is connected that are not IBM operating systems.

- A **message** is a one line communication that is displayed on the recipient's terminal. Exchanging messages with another user is similar to carrying on a conversation: upon receiving a message, the recipient can respond by sending you a message.

  - Use the **MESSAGE** command to send a message to a single user on your system.

  - Use the **TELL** command to send a message to one or more users on your system and other VM/CMS systems to which yours is connected.

RDRLIST is a facility on VM/CMS that enables you to manage and work with the files and notes that other computer users send you.

Most of the facilities discussed in this chapter require an understanding of XEDIT. Before reading this chapter, you should be familiar with XEDIT.

The terminology and concepts concerned with virtual devices and spooling in this chapter are discussed in detail in the chapter *Virtual Devices and Spooling*.

Consult with those who support your system to determine whether any of the facilities discussed in this chapter have been modified on your system and, if so, how.

11.1 The NAMES File

A NAMES file is a file containing entries for the computer users with whom you communicate. Each entry is identified by a **nickname** and contains **tags** that provide information necessary to communicate with either a single user or a list of users. Having a NAMES file makes it easier for you to communicate with others when you are using the NOTE, SENDFILE and TELL commands.

```
:Nick.KRYPTON    :Userid.KRYPTON   :Node.CMSA      :Notebook.KRYPTON
                 :Name.the Hidden
                 :Phone.QQQ-1111
                 :Addr.36 P Block

:Nick.NE         :Userid.NEON      :Node.CMSA      :Notebook.NEON
                 :Name.the New
                 :Phone.QQQ-9999
                 :Addr.10 P Block

:Nick.AR         :Userid.ARGON     :Node.CMSA      :Notebook.ARGON
                 :Name.the Inactive
                 :Phone.QQQ-5555
                 :Addr.18 P Block

:Nick.XE         :Userid.XENON     :Node.CMSA      :Notebook.XENON
                 :Name.the Alien
                 :Phone.QQQ-0000
                 :Addr.54 P Block

:Nick.CU         :Userid.COPPER    :Node.CMSA      :Notebook.COPPER
                 :Name.Cuprum
                 :Phone.ZZZ-1111
                 :Addr.29 D Block

:Nick.PB         :Userid.LEAD      :Node.CMSA      :Notebook.LEAD
                 :Name.Plumbum
                 :Phone.ZZZ-5555
                 :Addr.82 P Block

:Nick.SN         :Userid.TIN       :Node.CMSA      :Notebook.TIN
                 :Name.Stannum
                 :Phone.ZZZ-3333
                 :Addr.50 P Block

:Nick.ZN         :Userid.ZINC      :Node.CMSA      :Notebook.ZINC
                 :Name.the Dull
                 :Phone.ZZZ-9999
                 :Addr.30 D Block

:Nick.CU+SN      :Userid.BRONZE    :Node.CMSB      :Notebook.BRONZE
:Nick.CU+ZN      :Userid.BRASS     :Node.VMSA      :Notebook.BRASS
:Nick.SN+PB      :Userid.PEWTER    :Node.UNIXA     :Notebook.PEWTER

:Nick.GASES      :List.KRYPTON NEON ARGON ZENON
:Nick.METALS     :List.COPPER ZINC TIN LEAD
:Nick.ELEMENTS   :List.GASES METALS
:Nick.ALLOYS     :List.CU+SN CU+ZN SN+PB
```

Figure 11.1 A sample NAMES file.

The NAMES file must have a filetype of NAMES and a filename that is the same as your userid.

Entries can be added to, removed from and changed in the NAMES file either by editing the file with XEDIT or with the NAMES command, discussed in the next section.

Tags in a NAMES File

Tags provide information about each entry. Each tag has the general form:

    :tag.value

where **:tag.**   is the name of the tag.

      value   is the value assigned to the tag. A value can continue on one or more of the records that follow the tag.

Lines in the NAMES file have this format:

    :tag.value [:tag.value...]

These are the NAMES tags and the values assigned to them. The only tag that is required is :Nick.. All others are optional.

:Nick.value   identifies the beginning of an entry and specifies **value** as the nickname. It must be the first tag on a line. Never use TO, AT or CC: as nicknames.

:Userid.value   specifies **value** as the userid of the entry if it is that of a single user. If the entry is that of a list of users, omit this tag.

:Node.value   specifies **value** as the name of the computer system on which the entry has his userid. If the entry is on the same computer system that you are on or the entry is that of a list of users, omit this tag.

:Notebook.value   specifies **value** as the filename of the file where notes sent to and received from this entry are copied. The filetype is NOTEBOOK. If this tag is omitted, the filename is ALL.

:Name.value   specifies **value** as the person's name. If the entry is that of a list of users, omit this tag.

:Phone.value   specifies **value** as the person's phone number. If the entry is that of a list of users, omit this tag.

The NAMES File § 319

:Addr.value   specifies **value** as the person's postal address.   If the entry is that of a list of users, omit this tag.

:List.value   specifies **value** as a list of recipients. Specify the recipients in one of three formats:

- If the recipient is a user on your system, specify the recipient as that user's userid:

USERID

- If the recipient is on another system to which yours is connected, specify the recipient as that user's userid followed by the word AT and the name of the system he is on:

USERID AT SYSNAME

- If the recipient is a list of users for which there is a nickname entered in a NAMES file, specify the recipient as the nickname:

NICKNAME

Any name that is not a nickname is assumed to be a userid on your computer system.

All three formats can be mixed together in a list. If the entry is that of a single user, omit this tag.

Example:

Figure 11.1 shows an example of a NAMES file. The userids are the names of the some gases (KRYPTON, NEON, ARGON and ZENON), metals (COPPER, LEAD, TIN and ZINC) and alloys (BRONZE, BRASS and PEWTER). The nicknames assigned to the gases and metals are the symbols by which they are known, except in the case of KRYPTON which is the userid that owns this NAMES file. The nickname assigned to each alloy consists of the nicknames of the elements that comprise it joined by a plus sign. Thus, the nickname for BRONZE is CU (for COPPER) + (plus) SN (for TIN) = CU+SN.

Notice that four lists are also formed:

- GASES is a nickname that refers to the userids that are gases.

- METALS is a nickname that refers to the userids that are metals.

- ELEMENTS is a nickname that refers to the userids that are gases and metals. Notice how nicknames can also be used in a list.

- ALLOYS is a nickname that refers to the userids that are alloys.

Notice also that all userids are on a VM/CMS system called CMSA except the userids that are alloys.

- BRONZE is on another VM/CMS system called CMSB.

- BRASS is on a VMS system called VMSA.

- PEWTER is on a UNIX system called UNIXA.

This NAMES file will be used throughout this chapter to illustrate the use of the NAMES file in communicating with other computer users. All examples assume that the userid sending notes, files and messages is KRYPTON.

11.2 Creating and Modifying the NAMES File

While entries can be added to, removed from and changed in the NAMES file with XEDIT, a more convenient approach is to use the NAMES command which displays a menu, such as the one in Figure 11.2, in which you can supply values for an entry's tags. The only occasion you may need to edit the NAMES file with XEDIT is when the value to be added to a tag is too large to fit in the field provided in the NAMES menu.

Command Format:

> **NAMES**   [nickname]

where **nickname**   is the nickname for an entry in the NAMES file.

- If the nickname already exists, the information for that entry is displayed in the NAMES menu, which you can examine and change, if necessary.

- If the nickname is a new one, all fields in the NAMES menu are blank except the one for the nickname. Supply values for all relevant tags.

  If the nickname is omitted, all fields in the NAMES menu are blank. You *must* supply a value for the nickname. Values for all other tags are optional. (**Caution:** If duplicate entries exist in a NAMES file, only the first is normally found.)

```
 ====> userid   NAMES      <=========>  N A M E S   F I L E   E D I T I N G  <===
 Fill in the fields and press a PFkey to display and/or change your NAMES file.
 Nickname:            Userid:         Node:          Notebook:
                        Name:
                       Phone:
                     Address:
                           :
                           :
                           :
          List Of Names:
                           :
                           :
                           :

 You can enter optional information below. Describe it by giving it a ''tag.''

 Tag:                 Value:
 Tag:                 Value:

 1= Help      2= Add      3= Quit    4= Clear     5= Find      6= Change
 7= Previous  8= Next     9=         10= Delete    11=          12= Cursor

 ====>
                                              MACRO-READ 1 File
```

Figure 11.2 The NAMES menu.

Moving the Cursor in the NAMES Menu

The TAB FORWARD, TAB BACKWARD and PF12 keys provide convenient ways to move the cursor in the NAMES menu.

- If the cursor is on the command line:

  - TAB FORWARD moves the cursor to the first field in the menu.

  - TAB BACKWARD moves the cursor to the last field in the menu.

  - PF12 moves the cursor to its previous location in the menu.

- If the cursor is in the menu:

  - TAB FORWARD moves the cursor to the next field in the menu.

  - TAB BACKWARD moves the cursor to the previous field in the menu.

  - PF12 moves the cursor back to the command line.

Program Function Keys in the NAMES Menu

Program function keys are automatically assigned to execute some commonly used commands in the NAMES menu. These commands are assigned to PF1 through PF12 in NAMES. (The command name appears in parentheses followed by a brief description of what the command does):

PF1	(Help) Invokes the HELP facility to display information about NAMES.
PF2	(Add) Adds the entry to the NAMES file.
PF3	(Quit) Exits from the NAMES menu.
PF4	(Clear) Clears all fields in the menu.
PF5	(Find) Locates the first entry in the NAMES file that contains the value typed into the menu.
PF6	(Change) Changes the entry in the NAMES file.
PF7	(Previous) Displays the previous entry in the NAMES file.
PF8	(Next) Displays the next entry in the NAMES file.
PF9	Unassigned.
PF10	(Delete) Deletes the entry from the NAMES file.

PF11	Unassigned.
PF12	**(Cursor)** If the cursor is in the menu, move the cursor to the command line. If the cursor is on the command line, move the cursor to its previous position in the menu.

Notice that the commands assigned to the PF keys are also displayed below the menu.

Exercise:

Begin a NAMES file for yourself by making an entry for your own userid:

1. Enter the NAMES command to display the NAMES menu.

2. Enter an appropriate value after each relevant tag. Use your userid as the nickname for your tag.

3. Press PF2 to add the entry to your NAMES file.

4. If you wish to add an entry for another userid, clear the screen with PF4 and enter an appropriate value after each relevant tag.

5. When you are done adding entries, press PF3 to quit.

11.3 Sending a Note to Another User

NOTE is an Exec that prepares and sends a note to computer users on your system and on other systems to which yours is connected. A note is a usually a brief communication similar in format to that of a letter. Figure 11.3 shows the appearance of the screen in NOTE.

NOTE is an environment created by XEDIT. When you enter the NOTE command, XEDIT creates a file whose filename is your userid and whose filetype is NOTE. Once in the NOTE environment, you have all the capabilities of XEDIT at your disposal to create and edit the file.

NOTE is particularly convenient for sending mail for several reasons:

- If you have an entry in the NAMES file, a heading is automatically generated that includes information for your entry in the NAMES file.

- A heading identifying the recipients is generated.

- A note can be sent to a list of recipients if the list is an entry in the NAMES file.

- All the capabilities of XEDIT are at your disposal to edit the file.

- Program function keys are assigned to execute useful commands such as sending the note and canceling the note.

NOTE is also convenient for sending files to users on other computer systems connected to yours that are not IBM operating systems. There are, however, two limitations:

```
 KRYPTON   NOTE      A0   V 132  Trunc=132 Size=24 Line=12 Col=8 Alt=1
 OPTIONS: NOACK   LOG   SHORT   NOTEBOOK BRONZE

 Date:   9 May 1988,   11:30:45  PDT
 From:   the Hidden                QQQ-1111              KRYPTON at   CMSA
 To: BRONZE AT CMSB
 cc: COPPER TIN

 * * * End of File * * *




 1= Help      2= Add Line 3= Quit    4= Tab      5= Send      6= ?
 7= Backward  8= Forward  9= =        10= Rgtleft 11= Spltjoin 12= Power input

 ====> _
                                             X E D I T   1 File
```

Figure 11.3 A sample NOTE display.

Sending a Note to Another User § 325

1. The file must not be too large to fit in virtual storage where a note is created.

2. The record length of the file must not exceed that of the note, which is normally 132.

Use the GET subcommand in the NOTE environment to read an external file into NOTE.

Command Format:

      NOTE   **[recipients [CC: recipients]] (options**

where **recipients** are the names of computer users to whom the note is to be sent. Specify the names in one of three formats:

- If the recipient is a user on your system, specify the recipient as that user's userid:

  USERID

- If the recipient is on another IBM system to which yours is connected, specify the recipient as that user's userid followed by the word AT and the name of the system he is on:

  USERID AT SYSNAME

- If the recipient is a list of users for which there is a nickname entered in a NAMES file, specify the recipient as the nickname:

  NICKNAME

All three formats can be mixed together in a list.

CC: specifies the names of recipients who are to receive complimentary copies of the note.

options are discussed below.

NOTE Options

**[Ack|*NOAck*] [ADd] [Cancel] [NONotebook|NOTebook fn]
[NOLog|*LOG*] [LONg|*Short*] [Replace] [PROFile fn]**

Ack specifies that an acknowledgment be sent to you when the recipient receives or discards the note. Normally, no acknowledgment is sent.

ADd   adds the recipient to the current list of recipients. This option is only valid when used from within the NOTE environment. When this option is specified, no other options may be used.

Cancel   deletes the note you are currently editing. This option is only valid when used from within the NOTE environment. When this option is specified, no other options may be used.

NOTebook   adds the note to a file whose filename is **fn** and whose filetype is NOTEBOOK. If this option is omitted, the filename is ALL. Using this option is equivalent to substituting **fn** for the value of the :NOTEBOOK. tag in your NAMES file.

NONotebook does not add the note to a NOTEBOOK file.

NOLog   does not make a record of the note in a file whose filetype is NETLOG and whose filename is your userid. Normally, whenever you send a note, a record is added to this file that includes the recipients and time and date the note was sent.

LONg   uses the long form of the note header. This includes all the information available in the NAMES file for each recipient. Normally, the short form is used.

Replace   erases an unfinished *userid NOTE* file before entering NOTE.

PROFile   uses the XEDIT macro with the filename **fn** to establish the NOTE environment. If this option is omitted, the file called PROFNOTE XEDIT is used to set up the default NOTE environment.

Program Function Keys in NOTE

The program function keys are assigned to execute some commonly used commands in NOTE. These commands are assigned to PF1 through PF12 in NOTE. (The subcommand name appears in parentheses followed by a brief description of what the subcommand does):

PF1   **(HELP NOTE)** Displays the HELP information for NOTE.

PF2   **(LINEADD)** Adds a blank line immediately below where the cursor is located.

PF3   **(QUIT)** Leaves NOTE and returns to the environment from which you began the note.

PF4	**(TAB)** Moves the cursor to the next tab position.
PF5	**(SEND)** Sends the note.
PF6	**(?)** Displays the subcommand previously executed on the command line.
PF7	**(BACKWARD)** Scrolls the display backward one full screen.
PF8	**(FORWARD)** Scrolls the display forward one full screen.
PF9	**(=)** Executes the previous subcommand again.
PF10	**(RGTLEFT)** Shifts the display to the right if column 1 is the left-most column displayed. Shifts the display to the left if column 1 is not the left-most column displayed.
PF11	**(SPLTJOIN)** Splits a line where the cursor is located if the cursor is followed by characters other than blanks. Joins two consecutive lines if the cursor is followed only by blanks.
PF12	**(POWER INPUT)** Enters power typing mode.

Preparing and Sending a Note

When you enter the NOTE command, you are placed in an environment controlled by XEDIT where you can prepare your note. Use the command line in NOTE just as you do in XEDIT to enter XEDIT subcommands to create and edit your note.

- Use INPUT to put text into the file.

- Use DELETE to remove lines from the file.

- Use GET to read an external file into the note.

- Use UP to move the current line toward the top of the file.

- Use DOWN to move the current line toward the end of the file.

- Use LOCATE to find text.

Once you've finished the note, press the PF5 key to send the note.

Examples:

All examples in this section assume you have the NAMES file in Figure 11.1.

- Suppose you want to send a note to the userid ARGON. The following are equivalent:

```
NOTE   AR
NOTE   ARGON
```

- Suppose you want to send a note to the userid BRONZE with the userids COPPER and TIN receiving complimentary copies. The following are equivalent:

```
NOTE   CU+SN  CC: CU  SN
NOTE   BRONZE AT CMSB  CC:  COPPER  TIN
```

- Suppose you want to send a note to all the userids that are elements. The following are equivalent:

```
NOTE   ELEMENTS
NOTE   GASES  METALS
NOTE   KRYPTON NEON ARGON ZENON COPPER ZINC TIN LEAD
```

- Suppose you want to send a file called XMPL DATA to the userid BRASS on the VMSB system and the userid PEWTER on the UNIXA system. Since the systems to which you are sending the file are not IBM operating systems, use NOTE to send the file instead of SENDFILE:

  1. Begin the note in the usual fashion. The following are equivalent:

```
NOTE   CU+ZN  SN+PB
NOTE   BRASS AT VMSA  PEWTER AT UNIXA
```

  2. Once inside of NOTE, enter the XEDIT GET command on the command line to read the file into NOTE:

```
====> GET   XMPL   DATA
```

  3. Send the file by pressing PF5.

Exercise:

Prepare and send a note to yourself. Enter the NOTE command followed by your own userid.

Postponing a Note

Once you begin a note, you can postpone completing and sending it until some later time. This is convenient if you haven't sufficient information or time to complete the note.

- To save what you've done so far and return to CMS, enter the FILE subcommand on the command line:

```
====> FILE
```

The note is saved in a file with a filetype of NOTE and a filename that is your userid.

- To return to the note, enter the NOTE command without specifying the note's recipient:

NOTE

If you have an unfinished note, you cannot begin another until you do one of the following:

- Complete and send the unfinished note.

- Rename the *userid NOTE* file, giving it another filename and/or filetype.

- Begin the other note, using the REPLACE option on the NOTE command to delete the unfinished note.

11.4 Sending a File to Another User

SENDFILE (**SF** is a synonym) is an Exec that sends files to computer users on your system and on other IBM systems to which yours is connected.

Do not use SENDFILE to send files to users on systems that are not IBM operating systems, such as VMS or UNIX, since those systems may not have the facilities to read files sent by SENDFILE. Use NOTE instead.

Command Format:

SENDFile [fileid [TO] recipients] (options

where **fileid** is the fileid of either a file to be sent or a list of files to be sent. If the fileid is omitted, the menu in Figure 11.4 is displayed where you can enter one.

recipients are the names of computer users to whom the file is to be sent. Specify the names in one of three ways:

- If the recipient is a user on your system, specify the recipient as that user's userid:

  USERID

- If the recipient is on another IBM system to which yours is connected, specify the recipient as that user's userid followed by the word AT and the name of the system he is on:

  USERID AT SYSNAME

- If the recipient is a list of users for which there is a nickname entered in a NAMES file, specify the recipient as the nickname:

  NICKNAME

  All three formats can be mixed together in a list.

options are discussed below.

SENDFILE Options

[Ack|*NOAck*] [Filelist|*NOFilelist*] [NOLog|*Log*] [NOType|*Type*]

Ack specifies that an acknowledgment be sent to you when the recipient receives or discards the note. Normally, no acknowledgment is sent.

Sending a File to Another User § 331

Filelist   indicates that file **fileid** is a list of files created either by the EXEC option on the LISTFILE command or by writing the FILELIST display to a disk file.

NOLog   does not make a record of the files sent in a file whose filetype is NETLOG and whose filename is your userid. Normally, whenever you send a file, a record is added to this file that includes the recipients and time and date the file was sent.

NOType   displays nothing on the terminal when the files are sent. Normally, when each file is sent, the userid and node to which the file was sent is displayed.

Examples:

- Suppose you must send copies of all files with a filetype of DATA on your A-disk to the userid ARGON. Rather than using a separate SENDFILE command for each file:

    1. Use the EXEC option on the LISTFILE command to create a CMS EXEC file:

       LISTFILE * DATA (EXEC

    2. Use the FILELIST option on the SENDFILE command to indicate that the CMS EXEC file contains a list of files to be sent:

```
---------------- SENDFILE -----------------
File(s) to be sent     (use * for Filename, Filetype and/or Filemode
                         to select from a list of files)
Enter filename :
      filetype :
      filemode :

Send files to  :

Type over YES or No to change the options:

  NO    Request acknowledgement when the file has been received?

  YES   Make a log entry when the file has been sent?

  YES   Display the file name when the file has been sent?

  NO    This file is actually a list of files to be sent?


  1= Help        3= Quit          5= Send          12= Cursor

====>
                                        MACRO-READ 1 File
```

Figure 11.4 The SENDFILE menu.

332   §   **Communicating with Other Computer Users**

```
SENDFILE  CMS  EXEC  ARGON  (  FILELIST
```

- Suppose you have the NAMES file in Figure 11.1 and want to send a file called XMPL DATA to the userids that are metals. The following are equivalent:

```
SF  XMPL  DATA  TO  METALS
SF  XMPL  DATA  TO  CU  PB  SN  ZN
SF  XMPL  DATA  TO  COPPER  LEAD  TIN  ZINC
```

The SENDFILE Menu

If you enter the SENDFILE command omitting the fileid and the recipients, the system displays a menu, as in Figure 11.4, in which you can enter them.

1. Specify the fileid(s) of the file(s) to be sent.

    - Substitute an * for the filename to use *all* filenames with the specified filetype and filemode.

    - Substitute an * for the filetype to use *all* filetypes with the specified filename and filemode.

    - Substitute an * for the filemode to use *all* filemodes with the specified filename and filetype.

    If you use an * for the filename, filetype or filemode and more than one file is to be sent, FILELIST is used to display a list of those files. You must indicate which files are to be sent:

    a. Place an 'S' next to each file in FILELIST.

    b. Press ENTER.

2. Specify the recipient(s) of the file(s).

3. If the default value for an option is not desirable, type in the desired value.

4. When you've entered values in all appropriate fields, do one of the following:

    - To send the file(s) and leave the SENDFILE menu, press PF5.

    - To leave the SENDFILE menu and not send the file(s), press PF3.

Exercise:

In the chapter *Becoming Acquainted with XEDIT* you created one file called QUERY MEMO and another called QUERY DATA. Use the SENDFILE menu to send those files with a filename of QUERY to yourself:

Sending a File to Another User § 333

1. Enter the SENDFILE command without specifying the file to be sent or the recipient:

    SENDFILE

2. Specify QUERY as the filename and * as the filetype.

3. Specify your userid as the recipient.

4. Press ENTER.

5. In FILELIST, place an 'S' next to each file to be sent and press ENTER.

6. Leave FILELIST by pressing PF3.

7. Leave SENDFILE by pressing PF3.

11.5 Working with Virtual Reader Files

When other computer users send you files or notes, those files and notes are stored in your virtual reader until you read them onto disk or discard them.[1]

RDRLIST (**RL** is a synonym) is a *full screen* facility that displays a list of reader files and their characteristics. RDRLIST is an environment created by XEDIT to facilitate the management and use of reader files. When you enter the RDRLIST command, XEDIT creates a file whose filename is your userid and whose filetype is RDRLIST. Once in the RDRLIST environment, you have all the capabilities of XEDIT at your disposal to manipulate the display of files by entering commands from the command line. RDRLIST is particularly convenient to work with reader files for two reasons:

- RDRLIST allows you to use certain abbreviations for spoolids that save you from having to type out the spoolids.

- Program function keys are assigned to execute useful commands.

Command Format:

>   RDRList   [Append] [PROFile fn]

```
KRYPTON   RDRLIST   AO   V 109   Trunc=109 Size=3 Line=1 Col=1 Alt=0
Cmd    Filename Filetype Class User  at Node    Hold  Records  Date      Time
 _     ARGON    NOTE     PUN A ARGON    CMSA     NONE      34  2/02/88 12:36:46
       BRONZE   NOTE     PUN A BRONZE   CMSB     NONE      51  2/02/88 14:11:36
       PEWTER   MAIL     PUN A PEWTER   UNIXA    NONE      87  2/02/88 15:21:34




















 1= Help      2= Refresh  3= Quit    4= Sort(type)  5= Sort(date) 6= Sort(size)
 7= Backward  8= Forward  9= Receive 10=            11= Peek         12= Cursor

====>
                                            X E D I T   1 File
```

Figure 11.5 A sample RDRLIST display.

---

[1] Your system may limit the length of time a file can remain in your virtual reader. Files left in your reader longer than the limit are purged. Consult with those that support your system to determine if there is such a limit and, if so, what it is.

where **Append**   appends another list of files to be displayed to the present list. This option only works if used from within the RDRLIST environment.

      PROFile   uses the XEDIT macro with the filename **fn** to establish the RDRLIST environment. If this option is omitted, the file called PROFRLST XEDIT is used to set up the default RDRLIST environment.

The Areas of the Screen and Their Uses in RDRLIST

When you enter the RDRLIST command, the fileids are displayed in the format shown in Figure 11.5. Notice that the order in which the files are listed is by the time and date they appeared in your reader, with the file most recently written to disk listed last.

- Under **Cmd** is the Command Area.

- Under **Filename** and **Filetype** is the fileid of each file.

- Under **Class** is the type and class of virtual device that sent each file.

- Under **User** is the userid that sent each file.

- Under **Node** is the name of the system from which each file was sent.

- Under **Hold** is whether there is a hold on each file.

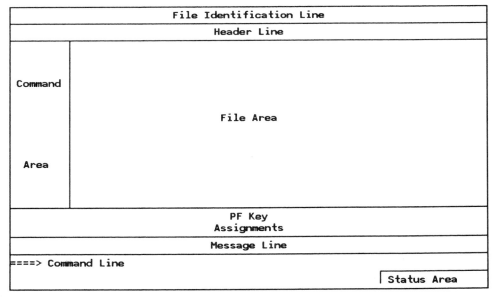

Figure 11.6 The areas of the screen in RDRLIST.

336   §   **Communicating with Other Computer Users**

- Under **Records** is the number of records in each file.

- Under **Date** is the month and day each file appeared in your reader.

- Under **Time** is the time of day each file appeared in your reader.

Figure 11.6 shows the areas of the screen in RDRLIST.

- The **File Identification Line** displays information about the *userid RDRLIST* file.

- The **Header Line** labels the areas in the file area below.

- The **Command Area** is where you enter commands to work with files.

- The **File Area** displays fileids and information about the files.

- The **PF Key Assignments** displays the commands assigned to PF keys.

- The **Message Line** displays messages issued in response to your commands.

- The **Command Line** is where you enter XEDIT commands to manipulate the display and CMS and CP commands to perform other tasks.

Working with Files in RDRLIST

Three commands, to be discussed in more detail later in this chapter, are especially useful in working with files in RDRLIST:

- PEEK displays a reader file.

- RECEIVE writes a reader file onto disk.

- DISCARD removes a reader file.

Once you enter the RDRLIST command to display a list of reader files, you can work with files in the display:

1. Position the cursor in the command area next to the file to be used.

2. Type the command that uses the file in the desired way, specifying one of these abbreviations:

/	represents the spoolid.
/n	represents the filename.
/t	represents the filetype.
/m	represents the type of device that sent the file.
/o	executes a command, omitting all parts of the fileid.

Any combination of **n**, **t**, and **m** up to seven characters can also be used:

/nt   represents the filename followed by the filetype.

/tn   represents the filetype followed by the filename.

If the command is longer than the command area, continue typing the command into the file area over the fileid. *You cannot enter a command in the command area if your terminal is in insert mode. If you try to do so, the keyboard will lock to prohibit you and the terminal may sound an alarm.* If necessary, use the RESET key to unlock the keyboard.

3.   Press the ENTER key to execute the command.

4.   When you've finished working with the files and want to leave RDRLIST, press PF3.

Exercise:

This exercise is designed to familiarize you with RDRLIST and how to use PEEK, RECEIVE and DISCARD to work with virtual reader files.

1.   In order that you have disposable reader files to work with, use the SENDFILE command to send yourself two copies of the file called QUERY MEMO that you created earlier.

       SF QUERY MEMO A TO *

2.   To display the list of files in your reader, enter the RDRLIST command:

       RDRLIST

       When you enter RDRLIST, the cursor is normally located in the command area next to the top-most file in the display.

3.   PEEK allows you to examine a reader file to decide whether you want to save the file on disk or discard it. PEEK is assigned to PF11.

       Use PEEK to examine the file called QUERY MEMO:

    a.   Move the cursor to the command area next to the file if it is not located there already.

    b.   Press PF11.

       While inside of PEEK, the PF keys are assigned to perform some useful tasks:

    •   PF8 scrolls forward in the file.

    •   PF7 scrolls backward in the file.

- PF3 leaves PEEK and returns you to RDRLIST.

4. DISCARD removes a file from your virtual reader. Suppose you've examined QUERY MEMO and now you want to remove it:

   a. Move the cursor to the command area next to the file if it is not located there already.

   b. Type the DISCARD command. The following are equivalent:

   ```
   DISCARD
   DISCARD  /
   ```

   c. Press ENTER.

5. RECEIVE writes a file in your virtual reader onto disk. Suppose you've examined QUERY MEMO and you want to write it onto disk. Normally, you position the cursor to the left of the file to be received and press PF9. If you do this in the case of QUERY MEMO, however, you'll receive an error message indicating that the file already exists:

   ```
   File 'QUERY MEMO A1' already exists -- specify 'REPLACE' option.
   ```

   This is meant to protect you from inadvertently destroying a disk file that may be of value. If you have a file in your reader that you want to receive that has the same fileid as another file on your A-disk, you can do one of three things:

   - Receive the reader file with a fileid that differs from that of the disk file.

   - Rename the disk file and receive the reader file.

   - Use the REPLACE option on RECEIVE to replace the disk file with the reader file.

   Suppose you want to receive QUERY MEMO with a fileid of ELSE DATA:

   a. Position the cursor in the command area next to the file.

   b. Type the RECEIVE command followed by a / (to represent the spoolid) and the new fileid:

   ```
   RECEIVE  /  ELSE  DATA
   ```

   c. Press ENTER.

   Suppose you want to replace the disk file called QUERY MEMO with the reader file called QUERY MEMO:

   a. Position the cursor in the command area next to the file.

Working with Virtual Reader Files § 339

      b.   Type the RECEIVE command followed by a / (to represent the spoolid), a left parenthesis and the REPLACE option:

```
RECEIVE  /  (  REPLACE
```

      c.   Press ENTER.

  6.   To leave RDRLIST and return to CMS, press PF3.

Program Function Keys in RDRLIST

Program function keys are automatically assigned to execute some commonly used commands in RDRLIST. These commands are assigned to PF1 through PF12 in RDRLIST. (The command name appears in parentheses followed by a brief description of what the command does):

PF1	**(Help)** Invokes the HELP facility to display information about RDRLIST.
PF2	**(Refresh)** Updates the display to include files that arrived since you entered RDRLIST, remove discarded files and clean up‍ RDRLIST's responses to your commands.
PF3	**(Quit)** Exits from RDRLIST.
PF4	**(Sort)** Sorts the files in the display first by filetype and then by filename.
PF5	**(Sort)** Sorts the files in the display first by date and then by time of day, with the oldest files first.
PF6	**(Sort)** Sorts the files in the display by the user who sent the files.
PF7	**(Backward)** Scrolls the display backward one screen.
PF8	**(Forward)** Scrolls the display forward one screen.
PF9	**(RECEIVE)** Writes the file next to the cursor onto your A-disk using the same filename and filetype the file had in your reader. If the file has no filename and filetype, you must assign them. How to do so is discussed later.
PF10	Unassigned.
PF11	**(PEEK)** Displays the file next to the cursor.
PF12	**(Cursor)** If the cursor is in the file area, move the cursor to the command line. If the cursor is on the command

line, move the cursor to its previous position in the file area.

Notice that the commands assigned to the PF keys are also displayed below the file area.

How RDRLIST Responds to Your Commands

RDRLIST responds to the commands you enter in the command area by displaying one of these symbols:

*	indicates that the command was successfully executed.
*n	indicates that the command was not successfully executed and that the return code was **n**.
*?	indicates that the command was an unknown CP or CMS command.

Displaying or Executing the Previous Command

RDRLIST also allows you to execute the command previously executed or to display the command previously executed again in the command area without executing it.

= executes the command previously executed using the file in the display next to which the = is placed.

1. After executing a command that you want to execute again, place = in the command area next to the file to be used when the command is executed again. If you want to execute the command using several different files, place = in the command area next to each of the files.

2. Press ENTER.

? displays the command previously executed in the command area next to any file in the display but does not execute it. This is useful if the previous command did not execute due to an error, because now you can display the command again, edit the mistake using the edit control keys and the press ENTER. It's also useful if the command you now want to execute is a minor variation on the previous command.

1. After executing a command that you want to display again, place ? in the command area next to the file where you want the command displayed again. If you want to display the command in the command area next to several different files, place ? next to each of the files.

2. Press ENTER.

Working with Virtual Reader Files § 341

Moving the Cursor in RDRLIST

The TAB FORWARD, TAB BACKWARD and PF12 keys provide convenient ways to move the cursor in RDRLIST.

- If the cursor is on the command line:

  - TAB FORWARD moves the cursor to the first file in the file area.

  - TAB BACKWARD moves the cursor to the last file in the file area.

  - PF12 moves the cursor to its previous location in the file area.

- If the cursor is in the file area:

  - TAB FORWARD moves the cursor to the next file in the file area.

  - TAB BACKWARD moves the cursor to the previous file in the file area.

  - PF12 moves the cursor back to the command line.

The Command Line in RDRLIST

The command line is the second line from the bottom of the screen. It begins with the arrow:

====>

Use the command line to:

- Execute XEDIT commands to manipulate the display by:

  - Move the display up or down a specific number of lines.

  - Scroll the display up or down a specific number of screens.

  - Locate a specific file or position in the list, such as bottom or top.

- Execute CP and CMS commands.

Examples:

- Suppose you must move the display up five lines:

  ====> UP   5

- Suppose you must move the display down five lines:

  ====> DOWN   5

- Suppose you must search forward in the list for a file with a filename of XMPL:

```
====> /XMPL
```

- Suppose you must search backward in the list for a file with a filename of XMPL:

```
====> -/XMPL
```

- Suppose you want to send a message to another user using the CP MSG command. (Since XEDIT also has an MSG command, remember to precede MSG with CP):

```
====> CP  MSG  ARGON  blah  blah  blah
```

Writing the RDRLIST Display to a Disk File

In RDRLIST, as in XEDIT, the FILE subcommand writes a file being edited to disk and returns you to CMS. If you enter the FILE subcommand in RDRLIST, XEDIT writes the RDRLIST display to a disk file with a filename that is your userid and a filetype of RDRLIST.

11.6 Displaying a Reader File

PEEK (assigned to **PF11** in RDRLIST) displays a file or note that is in your virtual reader. PEEK is an environment created by XEDIT. When you enter the PEEK command, XEDIT creates a file whose filename is the file's spoolid and whose filetype is PEEK. Once in the PEEK environment, you have all the capabilities of XEDIT at your disposal to view and edit the file by entering commands from the command line and using PF keys.

This command is most convenient if used from RDRLIST, where PF11 is assigned to execute it.

    1.   Position the cursor in the command area next to the file to be displayed.

    2.   Press PF11.

PEEK can also be entered as a command either on the command line or in the command area next to the file to be displayed.

Command Format:

PEEK	[spoolid] ([FRom recnum] [FOr numrec] [PROFile fn]

where **spoolid** is the spoolid of the file to be displayed. If the spoolid is omitted, the *next* file in your reader is displayed.

        FRom specifies the first record to be displayed as **recnum**. If this option is omitted, the display begins at the first record.

        FOr specifies the number of records to be displayed as **numrec**. If this option is omitted, only the first 200 records can be displayed. Use an * to display all records.

        PROFile uses the XEDIT macro with the filename **fn** to establish the PEEK environment. If this option is omitted, the file called PROFPEEK XEDIT is used to set up the default PEEK environment.

Example:

Normally, PEEK only displays up to 200 records in a file. Suppose you want to use PEEK to display a file containing more than 200 records:

    1.   Type the PEEK command in the command area next to the file using a / to represent the spoolid and * after the FOR option to indicate that all records are to be displayed:

        PEEK / (FOR *

    2.   Press ENTER.

Program Function Keys in PEEK

The PF keys are assigned to execute some commonly used commands in PEEK. These commands are assigned to PF1 through PF12 in PEEK. (The command name appears in parentheses followed by a brief description of what the command does):

PF1	**(HELP PEEK)** Displays the HELP information for PEEK.
PF2	**(SOS LINEADD)** Adds a blank line immediately below where the cursor is located.
PF3	**(QUIT)** Leaves PEEK and returns to the environment from which you began displaying the file.
PF4	**(TABKEY)** Moves the cursor to the next tab position.
PF5	**(SCHANGE 6)** Assigns PF6 to execute the SCHANGE subcommand.
PF6	**(?)** Displays the subcommand previously executed on the command line.
PF7	**(BACKWARD)** Scrolls the display backward one full screen.
PF8	**(FORWARD)** Scrolls the display forward one full screen.
PF9	**(RECEIVE)** Writes the file next to the cursor onto your A-disk using the same filename and filetype the file had in your reader. If the file has no filename and filetype, you must assign them. How to do so is discussed later.
PF10	**(RGTLEFT)** Shifts the display to the right if column 1 is the left-most column displayed. Shifts the display to the left if column 1 is not the left-most column displayed.
PF11	**(SPLTJOIN)** Splits a line where the cursor is located if the cursor is followed by characters other than blanks. Joins two consecutive lines if the cursor is followed only by blanks.
PF12	**(CURSOR HOME)** Moves the cursor from the command line to the file area or from the file area to the command line, depending on its current position.

Displaying a Reader File § **345**

Editing a File with PEEK

While displaying a reader file with PEEK, you can edit the file using XEDIT the way you would normally edit a disk file. When you are finished editing the file, use the FILE command to write the file to disk. The reader file remains unchanged. If you don't specify a fileid on the FILE subcommand, the file is written to your A-disk with a filename that is the file's spoolid and a filetype of PEEK.

Customizing the PEEK Environment

There are several differences between the environment set up for PEEK and the normal XEDIT environment for creating and editing files. In PEEK, the prefix area and the scale line are removed and the current line is not highlighted. If you prefer to change these or any of the other functions of the SET subcommand, you can do so with the SET subcommand discussed in the chapter *Customizing the XEDIT Environment*.

11.7 Writing a Reader File to Disk

RECEIVE (assigned to **PF9** in RDRLIST and PEEK) is an Exec that writes a reader file onto a disk to which you have read/write access.

- If the file was sent by the NOTE command, it is added to a file with a filetype of NOTEBOOK and a filename of ALL unless you have a :NOTEBOOK. tag specifying another filename.

- If the file was sent by SENDFILE, PRINT, PUNCH or DISK DUMP, the disk file is given the same filename and filetype as the reader file.

- If the file has no filename and filetype, you'll have to assign them.

This command is most convenient if used from RDRLIST or PEEK, where PF9 is assigned to execute it.

- In PEEK, press PF9.

- In RDRLIST:

    1. Position the cursor in the command area next to the file to be received.

    2. Press PF9.

RECEIVE can also be entered as a command either on the command line or in the command area next to the file to be received.

Command Format:

      RECEIVE   **[spoolid] [fileid] (options**

where **spoolid**   is the spoolid of the file to be received. If the spoolid is omitted, the *next* file in your reader is received.

      fileid   is the fileid.

- If the filename is omitted, it becomes the filename of the reader file.

- If the filetype is omitted, it becomes the filetype of the reader file.

- If the filemode is omitted, it becomes A.

      options   are discussed below.

RECEIVE Options

      [NONotebook|NOTebook fn] [NOLog|*LOG*] [Replace] [NEwdate|*Olddate*]

NOTebook   adds the note to a file whose filename is **fn** and whose filetype is NOTEBOOK. If this option is omitted, the filename is ALL. Using this option is equivalent to substituting **fn** for the value of the :NOTEBOOK. tag in your NAMES file.

NONotebook does not add the note to a NOTEBOOK file.

NOLog   does not make a record of the note received in a file whose filetype is NETLOG and whose filename is your userid. Normally, whenever you receive a note, a record is added to this file that includes the sender and time and date the note was received.

Replace   writes over a disk file with the same fileid as the reader file. Normally, a disk file with the same fileid as the reader file is not replaced.

NEwdate   writes the file to disk with the current date and time. Normally, the file is written to disk with the time and date the sender last wrote the file to disk.

11.8 Removing a Reader File

DISCARD is an Exec that removes a file from your virtual reader. This command can be used in either RDRLIST or PEEK:

- In RDRLIST:

    1. Type DISCARD in the command area next to the file to be removed. The spoolid is automatically appended.

    2. Press ENTER.

- In PEEK:

    1. Type DISCARD on the command line. The spoolid is automatically appended.

    2. Press ENTER.

Command Format:

> **DISCARD**   [spoolid]

where **spoolid**   is the spoolid of the file to be discarded. If the spoolid is omitted, the *next* file in you reader is discarded.

11.9 Sending a Message to Another User

A message is a brief communication that you can display on the terminal of another user who is currently logged on. The length of a message is limited to the command input area. If the message goes beyond the first line of the command input area, continue it on the next line up to, but not into, the status message area.

There are several commands for sending messages on VM/CMS, but only two are available to general users:

- MESSAGE

- TELL

These are differences between MESSAGE and TELL:

- TELL sends messages to users on your system and on other VM/CMS systems to which yours is connected, whereas MESSAGE only sends messages to users on your system.

- TELL references your NAMES files so that you can use nicknames in sending messages and you can send messages to a list of users, MESSAGE only sends messages to a single user.

System Messages:

Before a message is displayed on the recipient's terminal, the time of day and the sender's userid are displayed:

Using MESSAGE to Send a Message

MESSAGE (**MSG** is a synonym) is a CP command that displays a message on the terminal of another user who is currently logged on.

If the user to whom you are sending the message is either not logged on or is not receiving messages, no message will be sent.

Command Format:

    MSG   userid text

where **userid**   is the userid to which the message is sent. To send a message to yourself, use an *.

    text   is the message to be sent. The message may continue up to the end of the command input area.

Example:

Suppose you want to send a message to the userid ARGON:

```
MSG  ARGON  THIS IS THE MESSAGE.
```

Using TELL to Send a Message

TELL is an Exec that uses the CP MESSAGE command to display a message on the terminals of one or more users who are currently logged onto your system and other VM/CMS systems to which yours is connected.

If a user to whom you are sending the message is either not logged on or is not receiving messages, no message will be sent.

Command Format:

> **TELL**   recipient text

where **recipient**   represents the computer user(s) to whom the message is sent. Specify the recipient in one of three formats:

- If the recipient is a user on your system, specify the recipient as that user's userid:

   USERID

- If the recipient is on another IBM system to which yours is connected, specify the recipient as that user's userid followed by the word AT and the name of the system he is on:

   USERID AT SYSNAME

   If the first word of your message is AT, you *must* use this form.

- If the recipient is a list of users for which there is a nickname entered in a NAMES file, specify the recipient as the nickname:

   NICKNAME

text   is the message to be sent. The message may continue up to the end of the command input area.

Examples:

- Suppose you have the NAMES file in Figure 11.1 and want to send a message to the userids that are gases.

```
TELL   GASES   THIS IS THE MESSAGE.
```

- Suppose you want to send a message to the userid BRONZE, which is on the CMSB system. The following are equivalent:

```
TELL   CU+SN   THIS IS THE MESSAGE.
TELL   BRONZE AT CMSB   THIS IS THE MESSAGE.
```

Handling Messages Sent to You

The section *Controlling Terminal Output* in the chapter *Customizing the CP/CMS Environments* discusses how you can use the CP SET command to control whether or not others can send you messages.

Example:

Suppose you don't want to receive messages from other users:

```
SET   MSG   OFF
```

Part V
Special Topics in VM/CMS

Chapter 12
Managing Your Virtual Machine

Introduction

When you log onto the system, a VM is configured for you according to the specifications of your entry in the CP User Directory. Your VM is set up to have:

- Virtual storage of a specific size.

- A virtual printer with certain characteristics.

- A virtual punch with certain characteristics.

- A virtual reader with certain characteristics.

- A virtual console with certain characteristics.

- The disks that belongs to your VM.

- The disks that belong to other VMs that you are authorized to access.

Making a Temporary Change to Your Virtual Machine

On occasion, you may find that the normal configuration of your VM is not adequate to accomplish some task. Accordingly, you will have to change the configuration of your VM temporarily. Common changes that amount to a re-configuration of your VM include:

- Increasing your virtual storage capacity.

- Changing the number of copies that your virtual printer produces.

- Changing a disk's access mode or access passwords.

- Accessing another user's minidisk.

- Accessing a temporary minidisk.

Making a Permanent Change to Your Virtual Machine

If you frequently must change the configuration of your VM in the same way, you should probably make the change permanent by changing your entry in the CP User Directory. Thereafter, the change becomes part of your normal VM configuration.

There are at least two facilities available for making a permanent change:

- DIRMAINT is a product from IBM that is primarily command driven and only allows you to conduct one transaction at a time.

- VMSECURE is a product from VM Software that can be used either by entering commands or by using menus. It also permits multiple transactions.

VMSECURE and DIRMAINT can both be used to:

- Obtain information about your entry in the CP User Directory.

- Change your entry in the CP User Directory.

One of these facilities is available on your system. Contact those who support your system to determine which is available. Both facilities are discussed in this chapter.

12.1 Using VMSECURE

VMSECURE can be used in one of two ways:

- The USER option provides a menu of selections, each of which performs one or more directory maintenance functions. The USER option
  can only be used in display mode with a display terminal.

- The MAINT option provides a set of commands that perform directory
  maintenance functions. The MAINT option can be used in either line
  mode or display mode with any type of terminal.

System Messages:

Whenever you use VMSECURE, the system requests that you enter your logon
password to verify that you are authorized either to make changes to or inquire about the CP User Directory.

    Enter your logon password:

The User Selection Menu in VMSECURE

USER is a VMSECURE option that displays the **User Selection Menu** shown in
Figure 12.1.

Command Format:

    VMSECURE [USER]

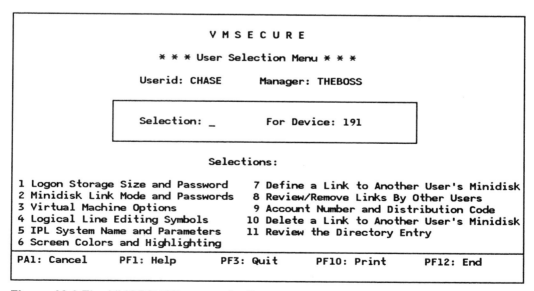

Figure 12.1 The VMSECURE user selection menu.

The cursor is positioned in the field following the word 'Selection'. The selection field is where you indicate what you want to do. Use the TAB keys to move from field to field:

- Use the TAB FORWARD key to move to the *next* field.

- Use the TAB BACKWARD key to move to the *previous* field.

The 11 selections available are displayed at the bottom of the screen.

- Selection 1 changes your logon password and/or the amount of virtual storage that your VM is defined to have when you log on.

- Selection 2 changes access modes and/or access passwords for disks that belong to you.

- Selection 3 changes various virtual machine options for your userid.

- Selection 4 changes the logical line editing symbols for your userid.

- Selection 5 specifies which operating system is loaded when you log on.

- Selection 6 changes the color and/or highlighting on your terminal.

- Selection 7 establishes an automatic link to another userid when you log on.

- Selection 8 reviews and optionally removes automatic links made to one of your disks by another userid.

- Selection 9 changes the account number that is billed for your use of the system and changes the distribution code for your spooled output.

- Selection 10 removes an automatic link to another user's disk.

- Selection 11 reviews your entry in the CP User Directory.

To use a selection:

1. Type the number with which it is labeled in the selection field. If the selection involves a disk whose virtual address is other than 191, enter the virtual address of the disk in the For Device field.

2. Press ENTER to display the selection. When a selection is displayed, the cursor is located in the first field.

3. Enter an appropriate value in each of the fields. Some fields are automatically supplied with a default value. If the default value suits your needs, leave it alone. Otherwise, type the desired value over the default.

4. When you have entered values in all the appropriate fields, do one of the following:

- End the selection and return to the User Selection Menu with EN-TER.

- End the selection and return to CMS with PF12.

- Cancel the selection and return to the User Selection Menu with PF3.

- Cancel the selection and return to CMS with PA1.

5. If you return to the User Selection Menu from a selection, you can choose another selection. To do so, repeat steps 1 through 4.

HELP is available for all selections and the User Selection Menu. If you make a mistake or are not sure what to do, press PF1 to display the online HELP. Once you have finished with HELP, press PF3 to return to the selection from which you entered HELP.

Commands in VMSECURE

MAINT is a VMSECURE option that performs the same directory maintenance functions with commands that can be performed with menus. Furthermore, there are some functions that can only be performed using the MAINT option.

Command Format:

VMSECURE MAINT function

These are some of the more useful VMSECURE options:

ACCOUNT changes the account number charged for system usage.

REVIEW obtains a copy of your own directory entry.

MDPW displays access passwords for one or all of your disks.

PASSWORD changes your logon password.

MINIDISK changes the access mode and access passwords for disks that belong to you.

DELETE removes an automatic link to another userid.

DEFINE changes the virtual address of one of your minidisks to a new address.

TERM adds, replaces, or deletes logical line editing characters.

LINK causes an automatic link to another user's disk when you log on.

RLINK   reviews automatic links made by other users to one of your disks and, optionally, removes them.

STORAGE   changes the virtual storage size of your VM.

DISTRIB   changes the distribution code for spooled output.

Among other topics, this chapter discusses the more useful VMSECURE options.

To display a complete list of the VMSECURE options and their syntax, enter the command:

VMSECURE MAINT HELP

12.2 Using DIRMAINT

These are some of the more useful DIRMAINT options:

REVIEW	obtains a copy of your own directory entry.
MDISK	changes the access mode and access passwords for disks that belong to you.
MDPW	displays access passwords for one or all of your disks.
PW	changes your logon password.
PW?	tells you how long ago your logon password was changed.
TERM	adds, replaces, or deletes logical line editing characters.
LINK	causes an automatic link, at logon, to another user's disk.
DLINK	removes links made by other users to one of your disks.
STORAGE	changes the virtual storage size of your VM.
ACCOUNT	changes the account number charged for system usage.
DISTRIB	changes the distribution code for spooled output.

Among other topics, this chapter discusses the more useful DIRMAINT options.

To display a complete list of the DIRMAINT options, enter:

DIRMaint   ?

To display the description of a DIRMAINT option and the command syntax, enter:

DIRMaint   ? option

To display only the command syntax of a DIRMAINT option, enter:

DIRMaint   ? option S

System Messages:

Whenever you use DIRMAINT, the system requests that you enter your logon password to verify that you are authorized either to make changes to or inquire about the CP User Directory.

ENTER CURRENT LOGON PASSWORD OR BLANK TO TERMINATE COMMAND:

Once DIRMAINT makes any change to your entry in the CP directory, it displays the message:

```
COMMAND DIRM option : SOURCE UPDATED AND CHANGE ONLINE.
```

12.3 Changing Your Logon Password

Unless you request a specific password when your userid is set up, the logon password initially assigned to your userid may be a random concatenation of letters and numbers. You may prefer to change it to something easier to remember. It is also good practice to periodically change your password.

There may be restrictions on what qualifies as a valid password on your system. Consult with those who maintain your system to determine what they are.

Using VMSECURE to Change Your Logon Password

Use Selection 1 in the VMSECURE User Selection Menu to change your logon password.

1. Enter the number 1 in the selection field.

2. Press ENTER to display the selection. VMSECURE will display a menu similar to that of Figure 12.2.

3. Carefully enter the new password in the password field and press ENTER. Normally, passwords are not displayed on the terminal screen in VMSECURE. If you prefer to have them displayed, press PA2.

4. Verify the new password by entering it again.

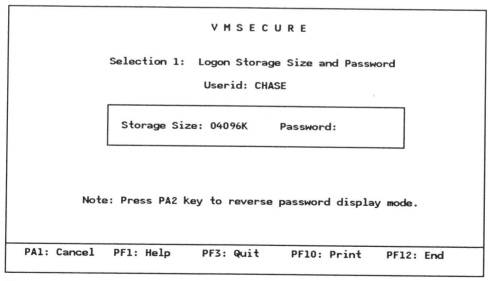

```
                          V M S E C U R E

            Selection 1:   Logon Storage Size and Password

                          Userid: CHASE


            ┌─────────────────────────────────────────────────┐
            │  Storage Size: 04096K       Password:           │
            │                                                 │
            └─────────────────────────────────────────────────┘



        Note: Press PA2 key to reverse password display mode.

 ┌──────────────────────────────────────────────────────────────────┐
 │ PA1: Cancel    PF1: Help     PF3: Quit     PF10: Print   PF12: End │
 └──────────────────────────────────────────────────────────────────┘
```

Figure 12.2 The VMSECURE menu for changing virtual storage size and logon password.

5. When you have entered values in all the appropriate fields, do one of the following:

- End the selection and return to the User Selection Menu with EN-TER.

- End the selection and return to CMS with PF12.

- Cancel the selection and return to the User Selection Menu with PF3.

- Cancel the selection and return to CMS with PA1.

• • •

PASSWORD is a VMSECURE option that changes your logon password.

Command Format:

VMSECURE MAInt Password

System Messages:

After requesting the old logon password, VMSECURE requests the new logon password:

Enter a new logon password:

VMSECURE then requests that you enter the new password again:

Reenter your new logon password for verification:

Using DIRMAINT to Change Your Logon Password

PW is a DIRMAINT option that changes your logon password.

Command Format:

DIRMaint   PW

System Messages:

After you enter the command, the system requests the new password:

ENTER NEW LOGON PASSWORD.

DIRMAINT only requests the new password once. So, be *very careful* that you press only the keys that you intend to press. If you inadvertently press a key other than one you intend to press, you will change your password to something that you do not know. If you should do this, contact those who administer your system and ask them to set up a new password for you.

If you enter an invalid password, the system displays the message:

```
INVALID LOGON PASSWORD SPECIFIED.
ENTER NEW LOGON PASSWORD.
```

12.4 Changing a Disk's Access Mode or Access Passwords

The access mode of a disk that belongs to your VM indicates how *you* access the disk when you log onto the system. Access modes are discussed in more detail in the section *Characteristics of CMS Disks* in the chapter *CMS Disks and CMS Disk Files*.

A disk access password can be any combination of letters, numbers and the special characters that may be used in filenames and filetypes. No more than eight characters may be used.

A read password of ALL allows anyone to read files from a disk without specifying a read password. This is convenient when you want to permit other system users to access a disk without knowing what the read password is.

When your userid is set up or when a new disk is added to your userid, disk access passwords may or may not be set up. Furthermore, if they are set up, they may be a random concatenation of letters and numbers that you may want to change to something easier to remember. You may also want to add nonexistent disk access passwords or remove existing passwords.

Using VMSECURE to Change Access Mode and Passwords

Use Selection 2 in the VMSECURE User Selection Menu to change the access mode and/or access passwords.

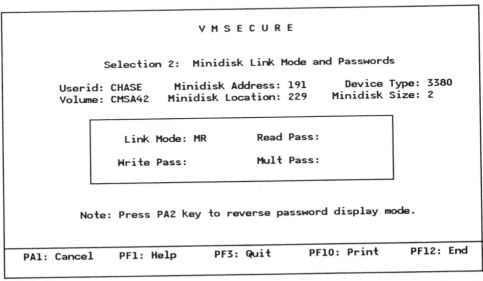

Figure 12.3 The VMSECURE menu for changing minidisk access mode and passwords.

364 § Managing Your Virtual Machine

1. Enter the number 2 in the selection field.

2. If the virtual address of the disk is not 191, enter the virtual address in the next field.

3. Press ENTER to display the selection. VMSECURE will display a menu similar to that of Figure 12.3.

4. Enter an access mode if the one supplied is not the one you want.

5. Add, change or remove the access passwords:

   - To add or change a password, position the cursor in the appropriate field and type in the password.

     - If you add a write password, you must also have a read password.

     - If you add a multiple password, you must also have a write password.

   - To remove a password, position the cursor in the appropriate field and type blanks in the field.

     - If you remove the read password, you also remove the write and multiple passwords.

     - If you remove the write password, you also remove the multiple password.

   Normally, passwords are not displayed on the terminal screen in VMSECURE. If you prefer to have them displayed, press PA2.

6. When you have entered values in all the appropriate fields, do one of the following:

   - End the selection and return to the User Selection Menu with EN-TER.

   - End the selection and return to CMS with PF12.

   - Cancel the selection and return to the User Selection Menu with PF3.

   - Cancel the selection and return to CMS with PA1.

· · ·

MINIDISK is a VMSECURE option that changes the access mode and/or access passwords.

Command Format:

   VMSECURE MAInt MInidisk vaddr

   Changing a Disk's Access Mode or Access Passwords § 365

where **vaddr**   is the virtual address of the disk.

System Messages:

After requesting the logon password, VMSECURE requests the new access mode and three passwords:

```
Enter new link mode value:

Enter read link password:

Enter write link password:

Enter mult link password:
```

- To leave a password unchanged, enter an equals sign (=).

- To remove a password, press ENTER without entering a password.

Using DIRMAINT to Change Access Mode and Passwords

MDISK is a DIRMAINT option that changes the access mode and/or access passwords for disks that belong to you.

Command Format:

    DIRMaint   **MDisk [vaddr mode [readpw [writepw [multipw]]]]**

where **vaddr**   is the minidisk virtual address.

    mode   is the access mode.

    readpw   is the read password.

    writepw   is the write password.

    multipw   is the multiple access password.

If the operands after MDISK are omitted, a menu is displayed in which you can enter them:

```
Minidisk Address: ===>
Access Mode:      ===>  =
Read Password:    ===>
Write Password:   ===>
Multi Password:   ===>
```

Do not press the ENTER key to move to the next area.

To move from field to field, use the TAB keys:

- Use the TAB FORWARD key to move to the *next* area.

- Use the TAB BACKWARD key to move to the *previous* area.

All fields except the minidisk address are set to =, which means that if you don't change the value in a field, it is left unchanged.

1. Enter the virtual address of the disk.

2. Enter the access mode if it is to be changed. If you change the access mode to either M, MR or MW you *must* also specify a multiple password.

3. Add, change or remove the access passwords:

    - To add or change a password, position the cursor in the appropriate field and type in the password.

        - If you add a write password, you must also have a read password.

        - If you add a multiple password, you must also have a write password.

    - To remove a password, position the cursor in the appropriate field and type a blank as the first character of the password.

        - If you remove the read password, you also remove the write and multiple passwords.

        - If you remove the write password, you also remove the multiple password.

4. Once you've entered values in all the appropriate fields, press ENTER.

12.5 Obtaining Your Disk Access Passwords

In order for another system user to access one of your disks, he must know the password corresponding to the access mode he intends to establish. The commands in this section allow you to obtain the access passwords for disks that belong to you.

Using VMSECURE to Obtain Access Passwords

Use Selection 2 in the VMSECURE User Selection Menu to obtain your access mode and/or access passwords.

1. Enter the number 2 in the selection field.

2. If the virtual address of the disk is not 191, enter the virtual address in the next field.

3. Press ENTER to display the selection. VMSECURE will display a menu similar to that of Figure 12.3.

4. Press PA2 to display the passwords.

5. Once you've determined what the access passwords are, do one of the following:

   • End the selection and return to the User Selection Menu with EN-TER.

   • End the selection and return to CMS with PF12.

• • •

MDPW is a VMSECURE option that obtains the disk access passwords for disks that belong to you.

Command Format:

VMSECURE MAInt MDpw [vaddr]

where **vaddr**   is the virtual address of the disk. If the virtual address is omitted, the passwords for all disks that belong to you are displayed.

System Messages:

VMSECURE displays the passwords in the format:

```
Minidisk 'vaddr' has passwords: readpw writepw multpw
```

Using DIRMAINT to Obtain Access Passwords

MDPW is a DIRMAINT option that displays the current disk access passwords for disks that belong to your VM.

Command Format:

DIRMaint   **MDPW [vaddr]**

where **vaddr**   is the virtual address of the disk. If the virtual address is omitted, the passwords for all disks that belong to you are displayed.

System Messages:

DIRMAINT displays your passwords in the format:

```
MINIDISK vaddr : READ= readpw  WRITE= writepw  MULTI= multpw
COMMAND DIRM MDPW COMPLETED.
```

12.6 Temporarily Changing Virtual Storage Capacity

On occasion, more virtual storage will be required to run a program or edit a file than your VM has at its disposal. The maximum virtual storage size that you can specify is recorded in your entry in the CP User Directory. If necessary, use the REVIEW option on the DIRMAINT and VMSECURE commands to determine what your limit is.

STORAGE is an option on the CP DEFINE command that changes your virtual storage. The virtual storage you define will remain available until you log off or change the storage capacity again.

Command Format:

> **DEFine**   **STORage size**

where **size**   is· the size of virtual storage. Specify the size in either kilobytes or megabytes.

System Messages:

After you enter the command, the system displays a message indicating your new virtual storage capacity and informs you that your VM in now in the CP environment in a disabled wait state:

```
STORAGE = nnnnnK
CP ENTERED; DISABLED  WAIT  PSW  '000200000 000000000'
```

Example:

Suppose you must increase your storage to one megabyte, which is the same as 1024K. The following are equivalent:

```
DEFINE STORAGE 1024K
DEFINE STORAGE 1M
```

Loading CMS Again

Once you've defined your storage, you must load CMS again, using the IPL command:

> **IPL CMS**

When CMS is reloaded by the IPL command, your VM is reconfigured according to your entry in the CP User Directory. What this means is that any disks, except temporary disks, that are not a permanent part of your VM will be released and all FILEDEFs will be cleared. Consequently, the ACCESS command must be used to reaccess those disks that were released and the FILEDEF command must be reissued for those FILEDEFs that were cleared.

12.7 Permanently Changing Virtual Storage Capacity

If you must regularly increase your virtual storage to run a program or edit large files, you should permanently change the virtual storage capacity your VM is defined to have when you log onto the system.

Using VMSECURE to Change Virtual Storage Capacity

Use Selection 1 in the VMSECURE User Selection Menu to change the virtual storage capacity that is defined when you log onto the system.

1. Enter the number 1 in the selection field.

2. Press ENTER to display the selection. VMSECURE will display a menu similar to Figure 12.2.

3. Enter the desired storage capacity expressing the size in either kilobytes or megabytes.

4. When you have entered values in all the appropriate fields, do one of the following:

   - End the selection and return to the User Selection Menu with ENTER.

   - End the selection and return to CMS with PF12.

   - Cancel the selection and return to the User Selection Menu with PF3.

   - Cancel the selection and return to CMS with PA1.

• • •

STORAGE is a VMSECURE option that changes virtual storage capacity.

Command Format:

VMSECURE MAInt Storage size

where **size**   is the amount of virtual storage to be defined when you log on. Express the size in either kilobytes or megabytes.

Example:

Suppose you must change the size of your virtual storage permanently to four megabytes. The following are equivalent:

```
VMSECURE  MAINT  STORAGE  4M
VMSECURE  MAINT  STORAGE  4096K
```

Using DIRMAINT to Change Virtual Storage Capacity

STORAGE is a DIRMAINT option that permanently changes the virtual storage capacity with which your VM is configured when you log onto the system.

Command Format:

DIRMaint   **ST**orage **size**

where **size**   is the size of virtual storage expressed in either kilobytes or megabytes.

Example:

Suppose you must change the size of your virtual storage permanently to four megabytes. The following are equivalent:

```
DIRMAINT  STORAGE  4M
DIRMAINT  STORAGE  4096K
```

12.8 Obtaining a Temporary Minidisk

The minidisks belonging to your VM are fixed in size and may not always have enough space for your needs. For example, some products generate intermediate files while they are working and erase those files when finished. Other products generate listing files which contain the results of some procedure. If there is insufficient space on your permanent disks for such intermediate files and listings, you may be able to access a temporary minidisk and use it for these files.

A **temporary minidisk** is a minidisk that you must explicitly request during a logon session. The files written to this disk are only present as long as you are logged on. When you log off the system, the temporary disk and the files on it are lost.

Most VM/CMS systems have an Exec that allows you to obtain a temporary disk quickly and easily. Consult with those who support your system to determine whether such an Exec is available and, if so, how to use it. Otherwise, obtaining a temporary minidisk is a two step process.

1. Use the CP DEFINE command to associate a virtual address with the disk and to identify the type of disk and its size.

2. Use the FORMAT command to initialize the disk, associate a mode letter with the virtual address and specify a blocksize.

Defining the Disk

DEFINE is a CP command that associates a virtual address with a temporary disk and identifies the type of disk and its size. While there are many different types of disks available for VM/CMS, your system probably has only a couple of different types. Consult with those who support your system to determine what types of disks are available to be used as temporary disks.

Command Format:

DEFine   Tnnnn [As] vaddr [CYL|BLK] size

where **nnnn**   (immediately after **T**) is the type of device.

vaddr   is the virtual address associated with the disk.

CYL   specifies the number of cylinders as **size** for count-key-data devices.

BLK   specifies the number of blocks as **size** for fixed-block-architecture devices.

Example:

Suppose your system has 3370 type devices available. The size on this type of disk is expressed in blocks. To assign the disk a virtual address of 91 and a capacity of 300 blocks:

```
DEFINE  T3370  91  BLK  300
```

Formatting the Disk

FORMAT initializes a disk, associates a mode letter with the virtual address and specifies a blocksize. The mode letter you use should be one not already associated with another minidisk. Otherwise, the other minidisk will be released.

(*Caution:* Formatting a disk erases all files on the disk. Consequently, you should never format a disk unless you really want to remove the files on it.)

Command Format:

    FORMAT   **vaddr mode ([BLksize size]**

where **vaddr**   is the virtual address of the disk.

    mode   is the mode letter to be associated with the virtual address.

    BLksize   specifies the blocksize to be **size**, which can be expressed in bytes as 512, 800, 1024, 2048 or 4096 or in kilobytes as 1K, 2K or 4K.

System Messages:

FORMAT warns you that all files on the disk will be erased:

```
FORMAT will erase all files on disk 'mode(vaddr)'.
Do you wish to continue? Enter 1 (YES) or 0 (NO).
```

If you indicate that you want to continue, FORMAT requests a label for the disk:

```
Enter disk label:
```

Example:

Suppose you've used DEFINE to obtain a temporary disk whose virtual address is 91. Now you want to initialize the disk, associate a mode letter of C with the virtual address of 91 and specify a blocksize of 4096:

```
FORMAT  91  C  ( BLKSIZE  4096
```

Thereafter, the disk is available as a C-disk. Remember that a temporary disk and the files on it are only available during the session that you obtained it. When you log off, the temporary disk and files on it are lost.

Temporary Disk: a Limited System Resource

Temporary disk is a limited resource shared by all system users. You should only request it when you need it and should only request as much as you need. If you consistently need temporary disk each time you log on, you should obtain more permanent disk space either by increasing the size of one of your existing disks or by adding another disk. Contact those who support your system to determine how to obtain more permanent disk space.

12.9 Temporarily Linking Another User's Disk

On VM/CMS, every minidisk belongs to a userid. The userid to which a mini-disk belongs is regarded as the *owner* of that minidisk. Two commands are necessary to access another user's minidisk:

- LINK identifies the disk to CP by associating a virtual address with the disk.

- ACCESS identifies the disk to CMS by associating a mode letter with the disk.

When you log off the system, any disk belonging to another VM that you ac-cessed by using the LINK and ACCESS commands is removed from your VM. Consequently, when you log on again and require access to the same disk again, you must use the LINK and ACCESS commands again.

Identifying a Disk to CP

LINK is a CP command that associates a virtual address with a disk belonging to some VM. To LINK another user's minidisk, you must know three things:

1. The userid that owns the minidisk.

2. The virtual address assigned to the minidisk by the owner. Determine this by asking the owner what the virtual address is.

3. The access password corresponding to the access mode you intend to establish. Access modes and passwords are discussed in the chapter *CMS Disks and CMS Disk Files*.

    - The **read password** allows you only to read files from the disk.

    - The **write password** allows you to read files from and write files to the disk.

    - The **multiple password** allows you to read files from and write files to the disk *even if* someone else has access to the disk.

    The access passwords for minidisks belonging to a VM can *only* be found out from that VM and by certain privileged system support per-sonnel.

    - To change a disk's access mode or access passwords, use one of the commands discussed in the section *Changing a Disk's Ac-cess Mode or Access Passwords*.

    - To find out what your disk access passwords are, use one of the commands discussed in the section *Obtaining Your Disk Access Passwords*.

Command Format:

LINK   userid vaddr1 vaddr2 [accmode]

where **userid**   is the userid of the owner of the minidisk. If you are the owner of the minidisk, use an * for the userid.

     vaddr1   is the virtual address given to the minidisk by the *owner's* VM.

     vaddr2   is the virtual address given to the minidisk by *your* VM. This can be any whole number from one to three digits that you are not already using as a virtual address.

     accmode   is the access mode. No link is established if you only specify a primary access mode and another user has *any* kind of access to the disk. Thus, to ensure at least a read link, include an R as the secondary access mode. If the access mode is omitted, the one used depends upon whether the disk being linked belongs to you or to another user:

- If the disk belongs to another user, the access mode defaults to R.

- If the disk belongs to you, the access mode defaults to how you normally link to the disk when you log on.

System Messages:

After you enter the LINK command, CP displays a message requesting that you enter the password corresponding to the access mode you specified.

- If the access mode is omitted or specified as R or RR, CP requests the read password:

ENTER READ PASSWORD:

- If the access mode is specified as W or WR, CP requests the write password:

ENTER WRITE PASSWORD:

- If the access mode is specified as M, MR or MW, CP requests the multiple password:

ENTER MULT PASSWORD:

If you enter the password incorrectly or enter the wrong access mode for the password specified, the system displays the message:

Temporarily Linking Another User's Disk   § 377

      userid vaddr NOT LINKED; MODE OR PASSWORD INCORRECT

Example:

Suppose you want to establish a read LINK to the minidisk belonging to CHASE at virtual address 191 and have your VM assign it a virtual address of 91:

      LINK CHASE 191 91 RR

Identifying a Disk to CMS

ACCESS is a CMS command that associates a mode letter with the virtual address of a disk belonging to some VM.

If you have read/only access to a disk to which another user has read/write access, you should periodically re-issue the ACCESS command to obtain the current version of the master file directory.

Command Format:

ACcess	**vaddr2 mode[/ext] [fn [ft [fm]]] (NOPROF ERASE NODISK**

where	**vaddr2**	is the virtual address given to the minidisk by *your* VM.
	mode	is the letter that identifies the minidisk to CMS.
	ext	is the mode letter of a parent disk of which the disk being accessed is to be a logical read-only **extension**. If **ext** is specified, no blank characters should appear between the **mode** and the **/** nor between the **/** and **ext**.
	fn ft fm	specifies the filename(s), filetype(s) and filemode of a subset of the files on the disk to be accessed. Not specifying a subset of files is equivalent to specifying an * for the filename and an * for the filetype which means that all files on the disk will be included.
	NOPROF	prevents execution of the PROFILE EXEC when ACCESS is the first command entered after the IPL CMS command.
	ERASE	removes all files on the disk. This option is only valid for read/write disks.
	NODISK	accesses the system with no disks except the system disk (S-disk) and its extensions. This option is only valid if ACCESS is the first command entered after the IPL CMS command.

Examples:

- Suppose you've established a read LINK to the 191 disk belonging to the userid CHASE with your VM, giving it a virtual address of 91. Now you want to assign a mode letter of C to the virtual address 91:

ACCESS 91 C

From this point on during this session, the 191 disk belonging to CHASE is available as a C-disk.

- When one disk is accessed as an extension of another disk, the files on the accessed disk are searched after the files on the parent disk are searched when a command is searching for a specific file. This is useful when you want to control the order in which disks are searched. Suppose, as in the previous example, that you want to assign a mode letter of C to the virtual address 91 and make the C-disk an extension of your A-disk.

ACCESS 91 C/A

- If you log on and another user has access to one of your disks you may be given read/only access to the disk even though you normally access it as read/write. If necessary, use the CP MESSAGE command to request that the other user detach your disk. Once the other user has detached your disk, use the LINK command to establish your usual access mode. To LINK to your own 191 disk, enter:

LINK * 191 191
ACCESS 191 A

Notice that when you link to one of your own disks you can specify the userid as * and do not have to specify the access mode or the access password.

12.10 Automatically Linking Another User's Disk

If you must regularly access a disk belonging to another user to share programs and/or data, you should set up an automatic LINK to the user's disk.

The automatic LINK only identifies the disk to CP. The disk must also be identified to CMS using the ACCESS command. For convenience, put the ACCESS command in your PROFILE EXEC so that the command is automatically executed whenever you log on.

Using VMSECURE to Automatically Link Another User's Disk

Use Selection 7 in the VMSECURE User Selection Menu to permanently access another user's disk.

1. Enter the number 7 in the selection field.

2. Press ENTER to display the selection. VMSECURE will display a menu similar to that of Figure 12.4.

3. Enter the userid of the owner.

4. Enter the virtual address by which the owner links to the disk.

5. Enter the virtual address by which you will link to the disk.

6. Enter the access mode you intend to establish.

```
                         V M S E C U R E


         Selection 7:   Define a Link to Another User's Minidisk

                         Userid: CHASE


         ┌─────────────────────────────────────────────────────────┐
         │                                                           │
         │  Ownerid:          Address:          Link Address:        │
         │                                                           │
         │  Link Mode:        Password:                              │
         │                                                           │
         └─────────────────────────────────────────────────────────┘



         Note: Press PA2 key to reverse password display mode.


   PA1: Cancel    PF1: Help      PF3: Quit     PF10: Print    PF12: End
```

Figure 12.4 The VMSECURE menu for defining a link to another user's minidisk.

7. Enter the password corresponding to the access mode you specified.

8. When you have entered values in all the appropriate fields, do one of the following:

- End the selection and return to the User Selection Menu with ENTER.

- End the selection and return to CMS with PF12.

- Cancel the selection and return to the User Selection Menu with PF3.

- Cancel the selection and return to CMS with PA1.

• • •

LINK is a VMSECURE option that performs an automatic LINK to another user's disk when you log on.

Command Format:

VMSECURE MAInt Link ownerid ownervaddr yourvaddr accmode

where **ownerid**   is the userid of the owner of the disk.

       ownervaddr is the virtual address by which the owner links to the disk.

       yourvaddr is the virtual address by which you will link to the disk.

       accmode   is the access mode you intend to establish.

System Messages:

After requesting the logon password, VMSECURE requests the access password corresponding to access mode you specified.

Using DIRMAINT to Automatically Link Another User's Disk

LINK is a DIRMAINT option that performs an automatic link to another user's minidisk when you log on.

Command Format:

DIRMaint   **Link [userid vaddr1 vaddr2 accmode|DELETE]**

where **userid**   is the userid of the owner of the minidisk.

       vaddr1   is the virtual address given to the minidisk by the *owner's* VM.

vaddr2   is the virtual address given to the minidisk by *your* VM.

accmode   is the access mode. If omitted, it is assumed to be RR.

DELETE   removes an existing automatic link to another user's minidisk.

If you omit all operands after LINK, a menu is displayed in which you can enter them:

```
owner userid:            ===>
owner minidisk address:  ===>
your link address:       ===>
your link access mode:   ===> RR   (or DELETE to delete)
owner's access password  ===>
```

Do not press the ENTER key to move to the next area.

To move from field to field, use the TAB keys:

- Use the TAB FORWARD key to move to the *next* area.

- Use the TAB BACKWARD key to move to the *previous* area.

All fields are left blank except the one where you specify the access mode you intend to establish:

1.   Enter the userid of the owner.

2.   Enter the virtual address by which the owner links to the disk.

3.   Enter the virtual address by which you will link to the disk.

4.   Enter the access mode that you intend to establish.

5.   Enter the access password corresponding to the access mode specified.

6.   Once you've entered values in all appropriate fields, press ENTER.

12.11 Removing an Automatic Link to One of Your Disks

When others frequently use programs and/or data on a disk that belongs to you, it is convenient for them to perform an automatic link to your disk when they log on. The time may arise, however, when it is no longer appropriate for one or more users to have access to your disk. When this is the case, use one of the commands described in this section to remove other user's automatic links to one of your disks.

Be aware that another user can still make a link if he knows your disk access passwords. If the disk access passwords are known to the user whose automatic link you've removed, you should also change your disk access passwords.

Using VMSECURE to Remove Another User's Automatic Link

Use Selection 8 in the VMSECURE User Selection Menu to review and/or remove automatic links made by other users to one of your disks.

1. Enter the number 8 in the selection field.

2. If the virtual address of the disk is not 191, enter the virtual address in the next field.

3. Press ENTER to display the selection. VMSECURE will display a menu similar to that of Figure 12.5.

```
                        V M S E C U R E

       Selection 8:   Review/Remove Links by Other Users

             Userid: CHASE              Minidisk: 191

        Userid    Vaddr        Userid    Vaddr         Userid    Vaddr




   Note: To remove another user's link to your minidisk, clear the
         corresponding field and press the ENTER key.

   PA1: Cancel    PF1: Help      PF3: Quit     PF10: Print     PF12: End
```

Figure 12.5 The VMSECURE menu for reviewing and/or removing automatic links by other users.

4. To remove another user's link, position the cursor on the line of the user to be removed and clear the corresponding field using the ERASE EOF key.

5. When you have entered values in all the appropriate fields, do one of the following:

    •   End the selection and return to the User Selection Menu with EN-TER.

    •   End the selection and return to CMS with PF12.

    •   Cancel the selection and return to the User Selection Menu with PF3.

    •   Cancel the selection and return to CMS with PA1.

• • •

RLINK is a VMSECURE option that reviews and/or removes an automatic link by another user to one of your disks.

Command Format:

    VMSECURE MAInt RLink vaddr

where **vaddr**   is the virtual address of the disk.

System Messages:

After requesting the logon password, VMSECURE displays the message:

```
Reply YES or NO to the following prompts.
Terminate Prompting by replying 'END'.
Remove link 'userid' 'vaddr'?
```

Using DIRMAINT to Remove Another User's Automatic Link

DLINK is a DIRMAINT option that removes an automatic link made by another user to one of your minidisks.

Command Format:

    DIRMaint   **DLink userid vaddr mode**

where **userid**   is the userid that makes the automatic link. Specify an *
    to remove all userids.

vaddr   is the virtual address at which your VM links the disk.

mode   is the mode with which the other user accesses the disk. Specify an * for mode to remove all modes.

12.12 Removing a Temporary Link to a Minidisk

Once you've finished using another user's minidisk and you want to remove it, both CP and CMS must be informed. Just as two commands are necessary to attach another user's minidisk, two commands are necessary to remove another user's minidisk from your VM:

- DETACH informs CP by removing the association between the virtual address and the disk.

- RELEASE informs CMS by removing the association between the virtual address and the mode letter.

Using DETACH to Inform CP

DETACH is the CP command that removes the association between a virtual address belonging to your VM from a virtual address belonging to another VM.

Command Format:

> **DETach**   **vaddr**

where **vaddr**   is the virtual address of the disk to be removed.

Using RELEASE to Inform CMS

RELEASE is the CMS command that removes the association between a mode letter and a virtual address.

Command Format:

> **RELease**   **mode|vaddr ([DET]**

where **mode**   is the mode letter of the disk to be removed.

       vaddr   is the virtual address of the disk to be removed. If a disk has been accessed with more than one mode letter, using the virtual address will remove all mode letters.

       DET   invokes the CP DETACH command.

Example:

Suppose you've LINKed and ACCESSed a disk belonging to the userid CHASE giving it a virtual address of 91 and a mode letter of C. To remove the disk from your VM:

```
RELEASE C
```

DETACH 91

Or, for convenience, you can issue the RELEASE command with the DETACH command as an option:

RELEASE C (DET

12.13 Removing an Automatic Link to a Minidisk

If you've set up an automatic link to another user's disk, you can remove it using one of the commands in this section.

Using VMSECURE to Remove an Automatic Link

Use Selection 10 in the VMSECURE User Selection Menu to permanently remove a link to another user's disk.

1. Enter the number 10 in the selection field.

2. Enter the virtual address with which you link to the disk in the next field.

3. Press ENTER to display the selection. VMSECURE will display a menu similar to that of Figure 12.6.

4. If you wish to delete the disk, enter YES. Otherwise, enter NO.

5. When you have entered values in all the appropriate fields, do one of the following:

   - End the selection and return to the User Selection Menu with ENTER.

   - End the selection and return to CMS with PF12.

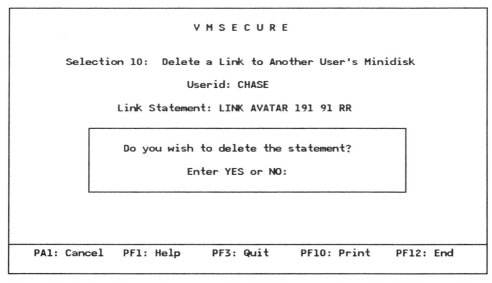

Figure 12.6 The VMSECURE menu for deleting an automatic link to another users' minidisk.

- Cancel the selection and return to the User Selection Menu with PF3.

- Cancel the selection and return to CMS with PA1.

● ● ●

DELETE is a VMSECURE option that removes an automatic link to another user's disk.

Command Format:

VMSECURE MAInt Delete vaddr

where **vaddr**   is the virtual address of the disk.

Using DIRMAINT to Remove an Automatic Link

LINK is a DIRMAINT option that removes an automatic link to another user's disk. This option is discussed in the section *Permanently Accessing Another User's Disk*.

12.14 Disconnecting the Terminal from Your VM

Using the LOGOFF command to leave the system has two consequences:

- Your VM ceases to run.

- Your terminal is disconnected from your VM.

There are two situations in which it is convenient for you to be able to *disconnect* your terminal from your VM and let your VM continue to run:

- If you have specially configured your VM and want to preserve that configuration until the next time you log on.

- If you enter a command that requires a long time to complete.

Preserving the Configuration of Your VM Until Your Next Logon

When you use the LOGOFF command to leave the system, any changes made to the configuration of your VM, such as a change in memory size or the addition of a minidisk, that are not made permanent in the CP directory, are lost.

DISCONN is a CP command that is useful if you have specially configured your VM and want to preserve that configuration until the next time you log onto the system but now want to leave the system. DISCONN removes the connection between your terminal and your VM, leaving your VM running in a **disconnected state**. When you log onto the system at a later time, the connection between the terminal and your VM is reestablished and your VM is configured just as it was when you left the system with the DISCONN command.

The only disadvantage in using DISCONN to leave the system is that your VM is still charged for connect time while it is in the disconnected state. So, whether DISCONN is worth the cost of connect time depends on how costly or inconvenient it is to reconfigure your VM in the desired fashion.

Command Format:

      DISCONN   **[HOld]**

where **HOld**   holds the connection to the system.

Running a Program While Your VM is Disconnected

If you enter a command that requires a long time to complete, you may wish to log onto another userid, if you have one, and work while the command on your primary userid completes. The DISCONN command can also be used to disconnect your terminal from your VM while it continues to run so you can use the terminal to log onto another userid.

Command Format:

#CP DISCONN   [HOld]

where **#CP**   executes the DISCONN command *immediately* regardless
of what your VM is doing.

HOld   holds the connection to the system.

System Messages:

The system responds to the DISCONN command by displaying a message
similar to the one displayed when you use the LOGOFF command.

Message Format:

DISCONNECT AT time zone weekday date

Logging Onto Your Disconnected VM the Next Time

When you log onto the system at a later time, your VM is placed in the CP
environment, as indicated by the status message:

CP READ

The system displays a message indicating the time and date that you are
logging onto the system.

Message Format:

RECONNECTED AT time zone weekday date

Furthermore, the system suspends the execution of any program that was
running while your VM was in the disconnected state.

BEGIN is a CP command that you should enter as your first command so that:

- Your VM resumes running any program that was running in the disconnected state but suspended when you logged on again.

- Your VM remains configured just as it was when you left the system
before. All disks, both permanent and temporary, are still there.

Command Format:

Begin

Chapter 13
Virtual Devices and Spooling

Introduction

When the use of an input or output device is restricted to a single computer user, that device is said to be a **dedicated device**. On a multi-user system such as VM/CMS, it is more convenient for users to be able to *share* certain devices such as card readers, card punches and printers. Thus, rather than dedicate a real device to any one user, VM/CMS creates **virtual devices** for each user in which the output from an output device is stored in a file on an auxiliary disk until it is processed by the *real* input or output device. This process of providing a **buffered interface** between the many virtual devices and the few real devices is known as **spooling** and the files created by this process are known as **spool files**. When a spool file is created, it is assigned an identifying number between 1 and 9900, known as the file's **spoolid**, that identifies the file.

Virtual Addresses: How Virtual Devices are Known to CP

When VM/CMS creates a virtual device, it defines the virtual device to exist at a virtual address indicated by a hexadecimal number:

- The virtual console is at 009.[1]

- The virtual reader is at 00C.

- The virtual punch is at 00D.

- The virtual printer is at 00E.

---

[1] On some systems, the virtual console is at 01F.

13.1 Characteristics of Virtual Devices

When VM/CMS creates your VM, it defines your virtual devices to have these characteristics:

- Each virtual output device has a destination.

- Each output device assigns a class to spool files.

- Each output device produces a specific number of copies.

- Each output device labels the output it produces with a distribution code.

- Spool files are either released to the real output device or held in the virtual output device.

- Spool files sent to a real output device are output either separately or as one continuous file.

Obtaining the Characteristics of Virtual Devices

Use the CP QUERY command to obtain the characteristics of all your virtual devices or of a specific virtual device.

Command Format:

Query   UR|vaddr

where **UR**   displays the characteristics of all **Unit Record (UR)** devices.[2]

vaddr   displays the characteristics of the virtual device at this virtual address.

Example:

Suppose you want to determine the characteristics of your virtual printer:

        QUERY E

In response, the system displays:

```
PRT 00E CL A  NOCONT NOHOLD COPY 001   READY FORM STANDARD
    00E FOR CHASE     DIST 36____36  FLASHC 000
    00E FLASH         CHAR       MDFY       0 FCB
```

---

[2] Printers, punches and readers are sometimes referred to as unit record devices because they operate on a single record at a time.

- CL A indicates the class is A.

- NOCONT indicates that files are to be output separately rather than as one continuous file.

- NOHOLD indicates that files are released to the real device rather than being held in the virtual device.

- COPY 001 indicates that one copy of each file is produced.

- FOR CHASE indicates that the file is being output for the userid CHASE.

- DIST 36___36 indicates that 36 is the distribution code used to file the output.

Changing Characteristics of Virtual Devices

SPOOL is a CP command that changes the characteristics of a virtual device. Use this command to change these characteristics of a device:

- The destination of an output device.

- The class of a device.

- The number of copies an output device produces.

- Whether a device processes files separately or together.

- Whether files are held in a virtual device or released to the real device.

13.2 Characteristics of Spool Files

Each spool file is assigned these characteristics:

- The origin of the file.

- A spoolid.

- The class of the virtual output device that sent the file.

- The type of virtual device that sent the file.

- The number of copies to be produced.

- The date and time the file was created.

- A filename and filetype.

- A label known as the distribution code.

- Whether the file is to be held in the virtual output device or released to the real output device.

Obtaining the Characteristics of Spool Files

Use the CP QUERY command to obtain the characteristics of spool files in a virtual device.

Command Format:

    Query   **device [ALL]**

where **device**   is the name (**PRINTER, PUNCH** or **READER**) of a virtual device.

    ALL   requests additional information.

Example:

Suppose you want to determine the characteristics of the files in your virtual reader:

    QUERY RDR ALL

The system displays information resembling this:

```
ORIGINID FILE CLASS RECORDS  CPY HOLD DATE  TIME     NAME    TYPE DIST
AVATAR   4587 A PUN 00000023 001 NONE 06/30 17:13:55 AVATAR NOTE 36____36
```

- AVATAR is the userid where the file originated.

- 4587 is the spoolid.

396 § Virtual Devices and Spooling

- A is the class.

- PUN (punch) is the type of device that sent the file.

- 23 is the number of logical records in the file.

- 001 is the number of copies.

- NONE indicates there is no hold on the file.

- 06/30 is the date the file was created.

- 17:13:55 is the time the file was created.

- AVATAR is the file's filename.

- NOTE is the file's filetype.

- 36 is the distribution code.

Changing Characteristics of Spool Files

CHANGE is a CP command that changes the characteristics of either individual spool files or of a class of spool files. Use this command to change these characteristics of individual spool files or a class of spool files:

- The class assigned to a file.

- The number of copies of a file to be produced.

- Whether a file is held in a virtual device or released to the real device.

- The filename and/or filetype.

13.3 The Destination of a Virtual Output Device

The destination of each virtual output device is defined when you log on. The destination of a virtual output device can be re-defined at any time, however, to be the userid of another VM.

SPOOL can be used to define the userid of another VM as the destination of files sent from a virtual output device.[3]

Command Format:

> SPool   device [TO] userid

where **device**   is the output device (**PRINTER** or **PUNCH**) whose destination is being changed.

      userid   is the destination of the output device. Use an * to make your userid the destination.

System Messages:

For each file sent to a virtual output device, CP displays the message:

> device FILE spoolid   TO   userid   COPY 001   NOHOLD

Example:

Suppose you want to send several files to another user whose userid is CHASE.

1. Make the userid CHASE the destination of your virtual printer:

   SPOOL PRINT TO CHASE

2. Use the PRINT command with each of the files to send them to CHASE's virtual reader:

   PRINT FILE1 DATA

---

[3] The SENDFILE command, discussed in the chapter *Communicating with Other Computer Users*, is usually more convenient to send a file to another user.

13.4 The Class of a Virtual Device

The class of a virtual device is indicated by a single character that can be a letter from A to Z or a digit from 0 to 9. Whenever you send a file to an output device, the current class of the output device is assigned to that file. Normally, all of your virtual devices are assigned a class of A.

The class of a virtual device becomes useful if you want to logically group files in a device and process all files in the same class in the same way. For example, the class of an output device can determine the destination of that device.

Changing the Class of a Virtual Device

CLASS is an option on the SPOOL command that changes the class of a virtual device.

Command Format:

> **SPool**   **device CLass c**

where **device**   is the name (**PRINTER, PUNCH** or **READER**) of the virtual device.

> **c**   is the class to be assigned to the device.

Changing the Class of Individual Spool Files

CLASS is an option on the CHANGE command that changes the class of individual spool files or of a class of spool files.

Command Format:

> **CHange**   **device   spoolids|Class c1   Class c2**

where **device**   is the virtual device (**PRINTER, PUNCH** or **READER**) the spool file is in.

> **spoolids**   are the spoolids of the spool files to be changed.

> **c**   is the class to be assigned to the spool files.

13.5 Processing Files Separately or as One Continuous File

CONT and **NOCONT** are options on the SPOOL command that control whether the files in a virtual device are processed separately or as one continuous file.

Command Format:

SPool   device **CONt**|*NOCont*

where **device**   is the name of a virtual device (**PRINTER, PUNCH** or **READER**).

CONt   processes spool files as one continuous file.

NOCont   processes spool files separately.

Example:

Normally, each file sent to the printer is preceded by a header page and followed by a trailer page. If you are going to print several files, you can save paper by using the CONT option to eliminate the need for header and trailer pages for each file.

```
SPOOL  PRINT  CONT
```

When you've sent the last file, restore the printer to its original condition:

```
SPOOL  PRINT  NOCONT
```

13.6 The Number of Copies a Real Output Device Produces

The number of copies of a file that are produced when the file reaches a real output device is normally defined to be one. You can, however, produce as many as you like.

Changing the Number of Copies a Real Output Device Produces

COPY is an option on the SPOOL command that specifies the number of copies that a virtual output device produces.

Command Format:

> **SPool**   device **Copy** n

where **device**   is the name of the virtual output device (**PRINTER** or **PUNCH**).

> **n**   is the number of copies to be produced.

Example:

If you print several copies of a file, you might also want to use the CONT option on the SPOOL command to output the files as one continuous file to avoid having each file preceded and followed by unnecessary paper. Suppose you must print 10 copies of a file.

1. Make the output from your virtual printer continuous:

    SPOOL PRINT CONT

2. Specify the number of copies that your virtual printer is to produce:

    SPOOL PRINT COPY 10

3. Enter the PRINT command for the file to be printed:

    PRINT FN FT

4. Restore the characteristics of your virtual printer to their original condition:

    SPOOL PRINT NOCONT COPY 1

Changing the Number of Copies of Individual Spool Files

COPY is an option on the CHANGE command that specifies the number of copies that are produced of individual spool files or of a class of spool files.

Command Format:

CHange   **device spoolids|Class c COpy n**

where **device**   is the name of a virtual output device (**PRINTER** or **PUNCH**).

     spoolids   are the spoolids of the files to be changed. Use **ALL** to change all files in the device.

     Class   changes class **c** spool files.

     COpy   changes the number of copies to be produced to be **n**.

13.7 Holding and Releasing Spool Files to a Real Device

Putting a *hold* on files sent to a virtual output device can be useful if you should decide later that some of those files shouldn't go the real output device. Files with a hold on them can be removed from a virtual device with the PURGE command, discussed later in this chapter.

Changing the HOLD/NOHOLD Status of a Device

HOLD and **NOHOLD** are options on the SPOOL command that control whether the spool files in a virtual device are released to a real device or kept in the virtual device.

Command Format:

SPool	device **HOld**|*NOHold*
where **device**	is the name of a virtual device (**PRINTER, PUNCH** or **READER**).
HOld	holds spool files in the virtual device.
NOHold	releases spool files to the real device.

Changing the HOLD/NOHOLD Status of Individual Spool Files

HOLD and **NOHOLD** are options on the CHANGE command that control whether individual spool files or a class of spool files are released to a real device or kept in a virtual device.

Command Format:

CHange	device **spoolids**|**Class c HOld**|**NOHold**
where **device**	is the name of a virtual device (**PRINTER, PUNCH** or **READER**).
spoolids	are the spoolids of the files to be changed. Use **ALL** to change all files in the device.
Class	changes class **c** spool files.
HOld	holds the spool files in the virtual device.
NOHold	releases the spool files to the real device.

Example:

Suppose you want 10 copies of a file being held in your virtual printer with a spoolid of 1357.

    1.   Change the number of copies to be produced:

      CHANGE PRT 1357 COPY 10

    2.   Remove the hold on the file so it can go to the real printer:

      CHANGE PRT 1357 NOHOLD

13.8 Transferring Spool Files between Virtual Devices

TRANSFER is a CP command that transfers spool files from one virtual device to another. This command will:

- Transfer a file from one of your virtual output devices to your virtual reader.

- Transfer a file from your virtual reader to your virtual output device of the same type that sent the file to your reader.

- Transfer a file that you sent to another user's virtual device from that virtual device to your virtual reader.

- Transfer a file in one of your virtual devices to a virtual device belonging to another user.

The only spool files that can be transferred are those still in a virtual device. The only spool files you can transfer from another user's virtual devices are those that you sent.

Command Format:

| TRANsfer | [fromdevice] spoolids\|CLass c [From\|To] userid [todevice] |

where **fromdevice** is the name of the virtual device (**PRINTER, PUNCH** or **READER**) from which the files are to be transferred. If this device is omitted, it is assumed to be **READER**.

spoolids are the spoolids of the spool files to be transferred. Use **ALL** to transfer all spool files.

CLass transfers class **c** spool files.

To transfers the spool files to the user **userid**. Use an * for **userid** to transfer the files to yourself.

From transfers the spool files from the user **userid**. Use **ALL** for **userid** to transfer files from all users.

todevice is the name of the virtual device (**PRINTER, PUNCH** or **READER**) to which the files are to be transferred. If this device is omitted, it is assumed to be **READER**.

System Messages:

After you enter the TRANSFER command, the system displays a message indicating the number of files transferred:

```
nn  FILES  TRANSFERRED
```

Examples:

- Suppose you've sent a number of files to the userid CHASE that you now want to retrieve:

  TRANSFER ALL FROM CHASE

- Suppose you have a number of files in your virtual printer that you would like transferred to your reader:

  TRANSFER PRINTER ALL TO *

- Suppose you have a file whose spoolid is 1234 in your virtual reader and want to send the file to the user AVATAR. You could use the RECEIVE command to load the file onto disk and then use the SENDFILE command to send the file. A simpler solution, however, is to use TRANSFER:

  TRANSFER 1234 TO AVATAR

13.9 Removing Files from a Virtual Device

PURGE is a CP command that removes spool files from your virtual devices that haven't yet been processed by a real device. This command is useful for removing files from your virtual reader which you do not want to receive and files from a virtual output device that you do not want to go to the real output device as in the case where you used the HOLD option on a file.

Command Format:

> **PURge**   device [ALL|spoolids|CLass c]

where **device**   is the virtual device (**PRINTER, PUNCH** or **READER**) from which the spool file is to be purged. Use **ALL** to purge all reader, printer and punch spool files. If **ALL** is specified, all other operands are ignored. If all operands after the device are omitted, all spool files on the device are purged.

> **ALL**   purges all spool files from the device.

> **spoolids**   are the spoolids of the spool files to be purged. Use **ALL** for spoolid to purge all files from a device.

> **CLass**   purges class **c** spool files. This option can be specified more than once.

System Messages:

After you enter the PURGE command, the system displays a message indicating the number of files purged:

>   nn   FILES   PURGED

Examples:

- Suppose there is a file in your reader with a spoolid of 1234 that you must remove:

>   PURGE   RDR   1234

- Suppose you must remove all class A files from your virtual punch:

>   PURGE   PUNCH   CLASS   A

- Suppose must remove all files from your virtual reader. You could use the DISCARD command in RDRLIST for each of the files. If the number of files is large, however, using PURGE is more efficient:

>   PURGE   READER

Chapter 14
Customizing the CP/CMS Environments

Introduction

When you log onto VM/CMS, the system defines the characteristics of the CP and CMS environments based on the normal assignments of three commands:

- CP SET

- CMS SET

- CP TERMINAL

This chapter is a discussion of these commands and how you can use them to modify the CP and CMS environments so that they better suit your needs and preferences. The final section is concerned with how you can use your PROFILE EXEC to modify the CP and CMS environments automatically whenever you log onto the system.

While this chapter is intended primarily for those who need to modify the normal CP and CMS environments, these topics are of general interest:

- Creating new commands with Execs.

- Assigning commands to PF keys.

- Defining synonyms and abbreviations.

- Changing command defaults.

14.1 The CP SET Command

The **CP SET** command controls these kinds of VM functions:

- The use of line editing symbols.

- The kinds of CP messages displayed on the terminal.

- The assignment of commands to PF keys.

This chapter discusses some of the more useful CP SET functions. Use the HELP facility to obtain a complete list of the functions and what they do:

```
HELP CP SET
```

Obtaining the Assignments of CP SET Functions

The **CP QUERY** command determines the current settings of *all* the CP SET functions.

Command Format:

> **Query   Set**

Example:

When the QUERY SET command is executed, the system normally displays this:

```
MSG ON   , WNG ON   , EMSG ON   , ACNT ON , RUN OFF
LINEDIT ON , TIMER ON   , ISAM OFF, ECMODE OFF
ASSIST ON SVC    NOTMR, PAGEX OFF, AUTOPOLL OFF
IMSG ON   , SMSG OFF , AFFINITY NONE    , NOTRAN OFF
VMSAVE OFF, 370E OFF
STBYPASS OFF    , STMULTI 03/00 00/000
MIH OFF , VMCONIO OFF , CPCONIO OFF
```

Changing the Assignment of a CP SET Function

The assignment of a CP SET function can be changed at any time. Most CP SET functions are either engaged or disengaged and, therefore, have the general format:

> **SET   function   ON|OFF**

where **function**   is the name of the function.

> **ON**   engages the function.

410 § Customizing the CP/CMS Environments

OFF   disengages the function.

Example:

MSG is a function that controls whether you receive messages sent by other users with the MESSAGE or TELL commands. Normally, MSG is set to ON, which means that your VM receives messages. Suppose you want to stop the transmission of messages:

    SET MSG OFF

14.2 The CMS SET Command

The **CMS SET** command controls these kinds of VM functions:

- Command interpretation and execution.

- The use of synonyms and abbreviations for commands.

- How CMS messages are displayed on the terminal.

This chapter discusses some of the more useful CMS SET functions. Use the HELP facility to obtain a complete list of the functions and what they do:

        HELP CMS SET

Obtaining the Assignment of a CMS SET Function.

The **CMS QUERY** command determines the current assignment of a specific CMS SET function.

Command Format:

        Query   **function**

where **function**   is the name of the function whose current assignment is to be displayed.

Example:

RDYMSG is a function that controls whether the ready message is displayed in a long or short form. Normally, the long form is displayed. Suppose you want to determine the present setting of this function:

        QUERY RDYMSG

- If the RDYMSG function is set to display the long form, the system displays:

        RDYMSG   =   LMSG

- If the RDYMSG function is set to display the short form, the system displays:

        RDYMSG   =   SMSG

Changing the Assignment of a CMS SET Function

The assignment of a CMS SET function can be changed at any time. Most CMS SET functions are either engaged or disengaged and, therefore, have the general format:

SET   function   ON|OFF

where **function**   is the name of the function.

ON   engages the function.

OFF   disengages the function.

Example:

Suppose you want to change the form of the ready message from long to short:

SET RDYMSG SMSG

14.3 The CP TERMINAL Command

The **CP TERMINAL** command controls these functions of your virtual console:

- How information input to the terminal is interpreted.

- How information output from the terminal is displayed.

This chapter discusses some of the more useful CP TERMINAL functions. Use the HELP facility to obtain a complete list of the functions and what they do:

```
HELP CP TERMINAL
```

Obtaining the Assignments of the CP TERMINAL Command

Use the **CP QUERY** command to determine the current settings of all the CP TERMINAL functions.

Command Format:

> **Query**   **TERMinal**

Example:

When the QUERY TERMINAL command is executed, the system normally displays this:

```
LINEND  # , LINEDEL  ¢ , CHARDEL  @ , ESCAPE  " , TABCHAR ON
LINESIZE 080, ATTN OFF, APL OFF, TEXT OFF, MODE VM, HILIGHT OFF
CONMODE 3215, BREAKIN   IMMED , BRKKEY PA1 , SCRNSAVE OFF
```

Changing the Assignment of a CP TERMINAL Function

The assignment of a CP TERMINAL function can be changed at any time. Many CP TERMINAL functions are either engaged, disengaged or specify a new character to perform the function and, therefore, have the general format:

> **TERMinal**   **function   ON|OFF|char**

where **function**	is the name of the function.
ON	engages the function.
OFF	disengages the function.
char	is the character defined to perform the function, if necessary. If a character is specified, the function is engaged.

Notice that the TERMINAL command separates the *definition* of a character to perform a function from the *implementation* of the function. What this means is that a character defined to perform a TERMINAL function will do so only if the function is engaged.

Examples:

- The # character normally represents the logical line end. Suppose you want to turn off the logical line end function:

  ```
  TERMINAL LINEND OFF
  ```

  After that, the # character would no longer be interpreted as a logical line end even though it is still defined to be the logical line end character.

- Suppose you want to define a period to be the logical line end:

  ```
  TERMINAL LINEND .
  ```

14.4 Creating New Commands with Execs

An Exec is a file that contains a sequence of commands. The commands can be CP commands, CMS commands, Exec program statements and other Execs. An Exec is an executable file. When an Exec is run, the commands in it are executed in the order they occur in the file unless the flow of control is changed by an Exec control statement. Many of the commands you use on CMS are, in fact, Execs. FILELIST and SENDFILE are both Execs. Execs become useful if you must frequently perform a task in which you execute the same sequence of commands each time. You can automate the task by putting the commands into an Exec. Each time you want to perform the task, you run the Exec. Execs also allow you to make the command operands into variables that can change from one execution to another. These are prime candidates for Execs:

- Any sequence of commands executed more than once.

- Any sequence of commands executed repetitively.

- Any sequence of commands executed as part of another procedure.

- Any sequence of commands in which the arguments that commands take change from one execution to another.

The PROFILE EXEC, discussed in the chapter *Becoming Acquainted with VM/CMS* and later in this chapter, is an example of an Exec. It is special in that it is executed whenever the IPL CMS command is executed.

When an Exec is run, the commands in it are processed directly by a command interpreter, in contrast to other language processors that translate commands into machine code.

This text does not discuss the components of the Exec languages and the writing of Execs as such. Those topics are covered in another text, *VM/CMS: A Guide to Programming and Applications*.

Creating an Exec

You create an Exec using a text editor such as XEDIT. An Exec can have any legitimate CMS filename but it *must* have a filetype of EXEC.

Running an Exec

Under normal circumstances, to run an Exec in the CMS environment:

1. Type the Exec's filename followed by any arguments to be passed to the Exec.

2. Press ENTER.

Different Generations of Execs

VM/CMS supports three generations of Exec processors:

- The **REXX** (Restructured Extended Executor) processor is the newest and most sophisticated.

- The **EXEC2** processor was the second generation.

- The **EXEC** processor was the first generation.

The Exec processor that is invoked when an Exec is run depends on the contents of the first record of the Exec file:

- The REXX processor is invoked if the first record of the Exec begins with a REXX comment, which begins with a /* and ends with a */:

  ```
  /* this is a comment */
  ```

- The EXEC2 processor is invoked if the first record of the Exec begins with the EXEC2 command:

  ```
  &TRACE
  ```

- The EXEC processor is invoked if the first record of the Exec does not begin with a REXX comment or &TRACE.

14.5 Defining Synonyms and Abbreviations for Commands

Command names and abbreviations of your choosing can be used either in place of or in addition to the regular CP and CMS command names and their abbreviations. Defining synonyms and abbreviations is a two-step process:

1.   Create a file containing a table of synonyms.

2.   Implement the synonyms using the SYNONYM command.

The Synonym Table

The file containing the table of synonyms can have any legitimate CMS filename and can reside on any disk to which you have access, but it *must* have these characteristics:[1]

- A filetype of SYNONYM.

- A fixed record format.

- A record length of 80.

Each record in the file defines a different synonym in the format:

       command   **synonym [n]**

where **command**   is the name of the command for which the synonym is to be recognized.

      synonym   is the synonym.

      n   is the minimum number of characters that must be specified for the synonym to be recognized. If the number of characters is omitted, the whole synonym must be specified.

Example:

Suppose you create a file with a filename of XMPL and a filetype of SYNONYM and put the following lines into this file:

```
ERASE     ER        2
FILELIST  FL        2
XEDIT     YEDIT     1
```

- The first line defines ER to be an abbreviation for ERASE.

---

[1]   If the file is made with the XEDIT editor, it will automatically have a fixed record format and a record length of 80.

- The second line defines FL to be a synonym for FILELIST with no abbreviation.

- The third line defines YEDIT to be a synonym for XEDIT and specifies that the synonym may be abbreviated as Y, YE, YED or YEDI.

Implementing the Synonyms

SYNONYM is used to either implement a table of synonyms and abbreviations or to display those currently in effect.

- If the command is executed with the filename of the file that contains the table of synonyms and abbreviations, those synonyms and abbreviations are put into effect.

- If the command is executed with no operands, those synonyms and abbreviations currently in effect are displayed.

Command Format:

SYNonym	[fn [SYNONYM [fm]]] ([STD|NOSTD] [CLEAR]

where	**fn**	is the filename of the file containing the synonym table.
	fm	is the filemode of the file containing the synonym table.
	STD	recognizes standard command abbreviations.
	NOSTD	recognizes only complete command names and abbreviations.
	CLEAR	removes from definition any table of synonyms previously implemented by the SYNONYM command.

Examples:

- Suppose you want to implement the synonyms in the file XMPL SYNONYM:

```
SYNONYM XMPL
```

- Suppose you want to determine which synonyms and abbreviations are currently in effect:

```
SYNONYM
```

14.6 Controlling Command Interpretation and Execution

Understanding this section requires a prior understanding of computing environments, Execs, program function keys and command search order. These topics are discussed in the chapter *Becoming Acquainted with VM/CMS*.

Assigning Commands to and Removing Them from PF Keys

PF is a function of the CP SET command that assigns a command to a PF key. Which PF keys are assigned commands depends on the environment you are in:

- In CP and CMS, PF keys are not normally assigned commands, but those that support your system may have done so for you.

- In FILELIST, HELP, NOTE, PEEK, RDRLIST, SENDFILE and XEDIT, PF1 through PF12 are assigned commands that are covered in the sections that discuss these commands.

Command Format:

SET	**PFn [IMMed|***DELAYED***] [command]**

where	**n**	(immediately after **PF**) is a number between 1 and 24.
	IMMed	executes the command immediately when the PF key is pressed. Omitting this option can be useful if you want to display that part of a command, such as the command name, that does not change from execution to execution and then type in one or more operands that do change from execution to execution.
	DELAYED	displays the command assigned to the PF key in the command input area but does not execute the command until the ENTER key is pressed.
	command	is the command assigned to the PF key. If the command is omitted, the command previously assigned to the PF key is removed.

Examples:

- Suppose you want to have FILELIST display a list of all files on your A-disk when you press PF2:

```
SET PF2 IMMED FILELIST
```

- Suppose you want to display the FILELIST command in the command input area when you press PF4:

```
SET PF4 FILELIST
```

Thereafter, whenever you press PF4, the FILELIST command is displayed with the cursor positioned after FILELIST so that you can type in the specific filenames, filetypes or filemodes you want to display.

Determining Which PF Keys are Assigned Commands

PF is also an option on the CP QUERY command that displays what command is assigned to a PF key.

Command Format:

> **Query**   **PF[n]**

where **n**   is the number of the PF key whose command assignment is displayed. If the number is omitted, the assignments of all PF keys are displayed.

Changing Default Values on Certain Commands

DEFAULTS is an Exec that changes default values on certain commands. This is a list of those commands and their alternative values. The normal default alternative appears in ***bold italics***:

FILEList	**Profile fn|*PROFFLST*** **Filelist|*Nofilelist***
Help	**DETail|*Brief*** **DEScript Format Parms Options NOTes Errors|*All*** **NOScreen|*Screen***
NOTE	**Profile fn|*PROFFLST*** **LONg|*Short*** **NOLog|*LOG*** **Ack|*NOAck*** **NONotebook|*NOTebook* fn|*ALL***
PEEK	**Profile fn|*PROFPEEK*** **FRom recnum|*1*** **FOr numrec|*200***
RDRList	**Profile fn|*PROFRLST***
RECEIVE	**NOLog|*Log*** **NEwdate|*Olddate*** **NOTebook fn|*ALL***
SENDFile	**NOLog|*Log*** **Ack|*NOAck***

When the DEFAULTS command is executed, a file is created on your A-disk called LASTING GLOBALV which contains a list of the current default values for each command under the control of DEFAULTS. Do not edit or change the LASTING GLOBALV file.

Command Format:

> **DEFAULTS**   **[*List*|Set command options...]**

where **List**   displays the current defaults values for the command specified. If no command is specified, default values for all commands are displayed.

      command   is one of the commands under the control of DEFAULTS.

      options   is one or more options associated with one of the commands under the control of DEFAULTS.

Examples:

- When you use PEEK to display a reader file, only the first 200 records are normally displayed. Suppose you would like to always display all records:

  ```
  DEFAULTS SET PEEK FOR *
  ```

- When you use NOTE to send a note, SENDFILE to send a file or RE-CEIVE to receive a note or file sent to you by another computer user, a record is normally made in the *userid NETLOG* file of the file that was sent or received. Suppose you do not want to keep such records in the *userid NETLOG* file:

  ```
  DEFAULTS SET NOTE NOLOG

  DEFAULTS SET SENDFILE NOLOG

  DEFAULTS SET RECEIVE NOLOG
  ```

- Suppose you want to display the current default values of all commands under the control of DEFAULTS:

  ```
  DEFAULTS LIST
  ```

Forcing CP to Execute a Command

CP is a CP command that either sends a command to CP to be executed or causes your VM to enter the CP environment. This command is useful if you want to force CP to execute a command with the same name as a CMS command or Exec.

Command Format:

> **CP**   **[command]**

where **command**   is the command to be executed by CP. If the command is omitted, you enter the CP environment. If you enter the CP environment, use the CP BEGIN command to return to the environment from which you entered CP.

Forcing CMS to Execute an Exec

EXEC is a CMS command that executes a command as an Exec. This command is useful if the IMPEX function of the CMS SET command is assigned to be OFF.

Command Format:

> **EXec**   **fn [args...]**

where **fn**   is the filename of the Exec to be executed.

       args   are any arguments to be passed to the Exec.

Example:

The FILELIST command is actually an Exec procedure. If the IMPEX function is assigned to be OFF, the FILELIST command would not be recognized as a command unless you preceded it with EXEC:

```
EXEC   FILELIST
```

Should CMS Send Unrecognized Commands to CP?

IMPCP is a function of the CMS SET command that controls whether a command not recognized by CMS is passed along to CP. Normally, commands not recognized by CMS are passed to CP.

Command Format:

> **SET**   **IMPCP ON|OFF**

where **ON**   passes commands on to CP.

       OFF   does not pass commands on to CP.

Example:

If IMPCP is set to OFF and CMS does not recognize a command, CMS displays the message:

Unknown CMS Command

Should Execs be Recognized as Commands?

IMPEX is a function of the CMS SET command that controls whether Execs are considered to be commands. Normally, Execs are considered to be commands.

Command Format:

SET	IMPEX ON|OFF

where **ON**   recognizes Execs to be commands.

OFF   does not recognize Execs to be commands.

Example:

The FILELIST command is actually an Exec procedure. If the IMPEX function is assigned to be OFF, the FILELIST command would not be recognized and the system would display the message:

Unknown CP/CMS Command

Should Abbreviations be Recognized?

ABBREV is a function of the CMS SET command that controls whether abbreviations for commands and Execs are recognized. Normally, abbreviations are recognized.

Command Format:

SET	ABBREV ON|OFF

where **ON**   recognizes abbreviations.

OFF   only recognizes the full command or Exec name.

Example:

FILEL is normally recognized to be an abbreviation for FILELIST. If the ABBREV function is assigned to be OFF, FILEL would not be recognized and the system would display the message:

Unknown CP/CMS Command

14.7 Controlling Terminal Input

This section describes commands that temporarily redefine line editing symbols. Procedures for permanently redefining line editing symbols are discussed in the chapter *Managing Your Virtual Machine*.

An understanding of this section requires a prior understanding of what line editing symbols are and what they do. These concepts are discussed in the section *Line Editing Symbols* in the chapter *Becoming Acquainted with VM/CMS*.

Defining a Logical Line End Symbol

LINEND is a function of the CP TERMINAL command that defines any character to be the logical line end symbol. Normally, the logical line end function is set to ON and the # character is defined to be the logical line end.

Command Format:

> **TERMinal   LINEND ON|OFF|char**

where **ON**   engages the logical line end function.

      OFF   disengages the logical line end function.

      char   is the character that performs the logical line end function. If a character is specified, the function is engaged.

Example:

You can assign two or more commands to be executed sequentially to a single PF key:

1. Turn off the LINEND function:

    ```
    TERMINAL LINEND OFF
    ```

2. Assign the commands to the PF key, separating each command from the next with a logical line end:

    ```
    SET PF2 IMMED QUERY DISK#QUERY DASD
    ```

3. Turn the LINEND function back on:

    ```
    TERMINAL LINEND ON
    ```

Defining a Logical Line Delete Symbol

LINEDEL is a function of the CP TERMINAL command that defines any character to be the logical line delete symbol. Normally, the logical line delete function is set to ON.

- On IBM display terminals, the character that represents the logical line delete is the cent character (¢).

- On ASCII terminals, the character that represents the logical line delete may be the backslash character (\).

Command Format:

      TERMinal   **LINEDel ON|OFF|char**

where **ON**   engages the logical line delete function.

       OFF   disengages the logical line delete function.

      char   is the character that performs the logical line delete function. If a character is specified, the function is engaged.

Defining a Logical Character Delete Symbol

CHARDEL is a function of the CP TERMINAL command that defines any character to be the logical character delete symbol. Normally, the logical character delete function is set to ON, with the @ character representing the logical character delete character.

Command Format:

      TERMinal   **CHardel ON|OFF|char**

where **ON**   engages the logical character delete function.

       OFF   disengages the logical character delete function.

      char   is the character that performs the logical character delete function. If a character is specified, the function is engaged.

Defining a Logical Escape Symbol

ESCAPE is a function of the CP TERMINAL command that defines any character to be the logical escape symbol. Normally, the logical escape function is set to ON, with the " character representing the logical escape symbol.

Command Format:

    TERMinal   **ESCAPE ON|OFF|char**

where **ON**   engages the logical character escape function.

      OFF   disengages the logical character escape function.

      char   is the character that performs the logical escape function. If a character is specified, the function is engaged.

Should Line Editing Functions be Used?

LINEDIT is a function of the CP SET command that controls whether *all* line editing functions are turned on or off. Normally, all line editing functions are turned on.

Command Format:

    SET   **LINEDIT ON|OFF**

where **ON**   engages line editing functions.

      OFF   disengages line editing functions.

Translating Characters Input from the Keyboard

INPUT is a function of the CMS SET command that defines some character to be translated to the hexadecimal code for another character when entered from the keyboard. This option is useful when a character to be entered from the keyboard is not available on your keyboard.

Command Format:

    SET   **INPUT [inchar outchar]**

where **inchar**   is the character used to represent **outchar**.

      outchar   is the hexadecimal code of the character to be translated. If both **inchar** and **outchar** are omitted, all characters are returned to their original translation.

Example:

The tab character has no corresponding key on the keyboard. You could enter tab characters from the keyboard, however, by translating a character that is on the keyboard, such as >, to the hexadecimal code for the tab character, which is 05:

```
SET   INPUT  >   05
```

14.8 Controlling Terminal Output

Understanding this section requires a prior understanding of what the different kinds of messages are. Messages sent by the CP MESSAGE and TELL commands are discussed in the chapter *Communicating with Other Computer Users*.

Controlling Messages from Other Users

MSG is a function on the CP SET command that controls whether your VM receives messages sent by the CP MESSAGE or CMS TELL commands. Normally, your VM receives messages.

Command Format:

	SET	MSG ON|OFF
where	**ON**	allows messages.
	OFF	rejects messages.

Controlling Messages from the System Operator

WNG is a function on the CP SET command that controls whether your VM receives warnings sent by the system operator. Normally, warnings are received.

Command Format:

	SET	WNG ON|OFF
where	**ON**	allows warnings.
	OFF	rejects warnings.

Controlling the Information Displayed When an Error Occurs

EMSG is a function of the CP SET command that controls which information is displayed when an error occurs. Normally, when an error occurs, a brief text message is displayed to describe the problem.

Command Format:

	SET	EMSG ON|OFF|CODE|TEXT
where	**ON**	displays both the error code and error text.
	OFF	suppresses the error message.

CODE   displays only the error code.

TEXT   displays only the error text.

Controlling the Form of the Ready Message

RDYMSG is a function of the CMS SET command that controls whether the ready message is displayed in a long or short form.

- The format of the long form is:

    Ready; T=s.mm/s.mm hh:mm:ss

- The format of the short form is:

    Ready;

Normally, the long form is displayed.

Command Format:

SET   RDYMSG LMSG|SMSG

where **LMSG**   displays the long form.

SMSG   displays the short form.

Controlling Whether Informational Messages are Displayed

IMSG is a function on the CP SET command that controls whether informational messages issued by the CP commands CHANGE, DEFINE, DETACH, IPL, ORDER and PURGE are displayed. Normally, the informational messages are displayed.

Command Format:

SET   IMSG ON|OFF

where **ON**   displays informational messages.

OFF   suppresses the display of informational messages.

Example:

Normally, when you use PURGE to remove files from a virtual device, CP displays a message indicating the number of files purged:

    0001 FILE PURGED

If IMSG is set to OFF, CP does not display this message.

430 § Customizing the CP/CMS Environments

Defining the Terminal Linesize

LINESIZE is a function of the CP TERMINAL command that controls the length of the lines output on the terminal. Normally, the maximum line length output on a display terminal is 80 columns. If a line is longer than 80 columns, it is split into two or more lines. This option is useful if you must print a file with records longer than 80 columns on a printer attached to your terminal.

Command Format:

> **TERMinal**   **LINESize nnn|OFF**

where **nnn**   is a number between 1 and 255 that specifies the maximum line length to be output on the terminal.

OFF   indicates that CP does not split a long line into two or more lines.

Example:

Suppose you have a file with a record length of 130 and a printer attached to your terminal capable of printing lines 130 columns wide.

1. To change the output line length to 130:

    TERMINAL LINESIZE 130

2. Use the TYPE command to display the file on the terminal and simultaneously print the file on the printer.

Translating Characters Output to the Screen

OUTPUT is a function of the CMS SET command that defines some character to be translated to the hexadecimal code for another character when displayed on the screen. This option is useful when a character to be displayed on the screen is not available on your keyboard.

Command Format:

> **SET**   **OUTPUT [inchar outchar]**

where **inchar**   is the hexadecimal code of the character to be translated.

outchar   is the character to be used to display **inchar**. If both **inchar** and **outchar** are omitted, all characters are returned to their original translation.

Controlling Terminal Output   § 431

14.9 Automatically Customizing the CP/CMS Environments

Any modification of the CP or CMS environment made by changing the assignments of the CP SET, CMS SET and CP TERMINAL commands only remain in effect until you log off the system. The next time you log on, the CP and CMS environments established are the *default* environments based on the *default* assignments of the CP SET, CMS SET and CP TERMINAL functions.

VM/CMS provides a convenient mechanism by which the CP and CMS environments are always customized in certain ways whenever you log onto the system. You can do this by adding the commands you use to customize the CP and CMS environments to a file with filename of PROFILE and a filetype of EXEC. Determine whether you already have a PROFILE EXEC. One may have been provided when your account was set up. If you have one, determine which generation of Exec it is written in by examining the first line of the file. If you add commands to your PROFILE EXEC, be sure that all commands in the file are written in the same generation of Exec. In an Exec, a CP command should be preceded by CP and the name of an Exec should be preceded by EXEC.

The PROFILE EXEC is special in that this Exec is automatically executed when you log on. Thus, you can always enter a CP/CMS environment that suits your needs and preferences by putting the commands that customize the environment into the PROFILE EXEC at the end of the file.

Example:

These lines might be added to the PROFILE EXEC:

```
CP SET PF3 IMMED LOG HO
SET RDYMSG SMSG
SYNONYM XMPL
EXEC DEFAULTS SET PEEK FOR *
```

Notice that:

- Line 1 assigns the LOGOUT command to PF3.

- Line 2 sets the ready message to the short form.

- Line 3 implements the table of synonyms in the file XMPL SYNONYM.

- Line 4 makes an entire file available when PEEK is being used.

Chapter 15
Diagnosing and Correcting Problems

Introduction

When you are using the system, problems are bound to occur for a number of reasons. Sometimes the fault lies with the hardware or software of the machine but more often than not the problem is due to something you did — or failed to do. Some of the more common problems include:

- A command is not recognized.

- A file cannot be found.

- A file already exists.

- A file cannot be written to or erased from a disk.

- A disk is full.

- A fileid is missing, incomplete or invalid.

- An operand is missing or invalid.

- An option is invalid or in conflict with another option.

- A parameter is invalid.

- The virtual storage capacity is exceeded.

- The terminal will only sound an alarm or not respond at all.

- The system malfunctions.

When one of these problems occurs, there is often a simple solution. The first thing you must do when a problem occurs is *diagnose* it — determine the nature of the problem. Once you've done this, you are then in a position to *correct* it.

All users, even the most sophisticated, make occasional mistakes. The number and nature of the mistakes made by novice users usually differ from those made by experienced users. New users make *more* mistakes than advanced users and new users make mistakes that are usually more conceptual in nature. Advanced users are more likely to make simple spelling mistakes, which are readily identified and corrected. Furthermore, a user becomes *advanced* partly because he has somehow succeeded in understanding the nature of the problem.

• • •

This chapter is primarily concerned with problems that are under your control, such as when you enter a command that cannot be executed for some reason. Little will be said about problems that occur when the hardware or software on the system malfunctions. Such problems are out of your control and should be reported as soon as possible to those people who maintain your system.

There are several kinds of mistakes you can make in entering a command. This chapter discusses:

- Some of the more common types of mistakes.

- *How* the system responds when you make them.

- *Why* the system responds the way it does.

- *What* you should do to redress the problem.

15.1 Diagnosing a Problem

If you enter a command that the system cannot execute, the system displays two sources of information that can be useful in determining why the command could not be executed:

- The Status Message

- System Messages

The Status Message

The status message is displayed in the lower right corner of the screen. This message indicates which environment your VM is in and what it is doing. The status message can be especially useful when you enter a command that is *unknown* to the system. The environment your VM is in determines:

- *Which* commands will be recognized.

- *How* commands should be entered to be recognized.

If a command is unknown to the system, you may be in the wrong environment to be using the command or may be entering the command incorrectly.

If you have forgotten what the different status messages are and what they mean or if you have forgotten what the different environments are and their significance for command recognition, you should review the sections on *The Areas of the Screen and Their Uses in CP and CMS* and *Environments in VM/CMS* in the chapter *Becoming Acquainted with VM/CMS*.

System Messages

System messages are displayed in response to the commands that you enter.

- If you enter a command correctly, the system message is limited to a ready message.

- If you enter a command that is incorrect in any way, the system message includes an error message and a ready message with a nonzero return code.

System messages are useful in diagnosing a problem when the command is recognized but cannot be executed for some reason, such as a missing or invalid operand. If the nature of the problem is not apparent from the message text, you can use the HELP facility for a more detailed explanation of the problem as well as the corrective action to be taken. System messages and how to use the HELP facility with error messages are discussed in the chapter *Becoming Acquainted with VM/CMS*.

Return Codes as Error Diagnostics

Rarely does a return code uniquely identify a problem. A return code of 28 from the CMS COPYFILE command can result from any of several unrelated reasons. Perhaps the only time a return code uniquely identifies a problem is when it is −3, which indicates that the command that generated the return code is unknown to the system.

15.2 Problems with Command Recognition

This section requires an understanding of what status messages are and what they mean and what the different environments are and their significance for command recognition. These topics are covered in the sections on *The Areas of the Screen and Their Uses in CP and CMS* and *Environments in VM/CMS* in the chapter *Becoming Acquainted with VM/CMS*. These messages indicate that the system does not recognize a command that you've entered:

    Unknown CP/CMS Command

    Unknown CMS Command

    Unknown CP Command

    No Such Subcommand

The first thing to do is to determine whether you've misspelled the name of the command, used an abbreviation or synonym that is either too short or just incorrect, entered a command name that simply does not exist on the system or lost access to the disk on which the command is stored.

Is the Command Spelled Correctly?

If you are unsure of the spelling of the command, use the HELP facility to display a menu of command names and try to recognize the command name from the menu.

Are You Using an Abbreviation?

If you are using an abbreviation, refer to the HELP file for the command to determine what the shortest allowable abbreviation is. Remember that HELP show the shortest allowable abbreviation as the capitalized portion of the command name.

Are You Using a Synonym?

If you are using a synonym and are unsure of what the actual synonym is, use the SYNONYM command to display both system-defined and user-defined synonyms:

    SYNONYM

Are You Unsure of the Command Name?

If you simply do not know the exact name of a particular command, use the HELP facility to display a menu of command names. The name of a command usually bears a strong resemblance to what the command does. Thus, if you

Problems with Command Recognition § 437

know that you want to make a copy of a file, you could browse through the menu of command names until you find a command whose name is COPYFILE and then have a look at the HELP file for COPYFILE and discover that it is just what you were looking for.

If the release of CMS you are using is Release 5 or later, use the TASKS component of the HELP menu, to display a menu of tasks and determine whether one of the tasks in the menu resembles what you want to do.

Are You in an Appropriate Environment?

If you determine that the command is valid, the next thing to do is to examine the status message to determine what environment your VM is in.

- In the CP environment, only CP commands are recognized. Any other commands result in the message:

  Unknown CP Command

  If the command you are trying to execute is a CMS command, an Exec or a module, return to the CMS environment and enter the command again. To return to CMS, enter:

  IPL   CMS

- In the CMS environment, CMS executes CMS commands and normally sends unrecognized commands to CP. If CP recognizes the command, it will attempt to execute it. If CP does not recognize the command, the system displays the message:

  Unknown CP/CMS Command

  If the IMPCP function of the CMS SET command is assigned to be OFF, however, CMS will not pass unrecognized commands to CP and un-recognized commands will result in the message:

  Unknown CMS Command

  If the command not being recognized is a CP command, be sure that the IMPCP function is assigned to be ON.

  If the IMPEX function of the CMS SET command is assigned to be OFF, Execs will not be recognized as commands. If the command not being recognized is an Exec, be sure that the IMPEX function is assigned to be ON.

- In the XEDIT environment, XEDIT executes XEDIT commands and normally sends unrecognized commands to CMS. If CMS recognizes the command, CMS executes it. If not, CMS sends it to CP. If CP does not recognize the command, XEDIT displays a message indicating that the command is not a CP, CMS or XEDIT command:

No such subcommand

If the IMPCMSCP function of the XEDIT SET command is assigned to be OFF, however, XEDIT will not pass unrecognized commands to CMS and unrecognized commands will also result in the message:

No such subcommand

Have You Lost Access to a Disk?

Many commands are stored in files on disk. If you haven't accessed the disk on which the file is stored or if you've lost access to the disk, the system will not recognize the command.

The file called PROFILE EXEC may normally provide you with access to disks with various commands and programs stored on them. If you modify the PROFILE EXEC or erase it, your VM may not be configured with access to these disks.

If you use the IPL CMS command to load CMS into virtual memory, any disk that you've accessed that is not a normal part of your VM configuration is released. You must access the disk again.

15.3 Problems with Record Length and Record Format

This section requires an understanding of record formats and record lengths. These topics are discussed in the chapter *CMS Disks and CMS Disk Files*.

Record Length Exceeds Allowable Maximum

Most printers are limited to printing 132 characters per line. If you use the PRINT command with a file whose record length is 133 or longer and whose filetype is not LISTING or LIST3800, the system displays a message indicating that the record length is longer than the maximum:

```
Record length exceeds allowable maximum.
```

- If the file has a record length of 133 and carriage control characters in column 1 but doesn't have a filetype of LISTING, use the CC option on the PRINT command.

- If the file has a record length of 133 or longer and you want to print the file, consider splitting the file into two or more parts, each of which has a record length short enough to print. The SPECS option on the COPYFILE command can be used to specify which columns in a file are to be copied.

Record Format and/or Record Length is Invalid

Many software products expect that the files they read as input have a specific record format and/or record length.

- If an input file is expected to have a fixed record format but does not, the system may display one of these error messages:

```
File 'fn ft fm' is not fixed length
```

```
Invalid record format
```

- If an input file is expected to have a variable record format but does not, the system may display one of these error messages:

```
File 'fn ft fm' is not variable record format
```

```
Invalid record format
```

- If an input file is expected to have a specific record format and/or record length but it does not, the system may display the message:

```
Open error code 'nn' on 'ddname'
```

Use the RECFM option on the COPYFILE command to change the record format from fixed to variable or variable to fixed, whichever is appropriate. Use the LRECL option on the COPYFILE command to change the record length to the appropriate length.

15.4 Problems with Files and Fileids

This section requires an understanding of CMS disk files and their character-istics. These topics are discussed in the chapter *CMS Disks and CMS Disk Files*.

A File Cannot be Found

If you specify the command name correctly but misspell any part of the fileid of a file that is to be manipulated, the system displays a message indicating that the file cannot be found:

```
File 'fn ft fm' not found
```

- Determine whether the filename and filetype are spelled correctly. If you are unsure of what the file is called, use FILELIST to display a list of files. Once you recognize the fileid of the file with which you want to work, either work with it in the FILELIST display or return to CMS and enter the command again, correctly specifying the fileid.

- Determine whether the filemode is correct. If you are unsure of what disk the file is stored on, use FILELIST to display a list of files, speci-fying an * for the filemode.

- Determine whether the disk on which the file is stored has been ac-cessed. If not, then access the disk.

- If the file is on a disk to which you have read/only access and the file has a mode number of 0, the file is not available to you. To make it available, you must establish read/write access to the disk.

Examples:

- Suppose you have a file called SPECIOUS DATA A and want to make a copy of the file, calling the copy BACKUP DATA A. You then enter the COPY command, specifying PRECIOUS as the filename instead of SPECIOUS:

```
COPY PRECIOUS DATA A BACKUP = =
```

The system displays the message:

```
DMSCPY002E INPUT file 'PRECIOUS DATA A' not found.
Ready(00028);
```

To obtain the HELP file for DMSCPY002E:

```
HELP DMS002E
```

- Suppose you have a file called SPECIOUS DATA A and want to rename the file, calling it BACKUP DATA A. You then enter the RENAME command, specifying PRECIOUS as the filename instead of SPECIOUS:

```
RENAME PRECIOUS DATA A BACKUP = =
```

The system displays the message:

```
DMSRNM002E File 'PRECIOUS DATA A' not found.
Ready(00028);
```

To obtain the HELP file for DMSRNM002E:

```
HELP DMS002E
```

- Suppose you want to erase SPECIOUS DATA but misspell the fileid:

```
ERASE PRECIOUS DATA
```

The system displays the message:

```
DMSERS002E File 'PRECIOUS DATA' not found.
Ready(00028);
```

To obtain the HELP file for DMSERS002E:

```
HELP DMS002E
```

- Notice that the message text is identical for the COPY, RENAME and ERASE commands and that the message identifier differs only in the module code, which means that the same HELP file applies to all three commands:

```
HELP DMS002E
```

This makes sense, since all three commands failed for the same reason.

A File Already Exists

Each file on a disk must have a *unique* fileid. Two different files on the same disk cannot have the same filename and filetype. When you use the COPYFILE or RENAME commands, CMS checks to determine whether a file being output has been given the same fileid as an existing file. If so, the system displays a message indicating that the file already exists:

```
File 'fn ft fm' already exists.
```

Problems with Files and Fileids § 443

This is done to protect you from inadvertently destroying the existing file.

- If you are using RENAME and no longer need the existing file, use ERASE to remove the existing file and then enter the RENAME command again.

- If you are using COPYFILE and no longer need the existing file, enter the COPYFILE command again and use the REPLACE option to replace the existing file.

- If you are using either COPYFILE or RENAME and don't want to replace the existing file, either rename the existing file or give the output file a different fileid.

Examples:

- Suppose that you have a file called SPECIOUS DATA A and want to make a copy, calling the copy BACKUP DATA A, but a file called BACKUP DATA A already exists.

```
COPY PRECIOUS DATA A BACKUP = =
```

The system responds with the message:

```
File 'BACKUP DATA A1' already exists - specify 'REPLACE'.
Ready(00028);
```

If you no longer need the file called BACKUP DATA A, use the RE-PLACE option on the COPY command:

```
COPY SPECIOUS DATA A BACKUP = = ( REPLACE
```

- There is no option on the RENAME command to replace an existing file. If you try to rename a file giving it the fileid of a file that already exists:

```
RENAME PRECIOUS DATA A BACKUP = =
```

The system responds with the message:

```
File 'BACKUP DATA A' already exists.
Ready(00028);
```

If you really want PRECIOUS DATA to be called BACKUP DATA and another file called BACKUP DATA already exists, either rename BACKUP DATA A or erase it. Then, rename PRECIOUS DATA A to be BACKUP DATA A.

444 § Diagnosing and Correcting Problems

A Fileid is Incomplete

Most commands that work with files require that you specify the fileid of the file to be manipulated. If you fail to specify all or part of the fileid, the system displays a message indicating that the fileid is incomplete or missing:

    Incomplete fileid specified

    No fileid(s) specified

    No filename specified

    No filetype specified

    No filemode specified

Enter the command again, specifying a complete fileid.

Invalid Characters in a Fileid

The characters that can be used in a fileid are letters, numbers and certain special characters. If you use a special character in a filename or filetype that is not one of those permitted, the system displays a message indicating that the character is invalid:

    Invalid character 'char' in fileid 'fn ft fm'

Enter the command again, specifying a fileid composed of valid characters.

Invalid Wildcards in Fileids

Some commands that work with files do not allow you to use asterisks as wildcards in fileids. If you do so, the system displays a message indicating that the * is invalid:

    Invalid * in fileid

Either enter the command once for each fileid or use the LISTFILE command to create a CMS EXEC file. For more information about creating and using a CMS EXEC file, refer to the LISTFILE command in the chapter *Managing Disk Files*.

15.5 Problems with Disks

This section requires an understanding of CMS disks and their characteristics. These topics are discussed in the chapter *CMS Disks and CMS Disk Files.*

A Disk is Full

The storage capacity of a minidisk is fixed and can only hold so many blocks of files. Minidisks do not expand in size to meet your file storage requirements. If you attempt to write a file to disk that is larger than the space available, the system displays a message indicating that the disk is full:

```
Disk 'mode(vaddr)' is full.
```

To correct the disk space problem, you must do one of four things:

1. Make some space available on the disk in one or more of these ways:

    - Erase any files that are no longer needed.

    - Transfer files that are seldom used to another storage medium, such as magnetic tape or a floppy disk, and then erase them from disk.

    - Use the PACK option on the COPYFILE command to compress one or more files.[1]

2. Increase the size of the disk.

3. Obtain another permanent disk and write the file to that disk.

4. If the file is a temporary one, obtain a temporary disk and write the file to the temporary disk.

Increasing the size of your disk or obtaining an additional disk may only be possible through the same people that set up your account in the first place.

Examples:

- Suppose you are writing a file to your A-disk and the file is too large to fit in the space available. The system displays the message:

```
DMSERD107S Disk 'A(0191)' is full.
Ready(00256);
```

If you use FILELIST to display a list of the files that are now on your disk, you will notice that there is a now a file with a filetype of CMSUT1.

---

[1] Once you've *packed* a file you should not edit the file or use it in any way. Before using it, use the UNPACK option to restore the file to its original state.

This is part of the file that you were writing to disk when CMS discovered that there was no more space to write the file. Since the file is incomplete, you should erase it.

• Suppose you're editing an existing file, enter the FILE subcommand to write the file to disk and XEDIT displays the message:

```
Disk is Full. Set new filemode or clear some disk space.
```

If you have another disk to which you can write the file, use the FM function on the XEDIT SET subcommand to change the filemode. Another alternative is to erase files that are no longer needed. As a last resort, use the ERASE command to remove the version of the file you're editing that is stored on disk and enter the FILE subcommand.

An Invalid Mode Change

Renaming a file changes a file's filename and/or filetype but not the filemode. If you specify a filemode in the output fileid that differs from the filemode in the input fileid of the RENAME command, the system displays a message indicating that the mode change is invalid:

```
Invalid mode change
```

• Changing the filemode is equivalent to copying the file. If you want to change the filemode, use COPYFILE instead of RENAME.

• If you just want to rename the file, enter the RENAME command again, specifying the same mode letter in both the input and output fileids.

A Disk is Not Accessed

If you enter a command that refers to a disk by a mode letter that is not accessed, the system displays a message indicating that the mode letter is not accessed:

```
DISK 'mode' not accessed
```

• If the mode letter was incorrect, enter the command again, specifying the correct mode letter.

• If the mode letter was correct, but the disk has not yet been accessed or you've lost access to the disk, access the disk and enter the command again.

Files Cannot be Written to or Removed from a Disk

The access mode you specify when you link to a disk determines what you can do with files on that disk:

- A read/write link allows you to read files from and write files to the disk. You can also erase files from the disk.

- A read/only link allows you to read files from the disk, but you cannot write files to or erase files from the disk.

If you try to write a file to or remove a file from a disk to which you have read/only access, the system displays a message indicating that you only have read access to the disk:

```
DISK 'mode' is read/only
```

- If you must write the file to or remove the file from the disk, you must first establish read/write access to the disk.

- If you have another disk to which you can write the file, change the filemode to be that of the disk to which you can write.

Example:

Suppose you establish read/only access to a disk belonging to another user and access it with a mode letter of B. If you then try to write a new file to that disk or change any file on that disk, the system responds with the message:

```
DMSERS037E disk 'B' is read/only.
Ready(00036);
```

This occurs because the link you've established to the B-disk only allows you to read files that are on that disk. You cannot make any changes to that disk by changing files that are already there or by writing new files to the disk. If you must change the disk, you have to link to it again establishing read/write access.

A Virtual Address is Missing or Invalid

If you enter a command, such as LINK, that uses a virtual address and either omit a virtual address or use one that is not an appropriate hexadecimal number, the system displays a message indicating that the virtual address is either missing or invalid:

```
VADDR MISSING OR INVALID
```

If you are unsure of what constitutes an appropriate hexadecimal number, refer to the section on *Hexadecimal Numbers* in the chapter on *CMS Disks and CMS Disk Files*.

A Virtual Address is Already Defined

If a virtual address is already in use and you use it again on a LINK command, the system displays a message indicating that the virtual address is already defined:

```
userid vaddr1 NOT LINKED; DASD vaddr2 ALREADY DEFINED
```

Enter the LINK command again, specifying a different virtual address. Use the CP QUERY command to determine whether some hexadecimal number is already defined.

An Access Mode or Access Password is Incorrect

When using the LINK command, if you enter an access password that is incorrect or wrong for the access mode specified, the system displays a message indicating that either the mode or the password is incorrect:

```
userid vaddr1 NOT LINKED; MODE OR PASSWORD INCORRECT
```

Make certain that you have the correct password for the access mode on the LINK command. Enter the LINK command again and carefully enter the password.

15.6 Problems with Options and Parameters

This section requires an understanding of command syntax and what options and parameters are. These topics are discussed in the section on *Command Syntax* in the chapter *A Conceptual Overview of VM/CMS*.

An Option is Invalid

If you misspell the name of an option or use what you believe to be an option but which really is not, the system displays a message indicating that the option is invalid:

```
Invalid option 'option'
```

Use the HELP facility to determine what options are valid for the command and how they are spelled.

An Option is Specified Twice

CMS only allows you to specify an option once. If you specify it more than once, the system displays a message indicating that the option has been specified twice:

```
'option' option specified twice
```

Enter the command again, specifying the option once.

Options Conflict

Commands often have options that are alternatives to each other: you can specify one of the alternatives or the other, but not both. Some commands also have options that are incompatible with each other when specified together. If you specify options that are either incompatible or in conflict with one another, the system displays one of these messages:

```
'option' and 'option' are conflicting options
```

```
Conflicting options
```

Enter the command again, specifying one option or the other, but not both.

A Parameter is Invalid

CMS refers to the arguments supplied to options as **parameters**. If you misspell the name of an parameter or use what you believe to be a parameter but which really is not, the system displays a message indicating that the parameter is invalid:

invalid parameter 'parameter' in the 'option' option field

Use the HELP facility to determine what parameters are valid for the option and how they are spelled.

Example:

Suppose you want to copy a file called XMPL DATA beginning with record 10. This can be done with the FROM option. However, instead of using the number '0', you use the letter 'O' in 10:

COPY XMPL DATA A PART = = (FROM 10

The system responds with the message:

Invalid parameter '10' in the 'FROM' option field

15.7 Problems with Your Terminal

This section requires an understanding of input areas, protected areas and insert mode. These topics are discussed in the chapters *Becoming Acquainted with VM/CMS* and *Becoming Acquainted with XEDIT*.

If your terminal only sounds an alarm when you press a key, the problem is usually one of two things:

- You are typing in a protected area.

- Your terminal is in insert mode and you are typing in an input area that is full.

Locate the cursor and determine whether it is in a protected area or an input area:

- If the cursor is in a protected area, use the cursor movement keys to move the cursor either to the command line or to an input area.

- If the cursor is in an input area, such as the prefix area in XEDIT or the file areas in FILELIST and RDRLIST, remove your terminal from insert mode and try again. If necessary, use the RESET key to unlock the keyboard.

If you are using an ASCII terminal, use one of the cursor movement keys to see if you can move the cursor. If you cannot, the connection between your terminal and the ASCII Controller may have to be *reset*. Consult with those who support your system to determine how to do this on your type of terminal.

15.8 Problems with Virtual Storage Capacity

This section requires an understanding of your virtual storage capacity and how to change it. These concepts are discussed in the chapters *Becoming Acquainted with CMS* and *Managing Your Virtual Machine*, respectively.

These messages indicate that the amount of virtual storage currently defined for your VM is insufficient for the task in which you are engaged and that you must increase your virtual storage:

    Virtual storage capacity exceeded

    File 'fileid' too large.

Diagnosing the Problem

When you begin editing an existing file, a copy of that file is read from disk into virtual storage. Consequently, if you attempt to edit a file that is too large to fit in the amount of virtual storage that your VM is defined to have, the system will display a message indicating that the file is too large:

    DMSXIN132S File 'fileid' too large.
    Ready(00088);

In a similar fashion, if you attempt to run a program that requires more virtual storage than your VM is defined to have, the system will display the message:

    DMSSMN109S Virtual storage capacity exceeded.

Correcting the Problem

The first step in correcting this problem is to use the STORAGE option on the CP QUERY command to determine how much memory or virtual storage capacity your VM is currently defined to have:

    QUERY   STORAGE

The storage will be displayed in *kilobytes*, that is, *thousands* of bytes. This message indicates that the virtual storage is 960K bytes where 960K = 960 x 1024 = 983,040 bytes:

    STORAGE = 960K

The second step is to use the STORAGE option on the CP DEFINE command to increase your storage capacity.

Example:

Suppose you want to increase storage to 1024K bytes. The following are equivalent:

```
DEFINE  STORAGE  1M
DEFINE  STORAGE  1024K
```

After the DEFINE command has executed successfully, notice that your VM is put into the CP environment in a 'disabled wait state'. To return to CMS, enter:

```
IPL  CMS
```

System Messages:

The maximum amount of storage that your VM is allowed to have is defined in the CP directory for your VM. If you attempt to define your storage as an amount which is greater than the amount allowed for your VM, the system responds with the message:

```
STORAGE EXCEEDS ALLOWED MAXIMUM
```

If the maximum amount of memory that your VM is allowed to have is still insufficient, there are several courses of action to be explored:

- If you are regularly going to need a storage capacity larger than that allowed for your VM, contact those who administer your system to ask about increasing your maximum storage.

- If you are exceeding storage capacity in trying to run a large program, find out if there is there is a batch facility available at your installation. If so, the batch facility will probably be better equipped to handle large programming problems. Running your program in batch will probably also cost significantly less than if it is run interactively on CMS. If there is no batch facility available or if you are simply intent upon running the large program interactively, you might be able to reduce the amount of memory the program requires by reducing the size of arrays, eliminating unnecessary variables, etc.

- If you are exceeding storage capacity in trying to edit a large file, you should:

  1. Use COPYFILE to break the large file into two or more smaller files.

  2. Edit the smaller files.

  3. Use COPYFILE to reassemble the smaller files into a single large file.

Example:

Suppose you have a file called HUMPTY DATA A containing 20,000 records and want to break it up into two smaller files, each having 10,000 records.

1. To produce the first file:

    COPY HUMPTY DATA A PART1 DATA A (FROM 1 FOR 10000

2. To produce the second file:

    COPY HUMPTY DATA A PART2 DATA A (FROM 10001 FOR 10000

3. After you've finished editing the two smaller files, they can be combined into a single file:

    COPY PART1 DATA A PART2 DATA A DUMPTY DATA A

    where DUMPTY DATA A is the new edited version of HUMPTY DATA A.

15.9 Problems with the System

Occasionally, you will be working on the system when your terminal will not respond. The cursor will not move and none of the keys will seem to work. Should this happen, wait for a few moments and try again to move the cursor. If it remains frozen, try to log onto the system.

- If you are able to log on again, enter BEGIN as your first command to return to what you were doing before the interruption.

- If the system doesn't respond in the usual manner, chances are the system has malfunctioned in some way.

When the system goes down unexpectedly, there is nothing you can do except hope that it comes back up again *soon*, because the sooner it comes back up, the more likely you will be able to recover any work you were doing and the sooner you can return to work. If the machine comes back up within 10 or 15 minutes, log on again and enter BEGIN as your first command to return to what you were doing before the interruption. If you were editing a file when the machine went down, you should now be back in XEDIT, just as you were before.

If the work load on your system is heavy, it may take several seconds for it to process one of your commands. When a command takes much longer than normal to complete, however, it is possible that the system has gone down. If you've entered a command that takes an inordinate amount of time to complete, press the PA1 key once to determine whether the system is up or down:

- If the status message changes to CP READ, the system is up.

  - Use the BEGIN command to resume execution.

  - Use the IPL CMS command to halt execution and return to CMS.

- If the status message does not change, chances are the system is down.

Index

WR access mode 87
WRAP function of SET (XEDIT) 239
Write access 76
Write password 88, 364

X (XEDIT) prefix command 200
XEDIT (CMS) command 96
   NOPROFILE option 276

WIDTH option 196
XEDIT editor 95
XEDIT macros 225, 276

Y-disk 82

ZONE function of SET (XEDIT) 239
Zone 129
   changing 239